Teacher Education in Sub-Saharan Africa: closer perspectives

M. Asselin (signature)

Teacher Education in Sub-Saharan Africa: closer perspectives

Edited by
ROSARII GRIFFIN

SYMPOSIUM
BOOKS

Symposium Books Ltd
PO Box 204, Didcot, Oxford OX11 9ZQ, United Kingdom
www.symposium-books.co.uk

Published in the United Kingdom, 2012

ISBN 978-1-873927-36-6

Printed and bound in the United Kingdom by Hobbs the Printers, Southampton
www.hobbs.uk.com

Contents

TEACHER EDUCATION AT THE CHALKFACE:
CLOSER PERPECTIVES

Dedication

In memory of my father, Mr Patrick (Paudie) Joseph Griffin.
'As long as we live, they too will live; for they are now a part of us, as we remember them.' (Anon.)

Acknowledgements

I wish to acknowledge and thank all those who contributed to this volume, often at short notice and in record time, making it the exciting and interesting volume that it is. *Go raibh mile maith agaibh go léir – thank you a thousand times.*

I would like to acknowledge the contribution of Irish Aid and the Higher Education Authority under the Programme for Strategic Cooperation between Higher Education and Research Institutes 2007-2011, in funding the research pertaining to certain chapters herein relating to Lesotho and Uganda. The views expressed are those of the project teams whose work was undertaken during my time as Director at the Centre for Global Development in Education, Limerick and do not purport to represent the views of Irish Aid or the Higher Education Authority. Such funding is essential for ongoing sustainable development and collaboration for teacher education in sub-Saharan Africa and I would like to thank Irish Aid and the Higher Education Authority for creating important opportunities for cross-national development.

I wish to thank Colin and Shirley Brock for their kind hospitality towards me during my visit to their home during the final compilation of this book, and Colin for his ever helpful advice and insights.

Special thanks are in order for our publisher, Mr Roger Osborn-King, who was extremely encouraging and patient during the editorial process. Roger, you are really an Irish man at heart!

Finally, but by no means least, I would like to acknowledge the support of my family, particularly my husband Fintan and my two daughters Catherine and Miriam, for your continuous support and emotional sustenance. Thanks, too, to my wider family and friends for your ongoing interest in my academic endeavours, particularly my mother and late father Patrick (Paudie) Griffin, who was always very proud of my achievements and to whom this volume is dedicated.

Ar dheis Dé go raibh a anam uasal.

Preface

JOHN MUSAAZI

The recent attention being given to the contributions of African nations' human resources to their development suggests that the roots of social change run deep, and creating modern nations means creating modern men and women. That is, the development process is an educational process. Trust in the ability of education to promote economic and social development is a common thing in Africa today.

The concept of education as reflected in this book is a broad one, including all the activities outside the family that are consciously planned and organized to achieve specific educational objectives. Education is both an end in itself and a means to attaining other ends.

Education has an obligation to transmit from one generation to the next the accumulated wisdom, knowledge, skills, values and attitudes and knowledge of the society, and to prepare the young people for their future membership of the society and their active participation in its development. Education, therefore, is in itself an aspect or object of development. It is an instrumental resource and a means of achieving the wider objectives of development. Education is believed to contribute to political development by creating an informed and participant citizenry and to socio-economic development by equipping people for new roles associated with an expanding range of occupations.

Teacher education therefore continues to be given a major emphasis in all educational planning efforts because no education system can rise above the quality of its teachers. The purposes of teacher education should be:

1. to provide highly motivational, conscientious and efficient classroom teachers for all levels of the education system;
2. to encourage further the spirit of enquiry and creativity in teachers;
3. to help teachers to fit into the social life of the community and society at large and to enhance their commitment to national objectives;
4. to provide teachers with the intellectual and professional background adequate for their assignment and to make them adaptable to any

changing situation not only in the life of their country, but in the wider world;

5. to enhance teachers' commitment to the teaching profession.

This book examines a range of issues within teacher education. It highlights many salient issues around the provisions of a quality education. Among other issues and challenges addressed are: teacher resources and practices, the need for further research capacity building within teacher education, the need to generate evidence-based research for good policy making; the need to improve pedagogical practices and the need to focus on pre-service and in-service teacher education, and the building of cross-national partnerships and collaborations between teacher educators from global north and south.

This book, which, as the first two sentences in the Introduction (by Rosarii Griffin) point out, 'emerges out of a lacuna in the literature relating specifically to teacher education ... with particular reference to sub-Saharan Africa ... [which] appears to be a neglected area' is thus more than timely. As Dr Griffin explains, the book is divided into three main sections, namely (i) international and national discourses on teacher education; (ii) case country research reports on aspects of teacher education in sub-Saharan Africa; and (iii) teacher education at the chalkface. In these respective sections, contributors look at various issues and challenges around the teaching profession, particularly in relation to resources and practices within sub-Saharan Africa. The contributors examine the issue of building capacity for educational research within teacher education colleges and explore the concept of education for sustainable development. In this volume, research reports are presented highlighting various challenges within the structure and provision of teacher education within the national contexts of Gambia, Kenya, Lesotho, Madagascar, Mozambique, South Africa, Tanzania, Uganda and Zambia.

With such a solid piece of work, I have the rare privilege of congratulating the Editor, Dr Rosarii Griffin, for a job well done. I also thank and congratulate the 32 contributing authors for being part of this academic endeavour. I commend the book for all those who are in one way or another connected with education in general, and teacher education in particular, as a 'must read'.

INTRODUCTION

Teacher Education in Sub-Saharan Africa: closer perspectives

ROSARII GRIFFIN

This book emerges out of a lacuna in the literature relating specifically to teacher education and interrelated issues in the developing world, with particular reference to sub-Saharan Africa. Teacher education appears to be a neglected area and is often an area that is least funded, unlike other areas of academic endeavour such as the pursuit of mathematics, science and technology programmes, including information technology-related services and business matters. Nevertheless, it goes without saying that if the quality of provision of education, particularly at the primary level, is not of a reasonably high standard and quality, the chances of students attending secondary or tertiary education to benefit from any such programmes will be lessened. In other words, educational attainment is without doubt a factor of the quality of education and instruction such students have been afforded during the period of compulsory universal primary education (UPE). The quality of this education largely depends on the quality of the teachers who teach at this crucial period of a child's educational and intellectual development: the formative years. For this reason, this book focuses on teacher education in particular and highlights recent research that has focused on various aspects of teacher education which have heretofore been overshadowed by other priorities. However, it is time that the international community – in pursuit of the internationally endorsed Millennium Development Goals (MDGs), especially Goal 2 (to achieve UPE) – takes a step back and asks: What *kind* of an education is appropriate, relevant and sustainable for a country's citizens? This volume might go some way in highlighting such central and crucial questions and, in doing so, examine the central role of the teacher as an agent of change within the complex process of using education as a transformative vehicle for sustainable development with a view to the elimination of poverty forever, especially within sub-Saharan Africa.

This book is thus divided into three main sections: 'International and National Discourses on Teacher Education', 'Case Country Research Reports on Aspects of Teacher Education in Sub-Saharan Africa' and 'Teacher Education at the Chalkface: closer perspectives'. This volume highlights salient issues in relation to teacher education, especially as education is considered one of the most important pillars of development, alongside nourishment, shelter and health (Midttun, 2000; Sinclair, 2001). Education is also a basic human right, enshrined in the Convention on the Rights of the Child (Articles 28 and 29). Above all, education brings hope to people – hope for a brighter and more prosperous future.

Brock opens this volume with his chapter on 'Education as a Humanitarian Response as Applied to Teachers and Their Training in Sub-Saharan Africa'. In this chapter, he examines briefly the 'legacies of indigenous and colonial education for the present day', examining current problems and initiatives, and gives some specific examples of projects within countries and progress, particularly from Sierra Leone. Having given a brief contextual analysis of where the international community is at in respect of the MDGs and the achievements of Education for All, Brock points out that 'education as a humanitarian response' embraces all three forms of education – formal, informal and non-formal – and that the integration of all three is essential for education to be both effective and meaningful within the developing world context. Brock proceeds to examine the various colonial legacies within sub-Saharan Africa and the vulnerability of education within conflict zones. Brock also highlights the 'capacity' issue, and especially the lack of it, as another major issue within teacher education which does not receive as much attention as it might. Brock expands upon some successful educational initiatives in operation in parts of Africa and the kinds of lessons that can be gleaned from these. These initiatives are partly successful because of the recognition of the significance of local communities, especially in the 'rural worlds of the marginalised majority of the population of sub-Saharan Africa', and because they bring together all three modes of education, engendering the social and cultural capital necessary both for survival and meaningful sustainable development.

Moon & Wolfenden, in their chapter entitled 'Teacher Education in Sub-Saharan Africa: issues and challenges around teacher resources and practices', highlight that there is currently a shortfall of 1.2 million qualified teachers in sub-Saharan Africa, and at least one-third of those who are currently teaching are unqualified and another third are poorly qualified. This does not bode well for the future of the pupils in their care, whose own future prospects are at stake. Similar to Brock, Moon & Wolfenden have also suggested that the current institutional model, based on the Western model, may be an outdated mode of teacher instruction, originating from nineteenth- and twentieth-century industrial demands in Europe, and that new opportunities for providing teacher education within the African context should be explored. Such opportunities include the promotion of flexi-learning courses, as well as the potential harnessing of modern and mobile technologies where possible. For instance, Moon & Wolfenden 'wholeheartedly [embrace] the increasingly significant ideas of the Open Educational Resource (OER) movement' of Teacher Education in Sub-Saharan Africa (TESSA), but they also highlight the importance that grass-roots and indigenous courses, resources and practices are strengthened and promoted, and highlight how the work of TESSA can and does promote this through its operations. TESSA's operations currently span Ghana, Kenya, Nigeria, Rwanda, South Africa, Sudan, Tanzania, Uganda and Zambia, and it is expected to have half a million users in sub-Saharan Africa by 2012.

One of the challenges posed about education in sub-Saharan Africa, particularly in relation to South Africa, highlighted in Clive Harber's chapter, 'Contradictions in Teacher Education and Teacher Professionalism in Sub-Saharan Africa: the case of South Africa', is that 'teacher education is a part of the problem of authoritarian education rather than the solution. This is because teacher education tends to perpetuate traditional, unreflective and teacher-centred pedagogy rather than challenge it', often resulting from the fact that the teacher education provided is itself an authoritarian and reproductive preparation for teaching in schools. However, as Harber is at pains to point out, this is not unique to sub-Saharan Africa, but is also a trend in Western democracies due to the prevalent influence of neo-liberal forces. Haber believes that, in Africa, the 'myth of the liberal college' in teacher education helps to perpetuate a cycle of authoritarian reproduction, highlighting a gap between what teacher educators say they do and the perceptions of student teachers about their experiences. Harber highlights the reality that the teacher education curriculum was often dominated by 'a conservative, authoritarian ideology where debate and critical reflection were not encouraged', in striking contrast to the principles of participatory, learner-centred and enquiring pedagogy frequently espoused in curriculum documents. The case of South Africa, especially in transition from being an authoritarian state to a democracy, has left South Africans both pining for a loss of traditional values (prior to apartheid) and with an ambition to embrace the (post-apartheid) future, which brings hope of a better life. Yet, it is difficult to navigate, within the education context, the desire for authoritarian and hierarchical systems verses the understanding of the need to take a different approach from the past. It may yet take generations of teacher educators to fully embrace more participatory forms of education.

In the chapter 'What Hope for the Dakar Goals? The Lower Levels of Education in Lesotho and Uganda since 2000', by Urwick & Griffin, with Opendi & Khatleli, the authors explore how the essentialist aims of the MDGs have somewhat undermined the aims and aspirations of *The Dakar Framework for Action* (UNESCO, 2000), which conceived of education in the broader sense and looked at the educational process as a whole, as opposed to achieving enrolment numbers and measuring that in terms of the attainment of UPE. This chapter argues that many other areas of education have been neglected as a result of this narrow approach – areas such as special educational needs (SEN), adult learning, non-formal and informal learning, and early childhood education, for instance. The authors argue for a more balanced and inclusive approach to developing educational systems in a more coherent and integrated fashion for the benefit of all, in order to alleviate poverty.

David Stephens' chapter, 'A Critical Overview of Education for Sustainable Development with Particular Focus upon the Development of Quality Teacher Education in Sub-Saharan Africa', focuses specifically on education for sustainable development (ESD), which is now part of a global educational discourse. Similar to the calls for the promotion and embedding of gender equality in the 1980s, teachers and students are exhorted to develop a 'green' lifestyle and to mainstream sustainability issues. Essentially, ESD has become a mantra of hope, or, in Stephens' words, 'a call for change in the way we educate our children and ourselves with the express purposes of ensuring a sustainable future'. Within ESD, it is clear that if the education sector is to come close to achieving and sustaining such a change, it will fall to teacher education to provide the necessary cadre of appropriately trained personnel through its pre-service and in-service training.

Stephens' chapter also provides a brief critical overview of ESD and discusses the challenges and possibilities of ESD for the development and sustainability of *quality* teacher education in sub-Saharan Africa. Given the importance of context within ESD – for example, 'think global, act local' – the chapter also attempts to critique the more general issues and practices promoted by organisations such as UNESCO through the evaluation of one ESD teacher education project in Madagascar. Importantly, Stephens also pays particular attention to issues of culture, context and indigenous knowledge in the development of quality ESD and teacher education within the Madagascar and sub-Saharan Africa context. The chapter concludes with lessons that have been learned from the case study and he makes some suggestions for the way forward.

Stephens' chapter is followed by 'Building Capacity for Educational Research in Sub-Saharan Africa: opportunities, constraints and lessons in the context of Mozambique, Tanzania and Uganda', by Cremin, Nakabugo & Barrett. These authors highlight the need for increased emphasis to be placed on building capacity for educational research to ensure that the lacunae that currently exist within sub-Saharan African countries' systems of education can be addressed internally, or in partnership with other countries. The emphasis that Cremin et al focus on is the support given to those involved in the third-level sector, so that teachers are given the best possible education in order to become reflective practitioners and 'that the capacity to engage in research is something that can be grown and nurtured, whether at the individual or institutional level'. They highlight the combined efforts of their organisation, the Irish-African Partnership for Research Capacity Building, which attempts to examine the opportunities and constraints in building capacity for education and research in Mozambique, Tanzania and Uganda by working in partnership with nine Irish higher education institutions and four African higher education institutions from the aforementioned countries. They call for the need for greater relevance, control and ownership over the research process by African countries. Citing Samoff (1999, p. 253), they highlight that where genuine partnership does not exist between donor agencies or countries and their African counterparts, there is 'less national ownership of their results', thus highlighting the need for greater partnership – a theme this book will return to later on in the final section.

The second section of the book examines case country research reports on aspects of teacher education in sub-Saharan Africa with particular reference to Lesotho and Uganda. Some of this research was funded by Irish Aid (a division of the Department of Foreign Affairs, Government of Ireland) and administered by the Higher Education Authority through its Programme of Strategic Cooperation between Irish Aid and Higher Education and Research Institutes 2007-2011. The research was coordinated by the Centre for Global Development through Education (CGDE), based in Limerick (of which I was Director), as the CGDE was the hub of a consortium of Irish and African higher education institutions involved in teacher education which collaborated to achieve certain research and policy goals to assist in the alleviation of poverty through education, especially within the sub-Saharan Africa region. The following chapters arose from the aforementioned research projects and activities of the CGDE and are a credit to the dedication and tireless work of the educational researchers and their home institutions, North and South, who participated in this cross-national collaboration.

An important research report to emerge from the CGDE, which the following chapter is based on, 'Towards a Holistic Understanding of Special Educational Needs: informing the context of teacher education in Lesotho', gives an indication of the state of SEN in Lesotho and the kinds of challenges Basotho teachers face when in the classroom. The authors – O'Riordan, Urwick, Long & Campbell – set the context, outlining the international efforts and agreements entered into which raise awareness and potentially provision for those with SEN within the sub-Saharan

15

Africa context. As referred to in the chapter by Urwick et al, SEN has often suffered in the face of developing countries trying to achieve UPE targets. Within the Lesotho context, the achievement of 'inclusive education' has been very limited. This is partly because of the dearth of resources, trained teachers, specific facilities and funding structures to support SEN within mainstream schools. This problem is common across sub-Saharan Africa and elsewhere. O'Riordan et al explore some cross-national examples of positive practice from South Africa and elsewhere as to how some strategies and synergies between special schools and mainstream schools can be developed which can be both a mutually beneficial and cost-effective way of sharing limited resources and expertise. They also advocate the enhancement of community-based rehabilitation in partnership with non-governmental organisations (NGOs), which can encourage capacity building on a community-wide basis.

The research project which O'Riordan et al were engaged in involved mapping capacity both in the formal and administrative education sectors of Lesotho, as well as in the local community and households, incorporating approximately 75 interviews of varying length to establish patterns. The research also covered a small cross section of Lesotho villages to get a sense of the challenges facing the community, including teachers in the lowlands, foothills and highlands of Lesotho. One outcome highlights the fact that funding is 'a critical issue for the assessment process and access to key medical, educational and psychological staff'. International NGOs have a potentially very important role to play in this regard. There is also insufficient training capacity for teachers' initial identification of specific SEN – notably, attention deficit hyperactivity disorder or autism. The Ministry of Education and Training is aware of the need for urgent attention to be given to such areas, including the formulation of national guidelines around school placements relating to SEN matters. With financial incentives and promotional opportunities, these matters could be addressed through the teaching profession in partnership with the wider community. Although there is plenty of evidence that the Ministry of Education and Training in Lesotho is aware of these issues, the authors of this chapter highlight that mobilising the necessary resources appears to be the main stumbling block to success, and not so much the dedication or awareness of such matters amongst key individuals.

Conway, Oldham, Urwick & Kisa's chapter on 'The Teaching and Learning of Mathematics in Ugandan Secondary Schools: poised for change?' focuses on the pedagogy of mathematics in Ugandan secondary schools, using this as a lens through which the education of mathematics teachers can be viewed. This chapter is based on empirical research focused on teacher effectiveness in both mathematics and the sciences, influenced by two major factors. Firstly, the authors describe the relatively poor results experienced in these subjects in the Uganda Certificate of Education examination. Secondly, the authors highlight that the Ugandan Ministry of Education and Sports (MOES) introduced in 2007 a new in-career development programme for teachers of secondary mathematics and science, and that the MOES is in the process of monitoring the effects of this new programme. The authors of this chapter explore international and national debates on mathematics teaching and learning, which informed their research design. They describe the research design within the context of Uganda. The research focuses on the classroom learning environment under four key headings: pedagogy; teachers' experiences and pedagogical aspirations; teachers' continuing professional development experiences and needs; and, finally, the backwash effect of state examinations on teaching and learning. Their findings are consistent with findings from other parts of sub-Saharan Africa which highlight the dominance of the teacher-led approach to pedagogy; general constraints typically experienced by teachers in the classroom; the need for further in-service and continuous professional development in respect of core aspects of the curriculum; and the powerful effect of state examinations on what goes on in the classroom. Recommendations that impact on government policy are offered.

Staying with Uganda, the following chapter, 'Implementing the Thematic Curriculum in Uganda: implications for teacher education', by Holland et al, explores the implementation of the new Thematic Curriculum (TC) in Uganda and its implications for teacher education. The TC was designed to be more contextually relevant for the youth of Uganda and, in order to make the curriculum more accessible, it was to be taught in the local language for the first few years of primary education. Whilst a number of their findings highlight similar issues arising in the previous Conway et al chapter – namely, the dominance of teacher-centred approaches to teaching and learning; the lack of resources, which constrains classroom activity; the prevalence of the summative mode of assessing, which often dictates classroom activity; and constraints in the usage and relevance of more formative assessment methodologies – a lot of positives have emerged from the implementation of the TC. These include the accessibility of the TC to young children when taught in their local language, in spite of the logistical difficulties this poses for teacher education, which are further explored in this chapter. Mostly, the TC is well received by both parents and teachers alike, and has resulted in increased enrolment rates, although it has many constraints in terms of resources and poses many issues for teacher education institutions. The demand for more continuing professional development is always there due to the demands of the TC itself, which requires more participatory methodologies and continuous assessment techniques. The authors of this chapter explore in some detail how these might be attained, including exploring the importance of the role of head teachers in these matters.

'How Much Is Enough? Investigating Mathematical Knowledge for Primary Teaching in Lesotho', by Corcoran & Dolan, explores the literature around concerns about 'deficits in teachers' mathematical knowledge', which 'led to the construction of survey instruments to measure the mathematics knowledge required of teachers'. Recent comparative studies show the Chinese understanding of mathematics to be more profound than that of their USA counterparts, despite the latter taking more courses in the domains tested. The research in this chapter undertook a 'voluntary audit' of first-year students in the Lesotho College of Education and compared it with their counterparts in a teacher education college in Ireland. The researchers assessed prospective teachers' mathematical knowledge through a mathematical booklet which students volunteered to fill in and which it was hoped would offer 'a series of "snapshots" of aspects of the mathematics subject knowledge of a small voluntary sample of first-year student teachers at the Lesotho College of Education'. Interesting comparisons are made between the Basotho and Irish students based on the results of this audit. Although no generalisations could be made as the audit number was too small, the 'results' were interesting insofar as they give a 'snapshot' of mathematical understandings and the contextual nature (such as language and culture, for instance) of the differences between the groups' respective understandings. While the comparisons are fascinating, it is noteworthy that concerns about mathematical understandings are a worldwide phenomenon. This is particularly true in this globalised world, and many tests, such as the Trends in International Mathematics and Science Study and the Programme for International Student Assessment, compare different countries' performances on similar tests. An important aspect of understanding these tests is to examine the teacher educators' pedagogical approaches in different cultures and countries, and how they come to impart such crucial mathematical knowledge, understanding and skills, ideally in an interactive and meaningful way. This is of universal concern to all progressive education systems.

The third section of this volume is entitled 'Teacher Education at the Chalkface: closer perspectives'. This section has three exciting chapters told from three different perspectives. The first chapter tells of a lone educator's experience of working with the Turkana nomads of Kenya, and how this transformed him as an educator. Grenham turned to, and relied upon, the work of Paulo Freire, whose pedagogical approach made sense within the barren context of his work. The second chapter in this section, by Baily & O'Rourke, examines the experiences of pre-service educators as they embark on the Alternative Education Experience (AEE) module in Zambia and the Gambia, and what findings arose out of this research project for the trainee teachers' own practice as well as the implications this had for the course coordinators of this module. The final chapter looks at an exciting teacher educator exchange programme between Irish teacher educators from different Irish higher education institutions and their counterparts at Makerere University and Kyambogo University, Uganda. Of particular interest here are the outcomes of their peer observation and reflection process, and the impact this cross-national and collaborative exchange had on their respective approaches to their own pedagogical practice.

The first chapter of this section is entitled 'Teacher Educators and Teaching, Learning and Reflective Practice among the Turkana Nomads of Kenya'. In this chapter, Grenham draws upon the writing of the well-known Brazilian educator Paulo Freire and illustrates, through personal examples, how Freire's concepts of education were adapted and applied to his understandings of the Turkana pastoralist people of north-west Kenya. In a narrative fashion, Grenham explores the dilemmas and contradictions of being a cultural stranger within the African context and examines, through the lens of Freire, the process of 'intercultural education' within the context of 'teacher formation'. 'Interculturation', writes Grenham, 'is about a process of education that envisions humanisation as a two-way process of interpretation and cooperation between diverse cultures to awaken consciousness' and is 'respectful of the dignity of the learner within a particular cultural world view'. Grenham gives a rich account of the Turkana people, describing Freire's concept of 'conscientisation' within this particularly impoverished and harsh cultural context where mere survival is the fulcrum around which all else must rotate. Grenham is somewhat critical of the formal schooling mechanisms imposed by the Kenyan government, noting the detrimental impact that using Kenya's official languages may have on the Turkana language, culture and way of life. Grenham leaves us with more questions than answers about education and the development process, providing us with 'food for thought' and highlighting the advantages of teachers (and teacher educators) adopting a Freirean approach to teaching and learning in order to assist people educationally in a meaningful way within their particular cultural context.

The following chapter, 'An Account of the Alternative Education Experience Africa Programme in Transition: Irish pre-service teachers' experience in Zambia and the Gambia', by Baily & O'Rourke, is based on findings from a research report which examined the impact of student teacher trainee placements in the developing world context – namely, the Gambia and Zambia. The chapter outlines the AEE option during the teacher formation period, which is a module students can opt for. The research findings of the evaluation report are of particular interest. The AEE occurs during the teacher formation period and increased the students' interest and participation in development education and education in development issues. Many new teachers reported having subsequently joined related charities or NGOs working in the field. Interestingly, however, the respondents realised they had a superficial understanding of the underlying causes of development and the structural nature of poverty. Therefore, one of the recommendations that emerged from the report was to encourage a deepening of students' understandings of the complexity of development issues through the provision of modules on, for example, theories of development and the interrelational nature of global poverty. This chapter provides plenty to reflect on in terms of the provision of AEE options during the formation period of pre-service teachers on a Bachelor of Education programme in the global North.

A chapter which takes a slightly different approach, and gives an insider perspective 'at the chalkface', is Kieran, Hinchion, Kaije, Kyambadde & Bradley's chapter on 'Teacher Educator Exchange Partnership in Uganda and Ireland: closer perspectives on teacher education in sub-Saharan Africa'. This involved a teacher educator exchange programme between Irish teacher educator subject specialists from different Irish higher education institutions and their African counterparts from Ugandan higher education institutions – namely, Makerere University and Kyambogo University in Kampala. The exchange appeared to be largely a positive experience, where professional exchanges of pedagogical knowledge and experiences were shared. Particular aspects of the teacher educator experience stood out, including that of the various uses of information and communications technology and the core space of the university library within the Western sphere, which were underdeveloped and often missing within the African context, challenging the Ugandan educators to work often under difficult circumstances. In spite of these shortcomings, there was much to be learned and gained from the exchange. For instance, one of the notable outcomes from the programme was the emphasis on capacity building in terms of pedagogical knowledge, resources and ideas, as well as cultural education – experiencing being a 'cultural stranger' and the privilege of being a peer observer in another teacher educator's classroom within an entirely different array of circumstances – which appears to have been mutually enriching for all parties participating in the programme. Further capacity building also appears evident as these links continue to develop and grow through further collaboration on papers, presentations and publications.

Overall, the array of chapters presented in this volume covers much of sub-Saharan Africa, including South Africa, Lesotho, Uganda, Tanzania, Mozambique, Kenya, Sierra Leone, Madagascar, the Gambia and Zambia. The range of issues within teacher education is also wide-reaching and highlights many salient issues around the provision of a *quality* education: the issues and challenges of teacher resources and practices; the hiatus in provision for those with SEN; the need for further research capacity building within teacher education; the need to generate evidence-based research for good policy making; the need to improve pedagogical practices, especially around the teaching of mathematics and science; the need to re-examine curricular and assessment issues and to contextualise the curriculum to enhance sustainable development; the need to focus on pre-service and in-service teacher education; and the building of cross-national partnerships and collaborations between teacher educators from the global North and global South. In short, this volume could be said to focus on the provision of, and capacity for, a quality education for those in the global South in partnership with the global North, not merely to access *an education*, but to access *a good-quality education*, as highlighted by Urwick et al in their chapter 'What Hope for the Dakar Goals?' It is therefore hoped that this volume will bring some clarity to the issues around the provision of a good-quality education, especially teacher education, to ensure sustainable development.

Teachers are often considered the 'agents of change' within society. Teacher education is one weapon in the fight against poverty that will strengthen a nation's children to assist themselves. Building up a robust education system with a highly qualified and nurtured teaching force can only serve to benefit sub-Saharan Africa. With the proper tools and resources, and with a sustainable and contextual education, education will work for the people of sub-Saharan Africa. As a very wise man once said: 'Education is the most powerful weapon which you can use to change the world'. This same wise man also said that 'it is not money that creates success, but the freedom to make it will'. Education will assist in assuring that freedom. That same wise man was Nelson Mandela. He should know.

References

Midttun (2000) *Education in Emergencies and Transition Phases: still a right and more of a need.* Oslo: Norwegian Refugee Council.

Samoff, J. (1999) Education Sector Analysis in Africa: limited national control and even less national ownership, *International Journal of Educational Development*, 19(4), 249-272.
http://dx.doi.org/10.1016/S0738-0593(99)00028-0

Sinclair (2001) Education in Emergencies, in J. Crisp, C. Talbot & D. Cipollone (Eds) (2001) *Learning for a Future: refugee education in developing countries*, pp. 1-83. Geneva: UNHCR.

UNESCO (2000) *The Dakar Framework for Action. Education for All: meeting our collective commitments.* Paris: UNESCO.

CHAPTER 1

Education as a Humanitarian Response as Applied to Teachers and their Training in Sub-Saharan Africa

COLIN BROCK

SUMMARY The idea of education as a humanitarian response adopted by the writer is that any form of education needs to be appropriate to the needs of the receiver at any given time or place. Indigenous education traditions in Sub-Saharan Africa underlay, but have been supplanted by, derived colonial legacies of teacher education and training that, except for a small elite, are neither appropriate nor effective in meeting the needs of untrained or trainee teachers in most countries of the region. Violent conflict in a significant proportion of the region and the relatively high incidence of HIV/Aids are major constraints, but responses to them may give opportunities for new approaches. There have been a number of relevant initiatives in the last 20 years that do represent effective humanitarian responses.

Introduction

Education as a humanitarian response is conventionally thought of as being to do with education in emergencies, where the lives of people have been severely disrupted by man-made or natural disasters. Here, as in *Education as a Global Concern* (Brock, 2011), education as a humanitarian response is conceived as being a fundamental requirement of all education if that learning experience is to be appropriate. After making this case here, it will then be applied to the education and training of teachers.

The discussion will then move more specifically to applying this view to the education and training of teachers in sub-Saharan Africa, looking at the legacies of indigenous and colonial education for the present day, current problems and initiatives in this area, and some specific examples of projects and countries. It will conclude with a résumé and return to the fundamental issue of education as a humanitarian response in the context of sub-Saharan Africa.

Education as a Humanitarian Response

At the turn of the millennium, the World Education Forum in Dakar, Senegal, in April 2000 gave momentum to the World Declaration on Education for All (EFA) made in 1990 at Jomtien, Thailand. This momentum has been maintained partly through the Millennium Development Goals, the second of which aims at EFA in terms of basic education by 2015, and by the EFA Global Monitoring Reports (GMRs) since 2002. Each GMR, while monitoring and generating statistics on EFA, also has a theme, the latest being *The Hidden Crisis: armed conflict and education* (UNESCO, 2011), but to date there has been no GMR with a focus on teachers. This seems curious since the thrust of EFA has been with regard to formal education, especially schooling, and teachers reside at the interface between those providing schools and those attending them. From traditionally being 'founts of knowledge', teachers have now in many countries become facilitators of the identification and acquisition of relevant knowledge. In the context of sub-Saharan Africa, the role of facilitator now increasingly operates through appropriate use of information and communications technology (ICT), but the scale of the digital divide in this vast region is greater than in any other part of the world (Pye & Stephenson, 2003).

This connects with my concept of 'education as a humanitarian response' as necessarily being one that embraces and interconnects all three forms of education – formal, non-formal and informal. Education involves both learning and teaching, but in the context of ICT and other sources of information than the teacher, there are many 'teachers' in many different forms. This is especially so in the informal mode of learning, which is that in which we acquire most of our knowledge over our whole lifespan. If the formal and non-formal modes do not take account of what is acquired in the ongoing informal domain, then they will be severely diminished and dysfunctional. They will not, in that sense, be humane. What is needed, therefore, is for formal and non-formal programmes of learning, and especially schooling in the compulsory years, to connect on an organised basis with the world of informal learning that is going on around them. Such informal learning is ongoing at many levels and scales, from the family and local community through cultural association and nationality, to the globalisation of which ICT and other media are significant components. To enable basic schooling – which is all the formal education most people in sub-Saharan Africa will get for the foreseeable future – to become functional and humane by connecting with the informal is a massive challenge. It is a challenge to the political control of the state over the curriculum, and it is a challenge to schools and teachers to capitalise on the informal learning that is going on anyway.

The Education and Training of Teachers

Any programme of formal teaching, if it is to have a chance to be effective, must begin 'where the learners are at'. This is just as true of a teacher training course as it is of every lesson in the school classroom. Good practice in the classroom will often include an initial stage of connecting back to the previous lesson, but what is meant here is more fundamental than that. It refers, rather, to taking time to discover the additional non-formal and informal learning of each student that is relevant to whatever is now being embarked upon.

In the case of those entering on a programme of teacher education and training, 'where a student is at' will depend on their prior *formal* education experience, their prior *non-formal* education experience and their accumulated *informal* learning. This may well include entrenched conceptions as to what being a teacher in school really means in the context of the place and time at which they are preparing to take up the formal role. Such conceptions may well be misconceptions, and will therefore need to be challenged. They rarely are, as programmes of teacher education and training are often as centrally politically controlled as are the school curricula they will soon be required to deliver. It is also advantageous for trainee teachers to gain some understanding of the way in which the school system they are about to enter has evolved, as well as the range of forces and factors that bear in upon schooling. This means having some regard for what used to be known as 'educational foundations', such as the history, philosophy, economics, politics and sociology of education. In an increasingly instrumental, technical and managerial approach to teaching required in more developed countries such as England, these foundations are sidelined or absent from training programmes. Also minimised are cross-cutting issues outside of classroom management and the requirements of examinations, such as gender, language of the home, multicultural context and special learning needs.

In the same way, as there are influential colonial legacies for teacher education and training in sub-Saharan Africa, as will be discussed below, so there are contemporary conventions being transferred from the so-called 'developed countries'. These operate through higher degree experiences in metropolitan universities as international students, the influence of academic journals largely derived from such countries, and international conferences dominated by 'First World experts'. As Teame Mebrahtu (1984) observed in *Learning from the South: what, why and how?*, there is much that can and should be gained from the reverse process, but rarely is.

As well as these limiting legacies and conventions, most of the sub-Saharan African countries have a high proportion of untrained teachers employed full-time in their schools. Given the limited formal educational experience of most of these untrained teachers, the proportion of their accumulating education that is informal in nature is relatively high. As such, they are in a position to connect the informal and the formal in their teacher training process, but rarely have the opportunity. Thus is lost a most valuable resource – the ability to accommodate education as a humanitarian response with the new skills and technicalities of their training experience and subsequent classroom careers.

Aspects of the Legacy of Teacher Training in Sub-Saharan Africa

The context of sub-Saharan Africa overall ranges from the highly advanced and sophisticated – in Western terms – teacher education and training programmes in the elite universities of the Republic of South Africa, as well as in a few well-established institutions elsewhere such as Makerere University, Uganda, to the norm of teacher training colleges mostly established in colonial times. The nature of the legacy is naturally dependent in part on the colonial power in question and its domestic model of teacher education and training. In some countries, such as Cameroon, Togo and Tanzania, more than one European colonial legacy is involved. Subsequent discussion here will be mostly confined to the anglophone former colonies of the region.

As is well known, Britain employed a so-called 'indirect rule' in its African colonies, in most cases leaving all matters educational to maritime trading companies and Christian missions. Although schooling in Scotland was developing early, in England and Wales it was left to the inclination of individual parish priests of the dominant Anglican Church. As during the nineteenth century the Catholic Church throughout Britain and Ireland became free to operate schools and the non-conformist denominations gained ground in the rapidly growing industrial conurbations, this led to the multi-denominational character of educational colonisation in sub-Saharan Africa. Due to a combination of serendipity and rivalry, the locational pattern of schooling that emerged was ill-connected to population distribution, some indigenous communities having several schools from rival denominations while others had no schools at all. This spatial irregularity became know as *Missiongeographie* (Johnson, 1967). As far as Africans becoming teachers was concerned, it was a matter of learning on the job for the relatively few who had such an opportunity. With the state in England and Wales itself not being involved in education, the churches established the earliest teacher training colleges, though the first of these, Chester Diocesan Training College founded in 1839, was preceded more than a decade earlier by the founding of Fourah Bay College in Freetown, Sierra Leone, in 1827. Fourah Bay was established by the Church Missionary Society for teaching and training in theology and education, and in effect became the first 'Western-style' university in sub-Saharan Africa.

Throughout the nineteenth and early twentieth centuries, different Christian missions began to set up teacher training colleges in Sierra Leone and other countries of sub-Saharan Africa. They mirrored the irregular distribution of mission schools, and in overall capacity were grossly inadequate in relation to the national need for trained teachers. For example, in Sierra Leone, by the late twentieth century, there were just five such colleges training teachers for primary schools (Brock, 1996). Fourah Bay College had become the University of Sierra Leone following the achievement of national independence in 1961, and an example of the colonial legacy of thinking was that the university sported both an Institute and a Department of Education. The former had oversight of the five primary teacher training colleges, plus the one college for secondary training. This type of systemic replication, common in other former colonies in sub-Saharan Africa, meant that inappropriate concentration was fixed on a few institutions of alien cultural origins.

This was, and is, hardly a humanitarian response, and the same can be said of the entry requirements, curricula and staffing of teacher training colleges in most of the former British colonies of the region. The conventional English curricular model for the training of teachers became part of the colonial legacy. It was tripartite, comprising a programme of study in a main subject, a programme of educational studies involving some of the foundations plus some cognitive psychology, and a period, or periods, of teaching practice in the school classroom. The whole was followed by formal written examinations, and the successful were awarded a Certificate of Education or a Postgraduate Certificate of Education, according to whether the programme had been concurrent (over several years) or consecutive (one year, following a Bachelor's degree in a relevant subject). As in England from the late 1960s, the Bachelor's degree, often the Bachelor of Education, replaced the old Certificate of Education, so this also transferred to many of the former colonies in sub-Saharan Africa.

As, in the interests of supposed credibility, entry requirements to both types of teacher training programme were set as near as possible to those of the metropole, it was extremely difficult for most school leavers to qualify for entry. In order to even sit the relevant examination – in those days, the General Certificate of Education of London or Cambridge – most candidates would have had to have been at a secondary school. In many cases, this meant an elite selective school in a major town or city or, for some, a rural boarding school. Either way, most of the prospective teachers would not come from the rural subsistence farming communities of the majority of their future pupils, and would not share the informal educational experiences and cultures of their communities.

Central to any culture is language. Throughout much of sub-Saharan Africa, nations are multilingual. In Nigeria, the most populous country in the region, there are hundreds of indigenous languages, three regional languages – Hausa, Ibo and Yoruba – and the overlay of the colonial language, English. The language of the home is rarely the language of the school, and many trained teachers would not be familiar with the local social language. So they begin, and often remain, alien. After the Biafran War of 1967-70, in order to try to engender national cohesion, an initiative was introduced whereby teachers would be deployed to major language areas other than their own. Not surprisingly, this resulted in many teachers being even more alien with regard to the cultures and communities of their students. Recognising the profound significance of the learner's social language is one of the essential features of education as a humanitarian response. It is the language in which much of their informal learning resides, and this means the majority of their learning, especially in the context of the rural majority of sub-Saharan Africa.

While the majority of trainee teachers at that time were relatively elite, this was even more true of the staff of the training colleges. Some would have been graduates of such colleges who had moved on to a university at home or abroad, but many would have been direct from university. In any case, during the colonial era and for some time thereafter, teacher training colleges were perceived as stepping stones to university or at least to a more prestigious occupation in the civil service or a bank. The majority of teacher trainers therefore had little or no experience in the classroom, and so were doubly alien with regard to the majority of the students and communities in which their trainees would soon be working. We will return to this issue below in relation to an attempted reform of teacher education and training in Sierra Leone.

While the majority of the discussion in this section has been with reference to a colonial legacy in terms of teacher education, it is an enduring one that carries a powerful inertia throughout the so-called 'developing world'. Another, more recently growing phenomenon with implications for education as a humanitarian response is that of violent conflict, especially within countries.

Education and Conflict in Sub-Saharan Africa

Responses to the incidence of violent conflict affecting education, especially schooling, are often humanitarian in nature, but not necessarily so. Schoolchildren may be abducted and trained as soldiers. This is as much a part of their overall education as anything else, and those who train them and perhaps also indoctrinate them to certain ideologies and wider objectives are their 'teachers' for that period of time. The incidence of violent conflict affecting education in sub-Saharan Africa is so great that it is necessary first to describe its scale, and some of the principal examples.

O'Malley (2007) composed a pamphlet on behalf of UNESCO under the title of *Education under Attack*, which is advertised on the cover as 'A global study on targeted political and military violence against education staff, students, teachers, union and government officials, and institutions'. This had immediate impact, prompting a much enlarged sequel (O'Malley, 2010) and a related volume, compiled by Mark Richmond of UNESCO, titled *Protecting Education from Attack* (UNESCO, 2010).

It is this immensely important work that has prompted the theme of 'education and conflict' for the 2011 EFA GMR, which, like the much enlarged second version of O'Malley's findings, shows the incidence of violence against education to be much greater than previously thought. It is also on the increase not only in absolute terms, but also in respect of the proportion of the world's countries in which this is happening: about one-third.

The 2010 edition of *Education under Attack* details sub-Saharan country reports from Burundi, Chad, the Democratic Republic of the Congo, Ethiopia, Kenya, Niger, Nigeria, Somalia, Sudan and Zimbabwe. This selection was made with current situations of conflict in mind, and one must not forget other major cases of violence against, or involving, education in, for example, Angola, Liberia, Mozambique, Namibia, Rwanda, the Republic of South Africa, Sierra Leone and Uganda. This is not the place to detail the various forms and dimensions of attacks on teachers and the appropriation of some of them in a subversive cause, but it must also be remembered that, in fragile states past and present, teachers are in a position where they may have to choose between being a collaborator of the state or a voice for the local community against the state (Dove, 1982). That education, and especially schooling, can be a negative influence with regard to conflict in a wider non-violent sense has also more recently been illustrated by Davies (2004, 2005).

An indication of the scale of devastation created by attacks on education can be gained from the following extract:

> The eastern region of the Democratic Republic of the Congo
> witnessed a significant number of attacks on education over

the reporting period. Sexual violence against schoolgirls was widespread. Both the military and armed rebels forcibly recruited child soldiers from schools, using trucks to take them away. Teachers and schoolchildren were also shot or abducted.

Schools were ransacked, and it is estimated that up to 100 schools a year were occupied by the military, armed groups or IDPs [internally displaced peoples] in the territories of Rutsuru and Masisi, north Kivu. (O'Malley, 2010, p. 184)

The widespread rape of women, including teachers, and girls in this region adds to the already high incidence of HIV/AIDS, which is as prevalent among teachers as in the population at large. According to Moon & O'Malley:

UNICEF has estimated that nearly a million children a year lose their teachers to HIV/AIDS. A recent South African report drew attention to its finding with the sobering headline 'A teacher dies every two hours'. In Kenya, more teachers are dying of AIDS annually than the output of the teacher training colleges. In Zambia, HIV/AIDS claims the lives of 2000 teachers a year, again more than the output of the teacher training colleges. (Moon & O'Malley, 2008, p. 6)

Such situations have at least two major implications: the need for an early understanding of the means of avoiding HIV/AIDS gained through the teacher education and training curricula, and the difficulty of planning and delivering the supply of teachers required for making progress towards the target of EFA.

Disasters facing education such as violent conflict, health pandemics and natural disasters necessarily disrupt all aspects of education, including the education and training of teachers. Although now conventionally classified as 'education in emergencies', responses to the effects of such disasters can be very salutary with regard to inducing innovation to reform the alien legacy of derived models of teacher training from colonial metropoles described above. Some such situations have become so long-standing as to be the norm as far as the experience of communities where average expectation of life is of relatively short duration anyway.

Along with related environmental degradation, they merge into the widespread poverty that in any case afflicts the marginalised rural majority of sub-Saharan Africa. Lack of capacity on behalf of many of the state education systems of the region to fund and administer basic schooling, let alone an adequate teacher education and training operation, is leading to devolvement by default to local communities, non-governmental organisations (NGOs) and medium-term projects. The responses of such bodies tend to be innovative and, at least to some degree, humanitarian in nature.

Humanitarian Dimensions of
Selected Teacher Education Initiatives

Despite the colonial legacies, problems of lack of capacity and the influence of violent conflicts in the region, there are examples of good advice and practice in respect of teacher education and training in sub-Saharan Africa. Some of these are the subject of other contributions to this volume, but a brief discussion of some others follows here.

In the early to mid 1990s, I was a member of a World Bank team working on the projected International Development Agency IDA-4 Project in Sierra Leone, and the technical editor of *Developing Basic Education and Training in Sierra Leone: a national education action plan 1995-2000* (Sierra Leone Department of Education, 1995). The innovative plan within this for addressing the arcane teacher education and training sector is also discussed as a chapter 'Changing Patterns of Teacher Education in Sierra Leone' in Brock (1996). Some aspects of the legacy of structures and practices of teacher education and training in England have already been mentioned above. The resulting arrangements as they stood in the early 1990s were clearly inappropriate and unsustainable. What was needed was a reform that would recognise the realities of a situation where over half the teaching force in the primary sector was both unqualified for the job and also unqualified to enter the teacher training institutions with their colonially derived entry requirements. As has already been mentioned, the majority of staff in those institutions were in any case totally inexperienced in the realities of the primary sector in the rural environment of the disadvantaged majority population. At the same time, there was a pool of inactive but very able and willing retired head teachers who represented an ideal resource for addressing the problem.

So a plan was devised for a four-year part-time in-service Primary Teachers Certificate programme that would: (a) enable all the unqualified primary teachers to reach the technical level of a qualified teacher; (b) utilise the staff of the training colleges only for the area in which they were actually experienced (i.e. the academic dimension); and (c) utilise the existing head teachers and the pool of retired head teachers as the training agents (Brock, 1996, pp. 117-118). As the derived metropolitan model was still in operation for those qualified for it by virtue of having been to secondary school, it was important for the acceptance of the innovative programme for it to have the same number of contact hours and certain other equivalences. Sadly, this initiative was abortive in that the Projected IDA-4 funding failed to materialise due to the civil war reaching its peak and progress having to await the return of democratic government in 2000, when new plans of a more orthodox nature were devised. The main point of mentioning the proposed initiative here is that it recognised the imperative of employing 'on the job' (OTJ) methods of initial teacher education and training in the context of primary sectors of schooling where the majority of teachers are untrained.

OTJ was also supported by the Multi-Site Teacher Education Research (MUSTER) project report, the synthesis report of which was authored by Lewin & Stuart (2003) of the University of Sussex in the United Kingdom. Four of the five other institutions involved were in sub-Saharan Africa – in Ghana, Lesotho, Malawi and South Africa. OTJ surfaced mainly in the fifth case of Trinidad and Tobago, but was nonetheless recognised as having wider potential application in the context of sub-Saharan Africa, especially in the form of a pre-initial teacher training orientation course. The authors' comments on this have a clear resonance with the principles behind the plan mentioned above for Sierra Leone, though there was no connection. Lewin & Stuart list the 'key elements' of OTJ as:

- the participation of the school principal and mentor in the training
- learning practical elements in the classroom, supported by more   theoretical elements at induction, in vacations, evenings and weekends
- a phased introduction to teaching, through observation and team   teaching before taking over the class
- an introduction which offers basic skills, strategies and confidence- building, which can be complemented later by more substantial   academic and professional training.
(Lewin   & Stuart, 2003, p. 95)

Apart from the practical reality that a large proportion of primary school teachers in sub-Saharan Africa are unqualified but engaged as full-time staff, OTJ engages the everyday understanding of such teachers of the communities of which their pupils are part. A fair proportion of primary school teachers in the poorer countries of the region originate from urban areas where success at primary level is greater and some experience of secondary schooling more likely. Even if such teachers are willing to work in rural schools, they may well be less likely than local OTJ unqualified teachers to be in tune with the realities and cultural nuances of the survival communities in which they find themselves. It is not just a question of basic literacy and numeracy, for as Dachi & Garrett point out in respect of rural Tanzania:

Given that the life of the child in Tanzania is closer to that of an adult than it is in metropolitan societies, it is, therefore, sensible to look at the techniques that have been developed for working adults to assist them in accessing further education,

rather than solely trying to emulate Western style school
education. (Dachi & Garrett, 2003, p. 68)

In relation to this, locating teacher education and training facilities in
urban areas when the marginalised majority are mainly rural may well
not be for the best. In Botswana, one of the more stable and relatively
well-off of the sub-Saharan countries – albeit half is in the Kalahari
Desert – Patrick van Rensburg pioneered the admirable Botswana
Brigades initiative in the 1960s, whereby technical and vocational skills
could be acquired *in situ* in local communities. Partly due to the
products of this initiative migrating to urban areas to use their new skills
in gainful employment, many of the Brigades were in decline. In the mid
1990s, the government entered on a policy to enhance technical and
vocational education by creating a technical and vocational teacher
education and training programme. For political reasons, this was to be
focused on a new residential college to be constructed in Francistown,
the second settlement of Botswana, located near the northern border with
Zimbabwe. I was part of a team carrying out a feasibility study for the
funding agency, the European Commission (Scottish Development
Overseas & European Commission, 1998). The existing element of
government technical and vocational teacher education in Gaberone was
part of the study, as were the Brigades and the site that would be the
location of the technical and vocational teacher education and training
college in Francistown. At the time, the extraordinarily high incidence of
HIV/AIDS victims of all ages in Botswana made projections of the school
age population very difficult to determine, as well as the number of
school pupils who would survive the primary and secondary cycles.
Taking all this into account, and given the still existing network of
Brigades, plus the relatively well-developed ICT capacity of the country,
it was recommended that a network of facilities be created to support the
technical and vocational teacher education and training rather than
focusing the effort on a residential facility in Francistown. In the event,
the college was constructed but, between 2007 and 2010, the Botswana
Ministry of Education took over the network of Brigades as well, so
something approaching what was recommended seems to have been
created. The point here is that the initiative of local 'home-grown'
technical and vocational training was clearly so humanitarian in its
appropriateness that, despite difficulties encountered along the way, it
had developed an inertia that hopefully has been incorporated
successfully into a national sector.

Fundamental to the argument for a humanitarian response to the
provision of educational needs everywhere is the recognition of the
significance of communities. This is especially so in the rural worlds of
the marginalised majority of the population of sub-Saharan Africa, and is
very well recognised by the outstanding Teacher Education in Sub-
Saharan Africa (TESSA) project that is discussed in detail by Bob Moon

elsewhere in this volume. Many of the countries in the region have, or are still suffering, the incidence of conflict mentioned above. As detailed by Sullivan-Owomoyela & Branelly (2009), communities are fundamental to educational success through their active involvement in bringing all three modes of education together: formal, non-formal and informal. They engender the social and cultural capital necessary not only for survival, but also for meaningful sustainable development. This will include what the authors describe as both *bonding social capital*, inherent in a true community, and *bridging social capital*, meaning connections with local and national politico-administrative networks through association with NGOs and other agencies (Sullivan-Owomoyela & Branelly, 2009, p. 28).

Teacher education and training in all parts of sub-Saharan Africa needs to be part of this community scale of operation. This can be achieved by ensuring that part, if not all, of the process is culturally embedded, while also recognising developmental opportunities. NGOs, such as the Borien Educational Foundation for Southern Africa, can help this vital connection.

Conclusion

As with other sectors of formal education, teacher education and training has emerged in developed metropolitan nations having little meaningful connection with those other sectors or with non-formal and informal education. The transmission of such a discrete identity and approach, through colonialism and its legacy, to much less developed regions such as sub-Saharan Africa makes it doubly removed from the response to harsh challenges (environmental, economic, political) that is necessary – that is to say, a localised, holistic, humanitarian response. On top of this, much of the region has had to face, or is still facing, violent conflict or its aftermath. Here again a humanitarian response is needed. In the field of teacher education and training, there are examples of the flexible, radical thinking that is required to make the most of the inherent talents of community members. It is to be hoped that the mode of operation pioneered by TESSA, and other initiatives that make imaginative use of the potential of ICT to bridge the global and the local, will become the norm rather than the exception for teacher education and training in sub-Saharan Africa.

References

Brock, C. (1996) Changing Patterns of Teacher Education in Sierra Leone, in C. Brock (Ed.) *Global Perspectives on Teacher Education*, pp. 103-122. Oxford: Triangle Books.

Brock, C. (2011) *Education as a Global Concern*. London: Continuum.

Dachi, H.A. & Garrett, R.M. (2003) *Child Labour and Its Impact: a case study from Tanzania*. DfID Educational Paper No. 48. London: Department for International Development.

Davies, L. (2004) *Conflict and Education: complexity and chaos*. London: RoutledgeFalmer.

Davies, L. (2005) Schools and War: urgent agendas for comparative and international education, *Compare*, 35(4), 357-372. http://dx.doi.org/10.1080/03057920500331561

Dove, L. (1982) The Implications for Teacher Training of Conflicting Models of Community Schooling, in R. Goodings, M. Byram & M. McPartland (Eds) *Changing Priorities in Teacher Education*, pp. 101-114. London: Croom Helm.

Johnson, H.B. (1967) The Location of Christian Missions in Africa, *Geographical Review*, 57(2), 168-202. http://dx.doi.org/10.2307/213158

Lewin, K.M. & Stuart, J.S. (2003) *Researching Teacher Education: new perspectives on practice, performance and policy*. DfID Educational Paper No. 49a. London: Department for International Development.

Mebrahtu, T. (Ed.) (1984) *Learning from the South: what, why and how?* Bristol: Bristol Classical Press.

Moon, R. & O'Malley, B. (2008) *Every Child Needs a Teacher: the primary teacher supply and crisis in sub-Saharan Africa*. London: UK National Commission for UNESCO.

O'Malley, B. (2007) *Education under Attack*. Paris: UNESCO.

O'Malley, B. (2010) *Education under Attack*. Paris: UNESCO.

Pye, D. & Stephenson, J. (2003) *Using ICT to Increase the Effectiveness of Community-Based, Non-Formal Education for Rural People in Sub-Saharan Africa*. DfID Educational Paper No. 50. London: Department for International Development.

Scottish Development Overseas & European Commission (1998) *Report on the Eighth Vocational Training Programme: Francistown VTT/VTC Feasibility Study, Botswana*. Glasgow: Scottish Development Overseas & European Commission.

Sierra Leone Department of Education (1994) *Developing Basic Education and Training in Sierra Leone: a national education action plan 1995-2000*. Freetown: Government of Sierra Leone.

Sullivan-Owomoyela, J. & Branelly, L. (2009) *Promoting Participation: community contributions to education in conflict situations*. Paris & Reading: International Institute for Educational Planning & CfBT Education Trust.

UNESCO (2010) *Protecting Education from Attack: a state-of-the-art revue*. Paris: UNESCO.

UNESCO (2011) *EFA Global Monitoring Report. The Hidden Crisis: armed conflict and education*. Paris: UNESCO.

CHAPTER 2

Teacher Education in Sub-Saharan Africa: issues and challenges around teacher resources and practices

BOB MOON & FREDA WOLFENDEN

SUMMARY This chapter looks at the logistical challenge presented by the rapid increase in teacher numbers to meet Education For All targets. The analysis suggests that the growth is of such a magnitude that, for the foreseeable future, existing campus-based teacher education and training institutions will be unable to meet demand, in terms of pre-service, upgrading and in-service professional development programmes. The chapter sets out, therefore, the conditions under which school-based teacher development programmes can be implemented, including support systems, resource provision (including the use of open educational resources) and the use of new communication technologies. The analysis is exemplified by discussion of the Teacher Education in Sub Saharan Africa (TESSA) programme.

Most sub-Saharan African education systems are creaking under the strains of rapid expansion. This is particularly true of the structures through which countries educate and train teachers. The main argument of this chapter is that there is an urgent need to rethink the present approaches to, and mechanisms for, teacher education. Amongst all the variables that impinge on schooling, teacher quality is probably one of the most important and one where governments can make a difference. One survey (Moon, 2003) has shown that, in Europe, the vast majority of countries have introduced legislation and regulation to try to improve the quality of teacher education. In the USA, President Obama's first Secretary of Education, Arne Duncan, has moved rapidly to address the perceived failings of the teacher education institutions. He was quoted in the *New York Times* as saying: 'Many if not most of the nation's 1450

Schools, Colleges and Departments of Education are doing a mediocre job of preparing teachers for the realities of the 21st century classroom' (10 April 2010).

Similar concerns have been expressed in other parts of the world. Yet, in sub-Saharan Africa, where the need to improve teacher quality is most evident, there have been few substantive challenges to the status quo around teacher education and training. The extensive Multi-Site Teacher Education Research (MUSTER) project, led from the University of Sussex in the United Kingdom, summarised in its executive summary some of the difficulties:

> Teacher education appears to be one of the most conservative parts of many education systems. It seldom is the source of curriculum innovation, theorised pedagogy, or radical reconceptualisations of professional learning. It often lags behind schools in the adoption of new practice and patterns of learning and teaching. This is a signifier that political will and bureaucratic courage may be needed for the implementation of real changes designed to improve efficiency and effectiveness. (Lewin & Stuart, 2003, p. xxv)

South Africa is, perhaps, one example of a country that has attempted to move towards a more practical, outcomes-focused model, although evidence as to whether this has had any impact on teacher quality is hard to find.

The chapter is in two parts. The first provides an overview of the context of teachers in sub-Saharan Africa and sets out the consequences of this analysis for education and training. The second part looks in some detail at the Teacher Education in Sub-Saharan Africa (TESSA) programme, an initiative across nine countries which seeks to address some of the challenges facing teacher educators and policy makers in the region.

Analysing the Context of Teacher Education and Training in Sub-Saharan Africa

The number of additional teachers needed to achieve Education for All (EFA) targets is formidable. UNESCO, in its 2008 and 2009 Global Monitoring Reports (UNESCO, 2007, 2008), estimates the figure globally at 18 million teachers. And these figures do not assume any improvement in pupil-teacher ratios. Sub-Saharan Africa has the biggest ground to make up. As the 2009 UNESCO report makes clear, the increase required represents 145,000 posts annually, a step up of 77% compared to the recruitment achieved between 1999 and 2006 (UNESCO, 2008, p. 188).

The 2010 UNESCO report indicates that 1.2 million additional teachers will be needed to achieve EFA in the region. This is in addition to the recruitment needed to replace teachers who retire or move out of teaching. The deployment and distribution of teachers is also a concern. One study (Pôle de Dakar, 2009) has shown how rural areas, often associated with high levels of poverty, are particularly disadvantaged. These figures are for the primary sector alone. The expansion plans for post-primary will require parallel increases in the supply of more highly qualified subject teachers.

Teacher recruitment, however, is a challenge. This is a global problem (Moon, 2007) but it is at its most acute in low-income country contexts. The decline in salaries, particularly in comparison to newly emergent knowledge economy occupations, and in the status of teachers has been well documented (Colclough et al, 2003). The provision of adequate teacher training places is also problematic, particularly high-cost residential campus training. Teacher recruitment and training trails massively behind the expanding EFA provision. This shortfall, which has been endemic for many years, has led to the employment of millions of unqualified para-professional teachers across the region (often referred to as 'contract teachers'). A survey of 11 eastern and southern African countries by UNESCO (2000) indicated that one-third of existing primary teachers were untrained. Lewin (2002) has documented the shortfall in trained teachers that has arisen, and will become greater, if expansion to meet EFA targets continues. The Global Campaign for Education argues that:

> The education system in West Africa is increasingly the
> domain of 'para-teachers', with pre-service training of only a
> few months or even weeks. This is a direct attack on the
> quality education which all aspire and are entitled to. With the
> teacher crisis, quality has often been a hostage of quantity. The
> trend is to recruit as many teachers as possible, even if they do
> not have the necessary qualifications in order to respond to
> expanding enrolment. (Global Campaign for Education, 2006,
> p. 26)

Teachers are frequently cast as the weak link in the push for EFA, not the least following research that clearly links pupil achievement to the level of education and training received by class teachers (for example, Van der Berg & Louw, 2007). The 2005 Global Monitoring Report gave prominence to teachers:

> Achieving UPE [universal primary education] alone calls for
> more and better trained teachers. Countries that have achieved
> high learning standards have invested heavily in the teaching
> profession. But in many countries teachers' salaries relative to
> those of other professions have declined over the last two

decades and are often too low to provide a reasonable standard of living. Training models for teachers should be reconsidered in many countries to strengthen the school-based pre- and in-service training rather than rely on lengthy traditional, institutional pre-service training. (UNESCO, 2004, p. 3)

This was also recognised in the position paper produced for the launch of UNESCO's Teacher Training Initiative for Sub-Saharan Africa:

It is only now that people are starting to listen to those who saw the shortage of qualified teachers as a major impediment to national development and that national and international authorities are beginning to realize that the achievement of the Millennium Development Goals and the Education for All objectives depends on the training of professionals capable of the long-term effort to promote education effectively, in particular through the training of teachers and managerial staff in the education system. (UNESCO, 2006, p. 2)

The report of the Commission for Africa (2005, p. 186) made investment in teacher training a major recommendation and, in doing so, said: 'the push to achieve EFA will certainly never succeed without substantial investment in teacher recruitment, training, retention and professional development'. The crisis around teachers, however, is more than one of recruitment and training. Working conditions for many teachers are poor. HIV/AIDS, for example, is disrupting schooling across the region. A recent South African report (Education in Labour Relations Council, 2005) drew attention to its findings with the eye-catching headline: 'A Teacher Dies Every Two Hours'. In Kenya, where 14,500 teachers are estimated to be HIV-positive, between four and six teachers die of AIDS each day (Bennell, 2005). In Mozambique, HIV/AIDS kills over 1000 teachers each year (UNESCO, 2008).

Absenteeism is also a major concern in many education systems. In Uganda, for example, the teacher absentee rate in primary schools runs at 27%. The 2009 UNESCO Global Monitoring Report said that research studies 'suggest that teacher absenteeism is more pronounced in public sector schools, in schools with poorer infrastructures, in rural areas, in poorer states and in schools serving children from lower socio-economic backgrounds', and it goes on to say that '[h]igh levels of teacher absenteeism directly affect learning time and outcomes as well as national education costs and spending' (UNESCO, 2008, p. 121).

The relationship between teaching strategies and learner achievement is difficult to establish. The Centre for the Study of African Economies at the University of Oxford has published a paper (Aslam & Kingdon, 2007) which suggests that teacher qualification levels alone do not identify the factors that impact on achievement. They suggest that the usually unmeasured teaching process variables have an important impact on levels of attainment. The data indicates that lesson planning, involving students by asking questions and quizzing pupils on past material are strategies that do make a difference. The research was carried out in Pakistan but has implications for raising quality in the basic education sector more widely.

There is now also significant research evidence that the quality of education, not merely the provision of education, has significant social and economic consequences (Ramirez et al, 2006; Hanushek & Wößmann, 2007). In addition to this direct link with poverty alleviation, a number of specific studies have looked at the impact of schooling on girls' life chances. Quisumbing (1996), for example, found in Kenya that increasing the education and input levels of female farmers compared to those of male farmers could increase yields by as much as 22%. And a number of studies have shown that better educational provision for girls leads to lower infant mortality rates and a lowered incidence of HIV/AIDS (UNICEF, 2004).

The crisis around teachers, however, represents a complex interplay of factors and issues, as a number of analyses suggest (see, for example, Crossley & Watson, 2003). A number of studies provide evidence that many countries face a crisis of teacher morale, with poor salaries and difficult working conditions affecting the recruitment and retention of teachers (Bennell & Akyeampong, 2007; Department for International Development & Voluntary Service Overseas, 2008). The nature and extent of education, training and professional development is also an issue identified not only by teachers, but also by increasingly concerned members of local communities (Nelson Mandela Foundation, 2005). The education and training response can only be made on the basis of a full understanding of the crisis affecting all aspects of teachers' lives.

A number of education and training consequences flow from the teacher context, most specifically:

- The scale of the training need is so great that the 'bricks-and-mortar' institutions created to train teachers in the twentieth century will be insufficient to meet the needs of the twenty-first.
- The majority of training will inevitably be work- and school-based.
- Existing course structures and design need significant alteration to ensure an equitable distribution of training that is practically relevant to contemporary classroom situations.
- Given the urgent need to support teachers working in challenging environments, a much bigger commitment to in-service continuing professional development is essential.

This is not to suggest, in questioning the primacy in policy making of campus institutions, that colleges and universities will become redundant. Rather, the argument is being made that there is a need for repositioning and rethinking conventional provision to extend access and to improve quality. More distributed models of teaching and learning still require 'hubs' to organise provision and supply the essential support that professional preparation and development require. The need to develop shorter forms of pre-service education and training alongside better organised induction and in-service provision is urgent. Successive UNESCO Global Monitoring Reports have supported this. The report for 2005, for example, which brought the 'quality' issue to the fore, suggests that: 'Training models for teachers should be reconsidered in many countries to strengthen the school-based pre- and in-service training rather than rely on lengthy, institutional pre-service training' (UNESCO, 2004, p. 3). Universities and colleges, however, sometimes supported by teacher unions, have generally been resistant to such proposals.

In some countries, therefore, there are a minority of teachers experiencing a 'gold standard' two-, three- or four-year training, with a majority of teachers entering the classroom wholly unqualified. Millions of unqualified teachers are already working in schools. They need training and access to qualifications. Additionally, amongst those already qualified, there is a pressing need for better organised and more relevant professional support. If that is to be school-based, then it follows that some form of supported self-study (on an individual or whole-school staff basis) seems the only feasible and appropriate way forward. Course structures built around campus training models lack the flexibility and modularity necessary in part-time study. The curriculum of initial and continuing education and training also needs reviewing. The move towards more practically focused, outcomes-based, school-focused training can be seen in many teacher training systems worldwide (Moon, 2003).

Training structures and curriculum must be seen in a national context. In looking towards new policy approaches, however, the following seem relevant to the requirements of most countries:

1. The need to rethink the balance of resource distribution – for example, between pre-service and in-service professional development training.
2. The extent to which part-time (school-based) study is learner- or teacher-centred.
3. The relevance of established forms of the teacher education curriculum for those already in schools.
4. The appropriateness of traditional forms of assessment, particularly formal examinations, for those undertaking part-time (school-based) study.
5. The 'portability' of study in ways that allow teachers to move from one community to another, whilst continuing professional development courses.

6. The advisability of rethinking the role and the training of those who become teacher educators.
7. The potential for seeing teacher education and training as a holistic part of the economic and social development of local communities, renewing or recreating the sense of moral purpose or vocation traditionally associated with a profession.

The United Nations Task Force on Education and Gender Equality, in looking at progress to EFA, suggested that: 'Insufficient education of inadequate quality cannot be effectively addressed solely by "business as usual", that is expanding existing systems' (Birdsall et al, 2005, p. 83). Teachers are key to any reform. But serious challenges remain. The rapid expansion of education systems is creating difficulties in establishing coherent teacher supply policies. Broader social and economic trends (for example, public sector salary levels and widening alternative employment opportunities) are impacting on teacher retention. In some parts of the world, HIV/AIDS is problematic. Teacher education systems are experiencing strains from these and other trends at a time when many countries are looking for pedagogic reforms and improvement. The interrelation of these factors within a context of rapid social change is creating a significant development problem for policy makers at all levels.

From this analysis a number of consequences grow. First, there is the issue of scale. The bricks-and-mortar institutions, created to train teachers in the twentieth century, can in no way meet the needs of the present century. That is not to say there is no place for 'campus' institutions. We believe there is, although the nature of the role needs, we believe, rethinking (Moon et al, 2000). Second, teacher training policies and systems have to embrace the concept of 'school-based' provision. There is an urgent need to improve the quality of teachers already in the schools. The data suggests that at least one in three teachers in the primary phase across sub-Saharan Africa is seriously underqualified (Lewin & Stuart, 2003). Many have had no training at all, coming into schools as volunteers to try to provide an adult presence in the expanding school system. Third, it follows that if there is a recognition that support for teachers already based in schools is important, then a curriculum of teacher education and training needs to be devised that acknowledges this. Across the world, there has been a move towards more practically focused teacher training (Moon, 2007), and the need for this in sub-Saharan Africa is of great importance. It is out of these considerations that the TESSA programme has developed.

The TESSA Programme

The TESSA idea grew from a number of collaborative initiatives that sought to improve the quality of school-based training programmes and respond to the challenges described in the first part of this chapter. The aim was, through cooperative endeavour, to provide resources and advice that could be used to expand teacher education and improve the quality of the programmes offered. TESSA's purpose is to provide a rich source of classroom and practically focused teacher resources allied to advice on the policy and practice issues associated with implementation. TESSA is, in one sense, a grass-roots consortium in that the initiative for collaboration was taken at the local institutional level. Strong links, however, are maintained with governments and international agencies, such as UNESCO and the United Kingdom's Department for International Development.

Members of the TESSA consortium were aware that expanding teacher education involves growing the number of teacher educators. There is very little preparation and training for this role. The provision of high-quality resources, therefore, would give essential intellectual supports to those training teachers. The resources, in one sense, act as a toolkit from which programme planners can develop programmes specific to context.

Pedagogic

The TESSA consortium, through a series of workshops, set out a number of parameters within which they wanted the pedagogic resources to develop. These included:

- a focus on the core teaching tasks of the primary teacher, making practice the prime curriculum focus;
- an emphasis on active learning on the part of the teacher with plentiful examples of classroom activities;
- a common structure to the study units, providing users with a familiar teaching and learning approach;
- the need to explicitly define expected learning outcomes;
- the importance of promoting collaborative working between teachers.

The first curriculum areas developed were in literacy, numeracy, science, life skills and social studies. All the study units incorporated activities that had to be practical and classroom-based.

The TESSA resources, particularly the teaching activities, take account of the lives and working contexts of teachers in many low-income countries. Large classes, for example, are likely to be a feature of school practice for some time. Teaching classes of 60 or 80 pupils involves some ingenuity if moves towards active pupil participation are to be embraced. The TESSA resources set out practical ideas as to how this can be approached. If space, for example, inhibits group work, then strategies involving pairs can be an alternative. The contrary situation of small, multi-grade classes equally presents a pedagogical challenge. The ways in which schools can use the local environment and local community as a resource are given special attention, which is essential where books and other resources are at a minimum.

TESSA has used over 100 African authors and academics to create the materials. From a generic framework, all of the resources have been adapted to local country needs. Such adaptation happens at a number of levels. At one level, the straightforward but important differences in names, flora and fauna across the continent need to be taken account of. At a deeper level, differences of pedagogic tradition or curriculum regulation have to be acknowledged. All the resources exist in four languages (Arabic, English, French and Kiswahili). Whilst the consortium does not have any mandated approach to teaching and learning, there is a broad recognition that active rather than passive learning is key. TESSA, therefore, seeks to promote this through the full range of pedagogic strategies and methods used.

Technical

From the outset, TESSA planned to create a web environment that could be easily accessed by teacher educators across the region. Connectivity and access, despite significant progress, still remain an issue, particularly for teachers. TESSA set out, therefore, to offer support through the latest technologies, but with a means of publishing resources in traditional formats. All TESSA resources are available online and in downloadable formats. Although the resources in the two forms address common issues, the content of each, given the medium of delivery, is slightly different. The TESSA website is aimed at teachers and teacher educators. The latter, currently, are the more likely to be accessing online, although increasing numbers of teachers can do so. The development of mobile technologies in the next few years is likely to rapidly expand online capacity.

TESSA wholeheartedly embraces the increasingly significant ideas of the Open Educational Resource (OER) movement. All resources are freely available for anyone to adapt, whether for profit or not, through the Creative Commons licensing process. Institutions within the consortium have already carried out significant adaptation and, in the process, created one of the world's largest OER sites dedicated to teacher education and training.

The design of the web environment involved extensive consultation and took place over a two-year period from 2005-07. There were a number of technical problems − for example, the design of a site that could adapt to multiple languages. The consortium was also committed to creating multimedia resources and these had to be made available in a variety of formats. This process is now complete and the TESSA website is open to anyone.[1] Each country has a dedicated place on the site and a variety of forums and idea-exchange activities are under way. The technical cost represents an investment that can support future development and is also available for replication by similar projects.

Take-up and Evaluation

TESSA, as an extensive OER environment, has another distinctive feature: the emphasis that is placed on take-up and implementation. From the outset, the TESSA consortium was determined to avoid the fate of other projects where resource production, rather than use, had dominated programme design. The consortium has therefore devoted considerable time to workshops, information exchanges, expert visits and a range of other activities to support the varied forms of implementation being adopted by the participating institutions.

At every meeting of the consortium, representatives share their use and implementation experiences, revisit progress and contribute strategies for future use. Table I gives some examples of the way TESSA is being used.

Country/ institution	Course	Pre-service or in-service	Delivery mode	Number of teachers
Ghana				
University of Cape Coast	Bachelor of Education	Pre-service	Campus-based	400
	Diploma in Basic Education	In-service	Distance learning with campus-based lectures	
University of Education, Winneba	Bachelor of Education	Pre-service	Campus-based	
	Professional Diploma in Mentoring	In-service	Self-study	
Kenya				
Egerton University	Bachelor of Education Primary	In-service	Distance learning with campus-based lectures	500

Nigeria

National Teachers' Institute	Millennium Development Goals Teacher Retraining	In-service	Face-to-face workshop	5000
	Teacher Orientation	In-service	Face-to-face workshop	45,000
	State Teacher Retraining	In-service	Variable, predominantly workshops	145,000
	Nigeria Certificate in Education (NCE)	In-service	Distance learning/face-to-face tutorials	80,000

Rwanda

Kigali Institute of Education	Bachelor of Education	In-service	Campus-based, face-to-face	370

South Africa

University of Fort Hare	School of In-Service Programmes (SISP): Advanced Certificate in Education (ACE)	Pre-service and in-service	Campus delivered	
	SISP: National Professional Diploma in Education (NPDE)	Pre-service and in-service	Campus delivered	
	SISP: Bachelor of Education	Pre-service and in-service	Campus delivered	
University of Pretoria	Bachelor of Education (on campus)	Pre-service	Campus-based, face-to-face	1800
	Bachelor of Education (distance)	In-service	Distance learning/CD-ROM	1700
University of South Africa (UNISA)	Bachelor of Education	In-service	Distance learning	

Bob Moon & Freda Wolfenden

Sudan				
The Open University of Sudan	Bachelor of Education Primary	In-service	Distance learning/study centres	1500/ 1400
Tanzania				
The Open University of Tanzania	Diploma in Primary Teacher Education	In-service	Distance learning	500
Uganda				
Kyambogo University	Diploma in Education Primary External	In-service	Distance learning with three fortnightly face-to-face sessions each year	First year: 858 Second year: 1493
Makerere University	Bachelor of Education (distance)	In-service	Distance learning	
Zambia				
University of Zambia	Bachelor of Education Primary	In-service	Face-to-face on campus but can do first year at distance	

Table I. Illustrative examples of TESSA implementation.
Source: TESSA Programme Office.

The building blocks – the study units represented by TESSA's open educational resources – can be used for many interrelated purposes. Pre-service, upgrading and in-service professional development programmes are all represented in the TESSA implementation programme. National teacher upgrading programmes – for example, in countries such as Sudan and Nigeria, which are now implementing TESSA – extend to hundreds of thousands of teachers. In Nigeria, the TESSA resources and approach have been incorporated into the manuals for use by students in all the colleges of education. It is important to stress that TESSA serves face-to-face as well as open and distance learning courses and programmes.

In 2010, over 300,000 teachers were using the TESSA programme. This is expected to rise to half a million in 2011. In addition to the core TESSA institutions, over 100 other teacher training institutions have become affiliates to the programme. Dissemination of the TESSA approach, resources and experience is being carried forward on a number of fronts. In 2009, TESSA won for The Open University in the United Kingdom the Queen's Anniversary Award for Higher Education.[2] As an OER initiative, the resources are freely available for anyone to use. Most recently, the consortium has seen take-up and adaptation for use in Togo.

Research

TESSA represents a large-scale research and development initiative. All aspects of the programme contribute to the research and publication profile. Much of the contextual conceptual thinking has been incorporated in policy papers prepared for a range of organisations (see, for example, Moon, 2007; Moon & Singh, 2010), which, building on the sort of analysis set out in the first part of this chapter, proposes a framework for rethinking the structure and curriculum of teacher education. The working of the consortium and the programme also constitutes an intervention process that requires reflection. This has been examined in a number of ways, including in a Commonwealth of Learning publication (Moon, 2010), upon which some parts of this chapter have been based. Aspects of the programme have been the subject of specific enquiries. The collaborative process of resource adaptation to local country contexts is one example (Thakrar et al, 2009).

From the outset, TESSA established a core research activity focused on depicting the way teachers in different parts of sub-Saharan Africa perceived their role, what their working lives were like and how these factors impacted on teacher motivation. There was a particular instrumental purpose in this. The consortium wanted the resource authors and programme designers to empathise with those they were writing and planning for. There was also an awareness, however, that the research around teachers tended to focus on macro-statistical analyses or single-issue problems (for example, absenteeism or HIV/AIDS). What is important in these studies is that they fail to create a holistic interpretation of the lives of teachers, hence the title 'Teachers' Lives' was given to this aspect of the activity. The first publication of the project, *Pride and Light: female teachers' experiences of living and working in rural sub-Saharan Africa*, involved an ethnographic study with the researcher spending extended periods of time in the schools, communities and homes of teachers in Ghana, Kenya, Nigeria, South Africa and Sudan (Buckler, 2009). The title, taken from the Nigerian proverb, 'An oil lamp feels proud to give light even though it wears itself away', reflects the outcomes of the study, which shows how motivated many teachers are, despite onerous working conditions.

The work on teachers' lives is now being taken further, including the building of a newly theorised basis to the work. The worlds of education research and development research tend to be rather separate.

Bob Moon & Freda Wolfenden

The Teachers' Lives project is seeking to build bridges between theoretical traditions and contemporary ideas. For example, whilst the education literature around teacher identity is rich, it has primarily concerned high-income countries. And the current interest in capability theory in development research has only recently been applied to education (Walker & Unterhalter, 2007; Tao, 2009). This perspective is important to the TESSA programme and has been the focus of a number of research papers and seminars. The most recent study (Buckler, 2011) took the lives of two teachers in Kenya and Nigeria (Esther and Bilkisu) as a starting point for analysis:

> capturing teachers' voices and capturing stories of teachers' lives, like Bilkisu's and Esther's, provides policy makers with valuable tools for advocacy and for the promotion of issues. Teachers' narratives, and the narrative of ethnographic description, can be at once simple and powerful. For those not directly involved with all the complexities of the teacher issue, teachers' voices bring numbers to life. Teachers' voices provide a lens through which to see the real heart of an issue. (Buckler, 2011, p. 212)

It is towards these purposes that the TESSA research programme is directed.

The TESSA consortium and programme are now well established and a range of further funded activities is being launched. These include:

- the development of TESSA resources for secondary science teachers;
- exploration of how TESSA can embrace the emergent world of mobile technologies more fully;
- a country-focused development seeking to attract women in rural communities in Malawi into teaching.

Perhaps most significantly, TESSA now has funding to work closely with a project, OER Africa [3], which is being run by the South African Institute for Distance Education, a member of the TESSA consortium. OER Africa seeks to help in the revitalisation of the higher education sector generally, within which teacher education now has a major role. TESSA, of its own accord, cannot meet the huge needs and demands of teachers for education and training, but it does provide one model, one part of a response to the challenge, within which, and from which, others can build.

Notes

[1] See http://www.tessafrica.net
[2] See http://www.royalanniversarytrust.org.uk/

[3] See http://www.oerafrica.org/.

References

Aslam, M. & Kingdon, G. (2007) *What Can Teachers Do to Raise Pupil Achievement?* Centre for the Study of African Economies, Working Paper Series No. 273. Oxford: University of Oxford.

Bennell, P. (2005) *Teacher Mortality in Sub-Saharan Africa.* Brighton: Knowledge and Skills for Development.

Bennell, P. & Akyeampong, K. (2007) *Teacher Motivation in Sub-Saharan Africa and South Asia.* DfID Educational Paper No. 71. London: Department for International Development.

Berg, S. van der & Louw, M. (2007) *Lessons Learnt from SACMEQII: South African student performance in regional context.* Department of Economics and Bureau for Economic Research Working Paper 16/07. Stellenbosch: University of Stellenbosch.

Birdsall, N., Levina, R. & Ibratim, A. (2005) *Towards Universal Primary Education: investments, incentives and institutions.* London: Earthscan.

Buckler, A. (2009) *Pride and Light: female teachers' experiences of living and working in rural sub-Saharan Africa.* Milton Keynes: Teacher Education in Sub-Saharan Africa.
http://www.tessafrica.net/images/stories/pdf/tessateacherslives.pdf

Buckler, A. (2011) Reconsidering the Evidence Base, Considering the Rural: aiming for a better understanding of the education and training needs of sub-Saharan teachers, *International Journal of Educational Development,* 31(3), 244-250. http://dx.doi.org/10.1016/j.ijedudev.2010.04.003

Colclough, C., Al-Samarrai, S., Rose, P. & Tembon, M. (2003) *Achieving Schooling for All in Africa.* Aldershot: Ashgate.

Commission for Africa (2005) *Our Common Interest.* London: Commission for Africa.

Crossley, M. & Watson, K. (2003) *Comparative and International Research in Education: globalisation, context and difference.* London: Routledge.
http://dx.doi.org/10.4324/9780203452745

Department for International Development (DfID) & Voluntary Service Overseas (VSO) (2008) *Listening to Teachers: the motivation and morale of education workers in Mozambique.* London: DfID & VSO.

Education in Labour Relations Council (2005) *The Health of Our Educators: a focus on HIV/AIDS in South African public schools.* Cape Town: Education in Labour Relations Council.

Global Campaign for Education (2006) *Teachers for All: what governments and donors should do.* London: Global Campaign for Education.

Hanushek, E.A. & Wößmann, L. (2007) *The Role of Education Quality in Economic Growth.* Washington, DC: World Bank.
http://dx.doi.org/10.1596/1813-9450-4122

Lewin, K.M. (2002) The Costs of Supply and Demand for Teacher Education: dilemmas for development, *International Journal of Educational Development*, 22(3/4), 221-242. http://dx.doi.org/10.1016/S0738-0593(01)00060-8

Lewin, K.M. & Stuart, J.S. (2003) *Researching Teacher Education: new perspectives on practice, performance and policy*. London: Department for International Development.

Moon, B. (2003) A Retrospective Review of the National Case Studies on Institutional Approaches to Teacher Education, in B. Moon, L. Vlasceau & L.C. Barrows (Eds) *Institutional Approaches to Teacher Education within Higher Education in Europe: current models and new developments*. Bucharest: UNESCO.

Moon, B. (2007) *Research Analysis: a global overview of current policies and programmes for teachers and teacher education*. Paris: UNESCO.

Moon, B. (2010) Creating New Forms of Teacher Education: open educational resources (OERs) and the Teacher Education in Sub-Saharan Africa (TESSA) programme, in A. Umar & P.A. Danaher (Eds) *Teacher Education through Open and Distance Learning*. Vancouver: Commonwealth of Learning.

Moon, B., Brown, S. & Ben-Peretz, M. (2000) *Routledge International Companion to Education*. London: Routledge.

Moon, B. & Singh, M. (2010) *Researching the Role of the University in Teacher Education in Sub-Saharan Africa*. Milton Keynes: Open University.

Nelson Mandela Foundation (2005) *Emerging Voices*. Cape Town: HSRC Press.

Pôle de Dakar (2009) *Universal Primary Education in Africa: the teacher challenge*. Education Sector Analysis. Dakar: UNESCO Regional Office for Education in Africa (BREDA).

Quisumbing, A.R. (1996) Male-Female Differences in Agricultural Productivity: methodological issues and empirical evidence, *World Development*, 24(10), 1579-1595. http://dx.doi.org/10.1016/0305-750X(96)00059-9

Ramirez, F.O., Luo, X., Schofer, E. & Meyer, J.W. (2006) Student Achievement and National Economic Growth, *American Journal of Education*, 113, 1-29. http://dx.doi.org/10.1086/506492

Tao, S. (2009) *Applying the Capability Approach to School Improvement Interventions in Tanzania*. EdQual Working Paper, Quality No. 11. Bristol: University of Bristol.

Thakrar, J., Zinn, D. & Wolfenden, F. (2009) Harnessing Open Educational Resources to the Challenges of Teacher Education in Sub-Saharan Africa, *International Review of Research in Open and Distance Learning*, 10(4). http://www.irrodl.org/index.php/irrodl/article/view/705.

UNESCO (2000) *Education for All 2000 Assessment: statistical document*. Paris: UNESCO.

UNESCO (2004) *EFA Global Monitoring Report 2005. Education for All: the quality imperative*. Paris: UNESCO.

UNESCO (2006) The Teacher Training Initiative for Sub Saharan Africa. Unpublished paper. Paris: UNESCO.

UNESCO (2007) *EFA Global Monitoring Report 2008. Education for All by 2015: will we make it?*. Paris: UNESCO & Oxford University Press.

UNESCO (2008) *EFA Global Monitoring Report 2009. Overcoming Inequality: why governance matters.* Paris: UNESCO & Oxford University Press.

UNESCO (2010) *EFA Global Monitoring Report 2010. Reaching the Marginalized.* Paris: UNESCO & Oxford University Press.

UNICEF (2004) *Girls, HIV/AIDS and Education.* New York: UNICEF.

Walker, M. & Unterhalter, E. (2007) *Amartya Sen's Capability Approach and Social Justice in Education.* New York: Palgrave Macmillan. http://dx.doi.org/10.1057/9780230604810

CHAPTER 3

Contradictions in Teacher Education and Teacher Professionalism in Sub-Saharan Africa: the case of South Africa

CLIVE HARBER

SUMMARY This chapter is primarily concerned with the processes and structures of teacher education in Africa and their relationship to desired outcomes in terms of democratic values and behaviour. Based on evidence from Africa, it argues that, rather than there being a gap between the more democratic practices learned in teacher education and the authoritarian realities of schooling itself, the former in reality is actually a congruent preparation for the latter. The chapter then puts forward three categories of teacher professionalism in Africa and argues that teacher education needs to move from its current emphasis on more restricted and authoritarian forms of professionalism to more extended and democratic forms.

Introduction

Schooling in Africa tends to be characterised by poor quality:

> On the face of it, the news on educational development in Africa, especially when assessed against indicators such as 'good quality of education for all', appears to be grim. Indeed, for many countries the sheer task of overhauling what are, to a large degree, dysfunctional systems of education is so overwhelming that it is difficult to think in terms of changes and progress. (Johnson, 2008, p. 7)

Both schools and teacher education in Africa face serious issues of resource input and learning outcomes (Lewin & Stuart, 2003; Verspoor,

2008). However, this chapter is primarily concerned with the processes and structures of teacher education and their relationship to desired outcomes in terms of values and behaviour. The dominant pattern of schooling in Africa is not only often of poor quality but its processes and structures, despite frequent aspirational government policy statements to the contrary, usually tend to be authoritarian in nature, being characterised by hierarchical organisation, transmission teaching and teacher-centred classrooms, often reinforced by corporal punishment (Harber, 2004, ch. 2, 5; 2009, ch. 15, 16).

This is despite the fact that many countries in sub-Saharan Africa now refer to themselves as democracies, however imperfect the transition from one-party and military rule has been in some contexts (Gyimah-Boadi, 2004). However, it has long been a theme of political science that democracy is only sustainable in a supportive political culture where a sufficient proportion of the population has a high commitment to democratic values, skills and, particularly, behaviours (Almond & Verba, 1963). Such an understanding is based on a view of democracy that goes beyond the minimum ritual of voting (or not voting) every four or five years in an election. While democracy does require an informed citizenry capable of making genuine political choices, it is reinforced by a fuller and deeper notion of democracy that forms the basis of a democratic *society* in which people actually behave in a democratic manner in their daily interactions (Carr & Hartnett, 1996, ch. 2).

Moreover, in a world where democracy is increasingly becoming a global phenomenon (Holden, 2000) and is recognised as a key aim of development (Sen, 1999), formal education should also be essentially democratic in nature, even though in practice it often is not. One key obstacle to schooling playing a greater role in education for democratic citizenship appears to be teacher education and, in many countries of Africa, as elsewhere, teacher education is a part of the problem of authoritarian education rather than the solution. This is because teacher education tends to perpetuate traditional, unreflective and teacher-centred pedagogy rather than challenge it. Over 30 years ago, Bartholemew (1976) put forward the idea of the 'myth of the liberal college' – that is, a myth that there is a contradiction between the liberal, progressive and democratic college or university, on the one hand, and the traditional, conservative and authoritarian school, on the other. This myth suggests that student teachers are exposed to the more radical, democratic forms of teaching and learning during their courses in higher education, with a high emphasis on learner participation, but are rapidly re-socialised into more authoritarian understandings and practices during their teaching practice and their subsequent employment in education. Rather than there being a contradiction between the two – in terms of power over what is taught and learned, how and when, let alone the contradiction between 'do as I say and do as I do' – it is argued that, in reality, teacher education is often an authoritarian and reproductive preparation for teaching in schools.

In Europe, North America, Australia and New Zealand, it has been argued that in recent decades this situation has hardened as teacher education has been subject to the increasing influence of a neoconservative ideology of control and a neo-liberal ideology of competition and accountability. The result is a combination of markets, standardisation, regulation and measurable outcomes. This, it is argued, has led to a situation of uniformity, conformity and compliance and the prescription of alignment, consensus and consistency through bureaucratic and authoritarian control, a position which is antithetical to democratic participation (Delandshere & Petrosky, 2004; but see also Griffiths, 2000; Hartley, 2000; Apple, 2001; Cochran-Smith, 2001). There have been a few exceptions to this model of teacher education that have tried to provide both a critical social and political perspective on education and more democratic and participatory experiences for student teachers (Harber & Meighan, 1986; Zeichner & Liston, 1987; Beyer, 2001; Bankov, 2007), but they remain a very small minority.

The Myth of the Liberal College in Africa

While much has been written on teacher education policy, official teacher education curricula, teacher supply and demand, and models of teacher education generally (on the United Kingdom and North America, see, for example, Hartley & Whitehead, 2006; on South Africa, see Lewin et al, 2003), we have relatively little systematic, reliable knowledge of the daily reality of teacher education – its internal practices and processes, consistencies and contradictions (Berry, 2004; Robinson & McMillan, 2006). In particular, we know little about the micropolitical dimension of teacher socialisation in relation to education for democracy – its daily practices, processes and relationships of curriculum, pedagogy, evaluation, and rewards and sanctions (Ginsburg & Lindsay, 1995, p. 8).

However, what we do know suggests that in Africa the myth of the liberal college in teacher education helps to perpetuate a circle of authoritarian reproduction, and there is evidence of a gap between what teacher educators say they do in their teaching and the perceptions of student teachers about their experiences. For example, one publication on Africa examined evidence from Botswana, Zimbabwe and Uganda. A detailed study of teacher education in Botswana, for example, found that students complained that time and again lecturers told them to use child-centred methods when teaching in schools but did not use the methods when teaching them. The students provided examples of lecturers who adhered to the lecture method as a matter of principle even when inappropriate because lecturing was the one method that epitomised the intellectual status of a tertiary institution. Another study of teacher education in Zimbabwe found that teaching in colleges of education was overwhelmingly lecturer-centred and authoritarian, with regular examples of dictation of notes word for word. As a result, there was little difference between the schools and teacher education. In a study of a teacher education college in Uganda, the students said that they most frequently experienced didactic teaching methods, whereas the tutors gave the opposite answer. As a result, teacher education is an un-virtuous circle of authoritarian reproduction (see Harber, 1997, ch. 7).

While there have been some attempts to introduce more democratic methods into teacher education, which are discussed below, elsewhere not much seems to have changed. The Multi-Site Teacher Education Research (MUSTER) project was the first major study of teacher education in developing countries – including Ghana, Lesotho, Malawi and South Africa – since the 1980s. Where its findings are relevant to the present discussion, they very much correspond with the above analysis (Lewin & Stuart, 2003). Teaching resembled traditional high school teaching methods and was lecture-based, with most teaching following a transmission style with question and answer. Overall, the studies found that the curriculum in teacher education was informed by a conservative, authoritarian ideology where debate and critical reflection were not encouraged. This reality was at odds with the principles of participatory, learner-centred and enquiring pedagogy often frequently espoused in curriculum documents of the teacher education institutions. Indeed, there seemed to be a kind of collusion between tutors and trainees, who knew little else from their schooling, to maintain the transmission mode because students found project work 'difficult' and group work 'less useful'.

The MUSTER project published three case studies from Africa. Without it being the central research focus, each of these commented on the seeming predominance of lecturer-centred, transmission teaching, an emphasis on recall, and a discouragement of independent learning and reflective practice. There is also a significant gap between the priority given to abstract academic theoretical knowledge in colleges and universities as opposed to the practical skills and application of knowledge also required to succeed in the reality of the classroom. The study on Ghana noted:

> Both student teachers and newly qualified teachers stressed
> that the most commonly used instructional approach in
> college was 'lectures with tutors dictating notes'. Rarely, it
> appears, were opportunities created for more interactive 'small
> group' work or discussions that would place much of the
> responsibility for developing personalised understanding of
> teaching on trainees. (Akyeampong, 2003, p. viii)

In teacher education in Malawi:

> Much learning is undertaken in a transmission style where
> information is projected with few opportunities for students to
> engage in debate and reflection. Questions were often
> informational and recall-based and much of the teaching
> appeared examination-driven, rarely departing from material
> likely to be found in assessment tasks. Few attempts seem to
> be made to capitalise on trainee insights into teaching and
> learning based on their experience in schools.
> (Kunje et al, 2003, p. xiii)

While in Lesotho:

> Classroom observation confirmed the conservative nature of
> the programme in that, in practice, most teaching at the
> College is transmission-oriented, and there is little emphasis
> on independent learning, critical analysis, creative thought or
> learning to exercise professional judgement. The interaction
> between students and tutors during lectures involves a
> question-answer approach but questions are restrictive and do
> not allow for full independent thinking for students.
> (Lefoka & Sebatane, 2003, p. x)

Lewin & Stuart make a distinction between teacher education as preparing the 'teacher as technician' and training the teacher as a 'teacher as reflective practitioner':

> The technician is seen as having a restricted role, her job being
> to deliver the curriculum – which is prescribed at a higher
> level – as effectively as possible, while the reflective
> practitioner is expected to play a more extended role, that may
> include developing the curriculum to suit the context,
> evaluating and trying to improve her own practice, and
> mentoring new teachers. (Lewin & Stuart, 2003, p. 63)

In practice, much of teacher education in Africa is currently not only aimed at producing the teacher as technician, but also still tends to be based on the one-way transmission of large chunks of predetermined academic knowledge rather than the exercise and practice of a range of classroom and whole-school skills. The main skill that is learned is being able to transmit in a didactic manner. Lewin & Stuart (2003, p. 73) also point out that gender issues were seldom foregrounded or discussed in teacher education, an issue of some importance given the levels of sexual harassment of girls that exist in African schools, further discussed below.

Teacher Professionalism

At the heart of teacher education, whether initial or in-service, should be shaping teacher professional identity and practice. In analysing and discussing observations of lessons and interviews in an evaluation of a quality education project in four African countries – Ethiopia, Zambia, Mozambique and Zimbabwe (Harber & Stephens, 2009) – three broad and overlapping categories of teacher professionalism in the African context emerged, based on an earlier study in the Gambia (Davies et al, 2005, pp. 35-39). These tend to have the following characteristics:

1. *Unprofessional*: absenteeism; unplanned lessons; the teacher has more than one job; instances of sexual abuse; strong use of corporal punishment; isolated; hostility to, and distance from, children.
2. *Restricted professional*: teachers are concerned with the mastery and exercise of technical skills in the classroom; a concern with basic competence; teacher-centred; a tendency to blame children for not learning; little continuing professional development; unimaginative or routine teaching; occasional use of corporal and psychological punishment; rigid; individualised; instrumental; rewards to teachers extrinsic.
3. *Extended professional*: teachers use autonomous and independent judgement to reflect on what they are doing; teachers do not just follow the rules but take active responsibility for themselves and their pupils; child-centred; a variety of methods; collaborative; trusting; very little or no corporal punishment; part of the continuing professional development support system; adaptive; flexible; rewards to teachers intrinsic.

It must be borne in mind, first, that this is a continuum of ideal types and that real classroom behaviour may have characteristics from one or more, and, second, that teachers can move up and down the continuum. However, there is much evidence that the critical mass of teachers in Africa tend to operate generally at the unprofessional or restricted level of professionalism in an occupation often hampered by poor training, lack of resources, low or unpaid salaries and low levels of continuous professional development (Harber & Davies, 1997; Harber & Stephens, 2009).

The shift from an unprofessional/restricted professional to an extended one also means a move from the present situation of authoritarian professionalism to a more democratic form of professionalism. Given the current, generally authoritarian nature of much schooling in Africa, a professional teacher is one who can perform his or her role according to the characteristics of this set of power relationships – controlling the classroom agenda and discourse; keeping control in the classroom and wider school; enforcing rules made without pupil consent; carrying out punishment; enforcing attendance at school;

implementing the curriculum as designed by a government; and ensuring uniform and uniformity in appearance. However, in Africa, while schooling tends to be bureaucratic and authoritarian in its formal organisation, this often actually operates in a messy and inefficient way because of the nature of developing societies (for a full discussion of this, see Harber & Davies, 1997). As a result, lip service may be paid to Western notions of 'professionalism' among teachers, but the reality is often very different.

However, the teacher is also sometimes a violent professional, being involved in both the active reproduction and perpetration of violence against pupils. For example, corporal punishment is still widely used in African schools, as in many countries elsewhere (Harber, 2004, ch. 5; 2009, pp. 124-128). The World Health Organization reports that corporal punishment in schools in the form of hitting, punching, beating or kicking remains legal in at least 65 countries, despite the fact that the United Nations Committee on the Rights of the Child has underlined that corporal punishment is incompatible with the Convention. It notes that: 'Where the practice has not been persistently confronted by legal reform and public education, the few existing prevalence studies suggest it remains extremely common' (World Health Organization, 2002, p. 64). In a further range of countries where it has been officially banned, such as South Africa (Nelson Mandela Foundation, 2005), it is still in use in many schools. This suggests that corporal punishment is regularly used in schools in between at least one-third and one-half of all countries in the world. In Africa, the same tensions exist around the question of abolition. In a survey of 45 educationalists at a seminar on education for democracy in the Gambia, the following statement about corporal punishment was included: 'Corporal punishment should be completely abolished.' Eighteen of the respondents agreed/strongly agreed with this statement whereas eleven disagreed/strongly disagreed, again suggesting that while the majority of this group (a group interested in, and generally supportive of, more democratic forms of education) were opposed to corporal punishment, a significant minority were not (Harber, 2006).

Sexual harassment and abuse of female pupils in schools is also a widespread problem in sub-Saharan Africa, or at least the problem is well documented for that region (Leach et al, 2003; Harber, 2004, ch. 6; Leach & Mitchell, 2006). Similar sexual harassment of female students by tutors was found in a study of teacher education in Ghana (Tengi-Atinga, 2006). The main cause of sexual harassment and violence in schools is that traditional gender stereotypes and unequal power relationships are not challenged but reproduced by the school and in teacher education. Moreover, the authoritarian, closed nature of much of schooling, meshed with patriarchal values and behaviours, provides a context in which the patterns of sexual harassment described above can happen. As a Plan (2008, p. 6) report on violence in schools says: 'Girls in societies where women are accorded a lower or more passive status (and where practices such as infanticide, female genital cutting and honour killings take place) are more likely to suffer sexual violence at school'. The report also points out that unless teachers themselves have been educated about gender and power issues, they are likely to model behaviour that reflects their own experiences and those of the wider community. It goes on to note that a South African survey found that 47% of female teachers in a pilot project had suffered physical abuse at the hands of an intimate partner, and 25% of male teachers admitted that they had been physically abusive to an intimate partner (Plan, 2008, p. 26). A survey of South African and English teacher education students found that few had studied or discussed gender issues, including the nature of masculinity, either at school or in their teacher education (Harber & Serf, 2006).

The Democratic Professional

What, then, if a society wishes to move away from authoritarian forms of teaching and learning and school organisation towards more democratic forms? Here, the problem is not just moving from unprofessional teachers to professionals who at least turn up and plan their lessons but operate in an authoritarian manner, but to create a new, democratic form of professionalism. There are important issues and lessons stemming from the notion of the democratic professional for all education systems or institutions genuinely interested in promoting democracy and human rights.

One five-year project in the Gambia tried to develop values and skills associated with education for democracy both at the pre-service level through the only teacher education institution and through the whole education system by working with inspectors in all six educational regions of the small state. The national policy context was favourable. The 2004 education policy document emphasises the importance of creating, through education, 'an awareness of the importance of peace, democracy and human rights, and the responsibility of the individual in fostering these qualities' (Department of State for Education, 2004, p. 13). While the project met with enthusiasm among participants overall and there was evidence of mixed success in terms of outcomes, it did reveal in considerable detail the kind of contextual cultural, historical and institutional tensions and barriers that would need to be worked through if more democratic forms of education were to be established in a sustained manner with full government and donor support in the long term (Schweisfurth, 2002b; Harber, 2006).

South Africa, however, is a country which since 1994 has attempted to create new, democratic forms of education in order to develop a political culture supportive of its democratic, post-apartheid constitution

(Harber, 2001). Post-apartheid education policy has been based on an explicit commitment to education for democracy. For example, the *Manifesto on Values, Education and Democracy* provides a comprehensive and detailed official account of how democracy can and should be applied to all sectors and modes of education across the system as a whole (Department of Education, 2001). The South African Department of Education is clear that the goal must be to create teachers who are democratic professionals:

> he or she is expected to play a community, citizenship and pastoral role, to practise and promote a critical and committed and ethical attitude towards developing a sense of respect and responsibility towards others, uphold the Constitution and promote democratic values and practices in schools and society. (Department of Education, 2001, p. 28)

The South African Council for Educators' code of conduct for South African teachers calls on teachers to

> acknowledge that the attitude, dedication, self-discipline, ideals, training and conduct of the teaching profession determine the quality of education; acknowledge, uphold and promote basic human rights ... act in accordance with the ideals of their profession ... In other words, to have internalised the ten fundamental values of the South African Constitution themselves and to act as role models for their students. (Department of Education, 2001, p. 29)

Commenting on the South African Council for Educators – a statutory body charged with regulating the teaching profession – two reviewers noted that:

> The locus of its strength lies in the drive for professionalism among educators, the sensitivity to the unequal power relations that exist between educators and learners (and among educators themselves) and the commitment to ideals of democracy and human rights. (Barasa & Mattson, 1998, cited in Jansen, 2004, p. 56)

However, democratic reform has not been introduced into a vacuum and there are important lessons to be learned in terms of teacher response based on notions of role, identity and professionalism. In 1997, the Deputy Minister of Education had this to say:

> In many of our education departmental offices, there is a chronic absenteeism of officials, appointments are not honoured, punctuality is not observed, phones ring without being answered, files and documents are lost, letters are not responded to, senior officials are inaccessible, there is

confusion about roles and responsibilities and very little
support, advice and assistance is given to schools ... Many of
our parents fear their own children, never check the child's
attendance at school, are not interested in the welfare of the
school, never attend meetings, give no support to the teacher
or principal ... Many of our teachers are not committed to
quality teaching, their behaviour leaves much to be desired,
are more interested in their own welfare, are not professional
and dedicated, are never at school on time, pursue their
studies at the expense of the children, do not prepare for
lessons ... Many of our children are always absent from school,
lack discipline and manners, regularly leave school early, are
usually late for school, wear no uniform, have no respect for
teachers, drink during school hours, are involved in drugs and
gangs, gamble and smoke at school, come to school armed to
instil fear in others ... Many of our principals have no
administrative skills, they are the source of conflict between
students and teachers, sow divisions among their staff,
undermine the development of their colleagues, fail to
properly manage the resources of their school, do not involve
parents in school matters. This has resulted in chaos, poor
decisions, lack of imagination and a total collapse of the
education system in many schools ... Many of our schools have
no electricity, no water, no toilets, no libraries, no laboratories,
no furniture, no classrooms, no teachers, no buildings, no
windows, no pride and no dignity. (Mkhatshwa, 1997)

As this suggests, the physical conditions in schools, the values and
behaviour of staff and students, and the intrusion of violence from the
wider society are not seen as conducive to an effective, safe and
professional school environment in which genuine transformation can
take place. Yet,

the entire edifice designed to transform South African
education will stand or fall on the basis of support offered to
teachers in the implementation of the policy as well as the
extent to which the support deals with teacher beliefs and
assumptions, and not only the outward signs of practice.
(Harley et al, 2000, p. 301)

Teachers are key actors in educational reform in South Africa and
elsewhere. Understanding teachers' present beliefs, understanding and
practices – their identity – is important if policy implementation is to be
successful and if in-service courses are to be suitably designed to
facilitate change. While some of these beliefs are discussed below, it is
important to bear in mind that a commitment to teaching as a profession
may not form a strong part of all teachers' personal identity. The

National Teacher Education Audit in 1994 stressed that many students in teacher education colleges did not have a genuine desire to teach and, similarly, in a study of teacher voice which included interviews from a sample of 68 South African teachers, more than half attributed purely instrumental reasons related to salary, status, the desire to urbanise and the attainment of qualifications to their choice of teaching as a career. For these teachers, 'the teacher was a person whom socio-economic circumstances had conspired to choose' (Jessop & Penny, 1998, p. 396).

The same study also found that there was considerable nostalgia for an imagined golden age in which children respected elders and certainty prevailed. For some South African teachers, nostalgia for the old order was coupled with suspicion of the new and radical democratic values accompanying the end of apartheid. There were difficulties for some teachers in reconciling the contradictions of the collapse of apartheid (a good thing) with the breakdown of traditional values (a bad thing). Evidence suggests that there remains quite a low level of critical consciousness among teachers. Under apartheid, teachers were expected to follow rules and implement prescriptive curricula established from above. Their job was to obey orders and not to be creative.

Related to the need for certainty is a tendency for South African teachers to see knowledge as composed of incontestable and objective facts to be transmitted for memorisation. Harley et al's study of ten 'effective' teachers at six 'resilient' schools in the Pietermaritzburg education authority in KwaZulu Natal suggested that as a result of this view of knowledge, the teachers were less likely to recognise learners' own experiences as worthwhile resources and to make use of interactive teaching methods such as classroom discussion and debate, therefore closing off most opportunities for developing critical and creative thinking: 'In short, teachers' own epistemologies left them rather uneasily at odds with the requirements of both curriculum and teachers' roles' (Harley et al, 2000, p. 295).

Finally, even when teachers are well aware of and understand the requirements of government policy, they may disagree with it and prefer their own views, beliefs and experience as a basis for behaviour and action. The study by Harley et al, for example, found that teachers' comments reflected some of the practical complexities arising from the contradictions between policy expectations and the culture and personal value systems of the teachers. When asked by a researcher whether he personally believed in gender equality, one teacher, a union official who was knowledgeable about the rights of teachers and learners, said: 'Never ever! As a man, I believe I am and will always be superior to a woman. Our culture is consistent with this view.' There was also some resistance to the government's promotion of the role of the teacher as a key person in community development, and six out of ten of the teachers taught at schools which still used corporal punishment, despite the fact that it was illegal. There was also some active resistance to the idea of pupils as critical learners: 'The new policy is good but there will be conflict between the government and the Zulu rural community. If children become more critical they will start to question their parents' authority and adopt values that conflict with their community' (Harley et al, 2000, pp. 295-296).

Schweisfurth (2002a, pp. 76-82) found that, in practice, South African teachers reacted in a number of ways to democratic reform:

- Reflective mediation, where teachers thought about the reforms and then decided on the degree and nature of their compliance.
- Personal identity crisis and protection, where teachers were going through a crisis as their personal and professional identities formed under the old regime were threatened under the new regime.
- Espoused theory and theory in use, where teachers were vocally supportive of the changes but this was not reflected in their practices.
- Persistent continuities and strange hybrids, where old habits died hard but where these were sometimes mixed with new approaches.
- Frustration and demoralisation, where teachers could not resolve competing imperatives of traditional professional identity, the cultural and resource issues they faced, and the demands of new legislation.
- The Ostrich response, where teachers denied the existence of reform.
- Strategic compliance, where teachers complied because they felt they had no choice and would be punished if they did not.

The consequence is that, overall, as another study concluded:

> teachers are caught in anxieties of transition, feeling trapped in the 'old' and wanting to work in the 'new' ways. They also lack the professional autonomy and competence to fulfil what is officially expected of them ... South African teachers do not currently see themselves as 'owning' the transformation of education in South Africa but as subjects of it. They also do not see themselves as formulators of policies but implementers of them, which are handed down to them from on top ... teacher education in South Africa would need to prioritise the sense of professionalism and autonomy of teachers as well as their role to inform and formulate policies as much as their own rights as human beings within a democracy are emphasised. Failure to achieve these aims in teacher development is likely to result in acute feelings of disempowerment and demoralisation of the teaching corps, albeit now ironically within a democratic educational dispensation. (Carrim, 2003, p. 319)

Finally, teacher education does not necessarily seem to help in a process of developing democratic professionalism as there is a wide gap between policy and practice. Educational policy documents are overt and explicit in their support for democracy. Yet a study of initial teacher education students (Harber & Serf, 2006) found contradictions between 'do as I say' and 'do as I do' – lecturers did not necessarily provide a good role model for the development of democratically professional teachers. Moreover, in a society openly seeking to transform its education system in a democratic direction, the failure of teacher education to work with students on teaching controversial issues in the classroom was particularly serious because all curriculum subject matter is potentially controversial and education for democratic citizenship cannot avoid the controversial. The study concluded that in South Africa, the implementation of a democratic policy framework seems hampered by inertia, inexperience and other priorities in the teacher education system, and argued that it was perhaps necessary to ask, 'Who educates the educators?' and 'Who trains the trainers?' – i.e. 'How can a sufficient cadre of teacher educators able to work in a more democratic manner be developed in South Africa?'

Conclusion

There is a need overall for more discussion of, and research on, both the purposes and goals of teacher education and the issue of their congruence with internal processes and practices. This chapter has identified the issue of the contradiction between the stated aims of teacher educators in terms of what should be happening in schools and their own practice. This has implications for teacher professionalism, particularly in relation to attempts to move from more restricted, authoritarian forms of professionalism to a more democratic professional. In Africa, there may well be a need for more and better managed resources in teacher education, but there is also a need to consider and provide for the type of teachers that a system wishes to produce, and therefore the skills and practices required of teacher educators.

References

Akyeampong, K. (2003) *Teacher Training in Ghana: does it count?* London: Department for International Development.

Almond, G. & Verba, S. (1963) *The Civic Culture.* Princeton: Princeton University Press.

Apple, M. (2001) Markets, Standards, Teaching and Teacher Education, *Journal of Teacher Education*, 52(3), 82-96.
http://dx.doi.org/10.1177/0022487101052003002

Bankov, K. (2007) The Influence of the World Educational Changes on the Teacher Education System in Bulgaria, *Oxford Comparative Studies in Education*, 17(1), 75-96.

Bartholemew, J. (1976) Schooling Teachers: the myth of the liberal college, in G. Whitty & M.F.D. Young (Eds) *Explorations in the Politics of School Knowledge*. Driffield: Nafferton Books.

Berry, A. (2004) Self-Study in Teaching about Teaching, in J. Loughran, M. Hamilton, V. LaBoskey & T. Russell (Eds) *International Handbook of Self-Study of Teaching and Teacher Education Practices*, vol. 2. Dordrecht: Kluwer.
http://dx.doi.org/10.1007/978-1-4020-6545-3_34

Beyer, L. (2001) The Value of Critical Perspectives in Teacher Education, *Journal of Teacher Education*, 52(2), 151-163.
http://dx.doi.org/10.1177/0022487101052002006

Carr, W. & Hartnett, A. (1996) *Education and the Struggle for Democracy: the politics of educational ideas.* Buckingham: Open University Press.

Carrim, N. (2003) Teacher Identity: tensions between roles, in K.M. Lewin, M. Samuel & Y. Sayed (Eds) *Changing Patterns of Teacher Education in South Africa*. Sandown: Heinemann.

Cochran-Smith, M. (2001) Constructing Outcomes in Teacher Education, *Education Policy Archives*, 9, 11. http://epaa.asu.edu/epaa/v911.html.

Davies, L., Harber, C. & Schweisfurth, M. (2005) *Democratic Professional Development*. Birmingham: Centre for International Education and Research & CfBT Education Trust.

Delandshere, G. & Petrosky, A. (2004) Political Rationales and Ideological Stances of the Standards-Based Reform of Teacher Education in the US, *Teaching and Teacher Education*, 20(1), 1-15.
http://dx.doi.org/10.1016/j.tate.2003.09.002

Department of Education (2001) *Manifesto on Values, Education and Democracy*. Pretoria: Government Printer.

Department of State for Education (2004) *Gambia Education Policy*. Banjul: Government Printer.

Ginsburg, M. & Lindsay, B. (1995) *The Political Dimension of Teacher Education: comparative perspectives*. London: Falmer Press.

Griffiths, V. (2000) The Reflective Dimension in Teacher Education, *International Journal of Educational Research*, 33(5), 539-555.
http://dx.doi.org/10.1016/S0883-0355(00)00033-1

Gyimah-Boadi, E. (Ed.) (2004) *Democratic Reform in Africa*. London: Lynne Rienner.

Harber, C. (1997) *Education, Democracy and Political Development in Africa*. Brighton: Sussex Academic Press.

Harber, C. (2001) *State of Transition: post-apartheid educational reform in South Africa*. Oxford: Symposium Books.

Harber, C. (2004) *Schooling as Violence*. London: RoutledgeFalmer.

Harber, C. (2006) Democracy, Development and Education: working with the Gambian inspectorate, *International Journal of Educational Development*, 26(6), 618-630. http://dx.doi.org/10.1016/j.ijedudev.2006.02.004

Harber, C. (2009) *Toxic Schooling*. Nottingham: Educational Heretics Press.

Harber, C. & Davies, L. (1997) *School Management and Effectiveness in Developing Countries*. London: Cassell.

Harber, C. & Meighan, R. (1986) Democratic Learning in Teacher Education: a review of experience at one institution, *Journal of Education for Teaching*, 12(2), 163-172.

Harber, C. & Serf, J. (2006) Teacher Education for a Democratic Society in England and South Africa, *Teaching and Teacher Education*, 22(8), 986-997.

Harber, C. & Stephens, D. (2009) *The Quality Education Project: an evaluation for Save the Children, Norway*. Oslo: Save the Children, Norway.

Harley, K., Barasa, B., Bertram, C., Mattson, E. & Pillay, S. (2000) The Real and the Ideal: teacher roles and competences in South African policy and practice, *International Journal of Educational Development*, 20(4), 287-304. http://dx.doi.org/10.1016/S0738-0593(99)00079-6

Hartley, D. (2000) Shoring up the Pillars of Modernity: teacher education and the quest for certainty, *International Studies in the Sociology of Education*, 10(2), 113-131. http://dx.doi.org/10.1080/09620210000200058

Hartley, D. & Whitehead, M. (2006) *Teacher Education: major themes in education*, 4 vols. London: Routledge.

Holden, B. (Ed.) (2000) *Global Democracy: key debates*. London: Routledge.

Jansen, J. (2004) Autonomy and Accountability in the Regulation of the Teaching Profession: a South African case study, *Research Papers in Education*, 19(1), 51-66. http://dx.doi.org/10.1080/0267152032000176972

Jessop, T. & Penny, A. (1998) A Study of Teacher Voice and Vision in the Narratives of Rural South African and Gambian Primary School Teachers, *International Journal of Educational Development*, 18(5), 393-404. http://dx.doi.org/10.1016/S0738-0593(98)00039-X

Johnson, D. (Ed.) (2008) *The Changing Landscape of Education in Africa: quality, equality and democracy*. Oxford: Symposium Books.

Kunje, D., Lewin, K. & Stuart, J. (2003) *Primary Teacher Education in Malawi: insights into practice and policy*. London: Department for International Development.

Leach, F., Fiscian, V., Kadzamira, E., Lemani, E. & Machakanja, P. (2003) *An Investigative Study into the Abuse of Girls in African Schools*. London: Department for International Development.

Leach, F. & Mitchell, C. (Eds) (2006) *Combating Gender Violence in and around Schools*. Stoke-on-Trent: Trentham Books.

Lefoka, J. & Sebatane, E. (2003) *Initial Primary Teacher Education in Lesotho*. London: Department for International Development.

Lewin, K.M., Samuel, M. & Sayed, Y. (2003) *Changing Patterns of Teacher Education in South Africa*. Sandown: Heinemann.

Lewin, K.M. & Stuart, J.S. (2003) *Researching Teacher Education: new perspectives on practice, performance and policy.* DfID Educational Papers No. 49a. London: Department for International Development.

Mkhatshwa, S. (1997) Speech delivered at Culture of Learning, Teaching and Service Campaign Consultative Conference, Johannesburg, 22-24 August.

Nelson Mandela Foundation (2005) *Emerging Voices.* Cape Town: HSRC Press.

Plan (2008) *The Global Campaign to End Violence in Schools.* Woking: Plan.

Robinson, M. & McMillan, W. (2006) Who Teaches the Teachers? Identity, Discourse and Policy in Teacher Education, *Teaching and Teacher Education*, 22(3), 327-336. http://dx.doi.org/10.1016/j.tate.2005.11.003

Schweisfurth, M. (2002a) *Teachers, Democratisation and Educational Reform in Russia and South Africa.* Oxford: Symposium Books.

Schweisfurth, M. (2002b) Democracy and Teacher Education: negotiating practice in the Gambia, *Comparative Education*, 38(3), 303-314. http://dx.doi.org/10.1080/0305006022000014160

Sen, A. (1999) *Development as Freedom.* Oxford: Oxford University Press.

Tengi-Atinga, G. (2006) Ghanaian Trainee Teachers' Narratives of Sexual Harassment: a study of institutional practices, in F. Leach & C. Mitchell (Eds) *Combating Gender Violence in and around Schools.* Stoke-on-Trent: Trentham Books.

Verspoor, A. (2008) The Challenge of Learning: improving the quality of basic education in sub-Saharan Africa, in D. Johnson (Ed.) *The Changing Landscape of Education in Africa: quality, equality and democracy.* Oxford: Symposium Books.

World Health Organization (WHO) (2002) *World Report on Violence and Health.* Geneva: WHO.

Zeichner, K. & Liston, D. (1987) Teaching Student Teachers to Reflect, *Harvard Educational Review*, 57(1), 23-48.

CHAPTER 4

What Hope for the Dakar Goals? The Lower Levels of Education in Lesotho and Uganda since 2000[1]

JAMES URWICK & ROSARII GRIFFIN with
VERONICA OPENDI & MATEMOHO KHATLELI

SUMMARY This chapter draws attention to the tendency for the 'Education for All' goals endorsed by the Dakar Forum to be overshadowed by the narrower agenda of the Millennium Development Goals (MDGs) as they relate to education. With reference first to Lesotho and then to Uganda, the chapter reviews progress made towards the educational MDGs of universal primary education and gender parity and then the relatively limited achievements in relation to the Dakar goals for early childhood education, quality in primary education and provision for special educational needs. The authors argue for a more comprehensive approach to educational development: one which recognises the important links between primary education and other sub-sectors.

Introduction: the Dakar goals and their context

The new millennium was the occasion for a reaffirmation of globalised development goals. In the year 2000, the Education for All (EFA) goals of *The Dakar Framework for Action* and the multi-sector Millennium Development Goals (MDGs) were endorsed in rapid succession by most of the world's governments (UNESCO, 2000; United Nations, 2000). However, the New York meeting somewhat overshadowed the one in Dakar and this chapter will argue that the same 'overshadowing' by the MDGs has continued to be one of the problems for the Dakar agenda in low-income countries. The MDGs select and restate the second and fifth EFA goals, concerned with universal primary education (UPE) and the elimination of gender disparities in education, but do not explicitly incorporate any of the others. Furthermore, references to quality and to 'children in difficult circumstances' are 'trimmed' from the UPE goal in the MDG context. While the other 'non-educational' MDGs all have important implications for educational development, these implications have not, as King (2009) points out, received the amount of analytical attention that might have been expected.

The MDGs have been said to reflect an increased degree of consensus among the major donor agencies – and especially between the World Bank and United Nations (UN) agencies – about development priorities and strategies (Robertson et al, 2007). The World Bank has widened its social agenda, while the UN agencies are said to have become more supportive of market strategies (Cammack, 2006). But such a consensus is less evident in some national settings. Lesotho and Uganda, on which we focus in this chapter, are both low-income countries: the gross national product per capita in 2006 is reported as US$980 for Lesotho and US$300 for Uganda (UNESCO, 2008).

We consider that in these two examples of low-income countries, international agencies have continued since 2000 to be somewhat divided, as they were in the 1990s, in their perspectives on educational goals. In practice, World Bank representatives and some bilateral aid agencies have tended to treat UPE and 'gender parity' in education (the latter lacking a clear definition) as the essential, minimum agenda for educational development, regarding the rest of the EFA goals as an idealist agenda of less practical importance. Representatives of UNICEF, UNESCO and some non-governmental organisations (NGOs) have shown more interest in the other EFA goals. The national ministries of education may have been under 'essentialist' pressures from their own ministries of finance as well as major aid donors of the first group.

While we accept that there has been considerable monitoring of progress towards the EFA goals vis-à-vis attention to their sustainability (King, 2009), we do not consider that the progress towards these goals in Lesotho and Uganda has been balanced or coherent. From our own experience in these countries, we are surprised by the optimism of King's (2009, p. 175) assertion that EFA Goal 3 (on meeting the learning needs of young people and adults) is the only one to have proved elusive. The evidence for our view will be apparent in the sections which follow. Insufficient or minimal progress towards several of the goals is linked to the way in which the UPE goal has been hastily pursued in both countries, through policies of free primary education (FPE), dating from 1997 in Uganda and 2000 in Lesotho. As Lewin (2007, p. 595) puts it: 'some targets interact in a zero sum way' to a certain extent. But in situations of great dependence on external funding, as in these two countries, much also depends on the willingness of donors to take on additional commitments and the ability of national governments to make the case for them. There have been great limitations in both respects.

In addition to the MDG problem already stated, a second contributory factor has been the lack of attention to the organic links between the EFA goals themselves. In the *Dakar Framework*, the goals, strategies and targets for each subsector of education are all stated discretely. This design responded to the demands of many agencies and NGOs with specific agendas of 'rights' and 'needs', but in the process the idea of planning a national system of education as a coherent whole seems to have been lost. If there was, in this respect, a collective retreat from rationality at the Dakar Forum, it may have been partly attributable to a loss of faith in earlier approaches to planning, especially those favouring 'user charges' for basic education. FPE policies were also introduced in Sierra Leone in 2000, Zambia in 2002 and Kenya in 2003 (Commonwealth Secretariat, 2003, p. 10).

There are potential developmental links between the education subsectors and between the EFA goals relating to each which, although widely known, should receive more attention from policy makers. Some progress has been made in the last few years in the study of the issues of coordination and interdependence of the expansion of primary education, on the one hand, and that of secondary, tertiary and non-formal education, on the other (see, for example, Lewin, 2005, 2008). In studying the prospects for education to contribute to poverty reduction, Palmer et al (2007, p. 92) make the general point that '[e]xcessive emphasis on the MDG target of Universal Primary Education (UPE) is not necessarily "pro-poor" or "anti-poverty" in the long run, given the crucial multi-way synergies between all levels of the education and training system'.

The present chapter focuses on a set of links between goals which have received rather less attention: those between the educational MDGs, on the one hand, and the EFA goals for early childhood education, quality in primary education and provision for special educational needs (SEN), on the other. Several considerations encourage this focus. Firstly, there is a growing body of research evidence that, in poorer as well as richer countries, more widely available early childhood education has the potential to increase the effectiveness of primary education. The evidence from Mwaura et al (2008) and Taiwo & Tyolo (2002) is relevant to eastern and southern Africa. Secondly, the recent UPE programmes spurred by international agreements have not avoided the problems of acute shortages of resources that were associated with previous UPE initiatives. Thirdly, there are grounds for supposing that investment in special and inclusive education helps to reduce wastage in primary education and encourages pedagogy that is useful for a wide range of learners. Many of the teaching strategies advocated for SEN have a wider application and do not necessarily depend on abundant resources (Baine, 1991; Mitchell, 2008). Overall, there is a case for more public investment in early childhood and special needs education within the general EFA framework, even if this entails more cost-sharing in other areas.

One can only have limited faith in policy documents, but, if the links between the EFA goals had been well articulated in *The Dakar Framework for Action*, it would have been more difficult for national governments and their 'development partners' to treat them as selectively as they have done. In the two sections which follow, we shall outline the problem of selective treatment in two low-income countries. The final section will reflect on the general implications for policy and planning.

Developments in Lesotho: progress towards the educational MDGs

Lesotho has been able to show impressive quantitative progress since 2000 in relation to the educational MDGs of UPE and gender parity. With regard to UPE, the 2009 Global Monitoring Report shows the gross enrolment rate (GER) for primary education in Lesotho to have increased from 102% in 1999 to 114% in 2006 and the net enrolment rate (NER) from 57% to 72% in the same period (UNESCO, 2008, p. 307). Among Commonwealth countries, this increase in NER was surpassed only by Tanzania, which abolished tuition fees in 2001. In presenting these figures, we are conscious of the work of Akyeampong (2009), which illustrates with reference to Ghana the problems that may accompany this kind of expansion.

The gender parity indices associated with the GER fell from 1.12 in 1999 to 1.04 in 2006, showing an improved share of participation for boys in a country where they have traditionally been diverted from school to carry out herding duties. In the same period, the gender parity index associated with the GER for secondary education fell from 1.35 to 1.27, indicating a more modest reduction in boys' disadvantage (UNESCO, 2008, pp. 307, 331). The latter may diminish further as a result of the change at the primary level.

From 2000 to 2006, tuition fees were removed incrementally, one grade at a time, in nearly all primary schools. This FPE programme resulted in a surge in participation, especially by boys, with a bulge of over-age children entering school in 2000. But there are two reservations to be stated. Firstly, the FPE policy was reinforced by a revival of free school meals in the lowlands (World Bank, 2005) and the surge in participation is likely to have been enhanced by this factor. Secondly, the apparent achievement of gender parity in relation to the GER for primary education conceals some complex imbalances. The gross intake rate has been higher for boys, at 105%, compared with 99% for girls in 2006 (UNESCO, 2008), and boys repeat grades more than girls do, but girls still complete primary education in larger numbers than boys. (The last two points are based on trends in the statistics of the Ministry of Education and Training for 2000-05.)

These minor imbalances notwithstanding, the most important types of disparity in Lesotho's primary education do not relate to gender, but to location within the country, especially according to the level of accessibility and to individuals with disabilities. Regional disparities in quality and outcomes are illustrated by Urwick (2011). The more mountainous districts, which were previously very disadvantaged with regard to access (Gay & Hall, 2000), have made great gains in GER, but may not compare well with other districts in NER. For lack of the necessary data, the differences between districts in NER cannot be measured at present. The gender parity index is the quotient of the statistics in question for females and for males, with the female statistic as the numerator. While the government of Lesotho has made commendable efforts to assist orphaned children (for example, a second meal is supplied to some of them through the school), children with disabilities remain very disadvantaged in terms of access even to primary education (Lesotho College of Education, 2007).

With the exception of the gender imbalance in secondary education, Lesotho's most serious educational problems lie not so much in the areas of the educational MDGs as in those of the EFA goals that are not explicitly supported by the MDGs. As we have indicated, three of these areas will be considered, both for Lesotho and for Uganda.

Early Childhood Education

The first EFA goal is the expansion and improvement of early childhood education, which in low-income countries has tended to be an 'orphan', neglected both by the state and by the household. In the period immediately after independence, this metaphor was relevant to Lesotho, but an administrative unit for early childhood care and development was established within the Ministry of Education and Training in 1985. In keeping with the holistic approach to child development favoured by the international agencies, the activity has now been renamed 'integrated early childhood care and development' (IECCD). (This is the name favoured by UNICEF in particular.) The approach implies a need to involve the health and social welfare authorities, as well as those of education.

In recent years, the policy of the Ministry of Education and Training for this level of the educational system (in principle for children aged three to five) has contained two, somewhat contradictory, strands. The first strand, represented in the *Education Sector Strategic Plan 2005-2015* (Ministry of Education and Training, 2005), is one of capacity-building and monitoring for community-based and home-based IECCD centres. The second, mentioned very briefly in the plan but now emphasised more, is one of attaching reception classes to selected primary schools. We shall comment on each of these strands.

There is a considerable demand for early childhood care and development in Lesotho, in rural as well as urban areas, enhanced by female employment in the textile industry and by the childcare problems occasioned by the HIV/AIDS pandemic. The level of participation is probably higher than the GER of 18% given by the 2009 Global Monitoring Report for 'pre-primary education' in 2006 (UNESCO, 2008, Table 3B), but not as high as the 33% claimed by the Ministry of Education and Training in that year – a claim made at a National Dialogue on Education in 2006.

Most of this participation has been in the IECCD centres and, for these, the IECCD Unit has been making a determined attempt to improve both access and quality, but with minimal resources. Until 2008, the government's role was limited to the provision of a curriculum, some monitoring and some in-service training. Community-based teachers receive very minimal pay from their communities, while home-based teachers work on a voluntary basis. There are between 1500 and 2000 of these teachers/carers, who are nearly all untrained and poorly educated. Of 1521 IECCD teachers for whom data were obtained in 2005, 53% had no more than a primary leaving qualification. Only 3.1% had a teaching qualification or a degree. As of 2008, according to the head of the IECCD Unit, these were supported by just 13 paid officers ('national teacher trainers'), 7 Peace Corps volunteers and about 40 volunteer resource teachers ('district teacher trainers').

The dearth of resources at this level is underlined by the funding gaps shown in the *Education Sector Strategic Plan* of the Ministry of Education and Training (2005, p. 39). For the year 2007-08, for example, if we exclude the proposed subsidies of M70 million for children with special needs, there are projected costs of M16.14 million (about US$2 million) and projected resources of M8.30 million (giving a gap of M7.84 million). In the costs, nothing is specified for teacher training or for subsidies to private providers.

In order to mitigate this situation, UNICEF has for some years provided financial support for in-service teacher training. Another intervention has been that of the Lesotho College of Education, which in 2007 started an in-service programme of training and certification for IECCD teachers. Since 2008, too, the government of Lesotho has begun to pay the fees of orphans and vulnerable children in the IECCD centres, though not all of them.

The actual focus of the government of Lesotho's policy for IECCD has been on the second strand: the establishment of reception classes, for children aged five to six, attached to primary schools. This began with 12 in 2006 and increased to 220 in 2009. This is, in itself, a positive development, especially as many children have hitherto entered primary education above the proper age of six. But the practice of funding this development from the IECCD budget (including donor contributions for that level), as opposed to that of primary education, is questionable. Another problem is that reception class teaching, which offers slightly higher pay, is absorbing the more successful teachers from the IECCD centres, including those receiving training at the Lesotho College of Education. Thus, the reception classes draw resources away from the IECCD centres, which are serving a wider age group. It is arguable that the reception classes should be funded as part of primary education and that, as they are established in all primary schools, the length of the main primary cycle should be reduced from seven years to six (the pattern in many other countries).

Another issue is the inequitable manner in which the reception classes have been distributed. They were piloted first in primary schools managed by the government (less than 10% of the total) and then mainly in 'community' primary schools (also a very small group), ostensibly on the grounds that this ensured control and quality. After this approach had been criticised, others (the last 100) were attached to church primary schools, which constitute nearly 90% of the total. Pupils admitted to the so-called 'community schools', some of which are fee-paying aided schools, are more likely in any case to have attended an early childhood centre beforehand.

These contradictory strands of policy have some parallels in Malawi (Kholowa & Rose, 2007), but the bias of policy and funding is clearer. The facts suggest that the government of Lesotho is more interested in making the start of primary education more effective, and in the process making its own primary schools more competitive, than it is in supporting child development generally at ages three to five. If the latter were the goal, the central policy issue for this level of education would be the type of partnership to be established between the state and the local community in order to provide a more comprehensive and effective service. But, contrary to the strategies recommended in the *Dakar Framework*, the government of Lesotho and its major development partners seem reluctant to engage in that kind of partnership.

Quality in Primary Education

The sixth EFA goal places emphasis on quality and on learners' achievement, but in Lesotho, as in a number of other countries, the FPE policy has not been compatible with this goal, at least in the short and medium term. Even though the government of Lesotho introduced FPE incrementally, one grade at a time, it has been a 'crash programme' involving greatly increased public commitments. As tuition fees were removed, the government took on new commitments to provide free school meals (in the lowlands), learning materials and (in principle) school maintenance, as well as paying for additional teachers. The effects of FPE on the quality of primary education in Lesotho have been similar to those of contemporary FPE policies in Malawi and in East Africa, and to those of earlier UPE schemes launched in countries such as Nigeria and Kenya. The pace of growth made it more or less inevitable that existing shortages of qualified teachers, classrooms, learning materials and supervisory support would become more severe. The outcomes were also disappointing for many pupils. In the context of FPE Lesotho's primary education system continued to have a very high level of wastage, with a weighted average repetition rate of 20% in the period 1999-2004 (analysis of Ministry of Education and Training, annual education statistics). The survival rate, to the end of primary education, of the first FPE cohort (of 2000) was the worst ever at 46.8% (data from the Ministry of Education and Training). The Southern and Eastern Africa Consortium for Monitoring Educational Quality (SACMEQ) II report (Mothibeli & Maema, 2005) showed the levels of literacy and numeracy of primary pupils in Lesotho to be rather low in the regional context.

Fundamentally, FPE has depended on a policy of recruiting a large number of unqualified teachers and gradually training them by in-service methods. Thus, the proportion of qualified teachers at the primary level declined from 78% in 1999 to 64% in 2004 (based on the Ministry of Education and Training annual educational statistics). UNESCO (2008, Table 10B) gives a 'trained proportion of 66% for 2006. For its policy of 'hire now and train later', the government of Lesotho was able to obtain important support, both technical and financial, from the World Bank. Perhaps encouraged by research which suggests that pupils' achievement at the primary level is not much affected by whether their teachers have a post-secondary education or not (Bruns et al, 2003), the World Bank financially supported, until 2007, the Distance Teacher Education Programme started at the Lesotho College of Education in 2002. This programme upgrades large numbers of unqualified teachers over a four-year period, using secondary school teachers as part-time academic tutors. Neither the Ministry of Education and Training nor the World Bank showed comparable interest in the expansion of pre-service teacher education, which remained at a modest level.

In the past few years, there has been a reduction of the shortage of classrooms at the primary level, but certain schools – usually in remote, rural locations – remain seriously disadvantaged in this respect, with two or more grades sharing the same room. The programme of school construction and maintenance has been substantial but not very equitable, owing to the government of Lesotho's emphasis on construction of new schools in order to increase the number under its own management. In the period from January 2005 to June 2006, for example, the number of government primary schools increased from 106 to 135, and, in 2009, the total number of government-owned primary schools was 168 (data from Ministry of Education and Training, Primary Field Inspectorate). While this reduced the government funds available for the maintenance and improvement of other schools, other sources of funds for this also diminished. By 2007, tuition fees had been completely phased out and the European Commission and Irish Aid had discontinued the micro-project grants that some schools had used. Only in 2008 did the government of Lesotho make a small allocation available to school principals for maintenance.

Partly as a result of the SACMEQ II report (Mothibeli & Maema, 2005), the Ministry of Education and Training commissioned a 'needs analysis' study of the teaching of key subjects at the primary level (Lesotho College of Education, 2006). The study was followed by some efforts to address the many problems of low quality which it documented, both in teaching itself and in the provision of resources and supervisory support for teaching and learning.

Provision for Special Educational Needs

A third area of relative neglect relates to the requirement, in EFA Goal 2, that primary education should be accessible to 'children in difficult circumstances'. The *Dakar Framework* further states that educational systems 'must be inclusive ... responding flexibly to the circumstances and needs of all learners' (UNESCO, 2000, p. 16). Here we shall consider the educational prospects in Lesotho for children with disabilities and other SEN in the context of FPE. The Ministry of Education and Training does have a Special Education Unit, whose report of 2001 shows that numerous pupils with SEN were enrolled in primary schools with no special provision (Ministry of Education and Training, Special Education Unit, 2001). This situation remained basically unchanged six years later (Lesotho College of Education, 2007, pp. 14-20). It is symptomatic, also, that a World Bank (2005) education sector review for Lesotho gives no attention at all to special or inclusive education. Officially, the Special Education Unit has a goal of 'integration' for disabled learners, whereas the primary issue is whether any appropriate provision, whether integrated or not, can be made for them.

Both the services of special schools and the mainstreamed provision for SEN pupils in regular schools are extremely limited in quantity and accessibility. At the primary level, there are four residential special schools for children with specific kinds of disability, with a total enrolment of 317 in 2009 (data from Ministry of Education and Training, Special Education Unit). Of these, only one (the Resource Centre for the Blind) is managed by the government. Some of these schools prepare their pupils for total or partial inclusion in nearby primary school classes. But only a minority of their teachers have any qualification in special education. All four institutions are located in the lowlands and in most cases parents have to pay boarding fees. There are also two residential homes for disabled children, whose inmates attend regular primary schools nearby.

In 2006, the mainstreaming of SEN pupils was being attempted in 82 primary schools (out of a total of about 1400). By 2008, the schools in the designated list had increased to 200 (data from Ministry of Education and Training, Special Education Unit). These efforts are being supported by just six 'itinerant' teachers for special education, in six out of the ten districts. In secondary education, there is no provision for SEN except for a unit for the blind in one school. In 2006, the Lesotho College of Education had just one lecturer for special education, and teacher training for this field was limited to one introductory course in the regular pre-service diploma programmes (primary and secondary). In the Distance Teacher Education Programme of the College, the exposure was even more limited. In 2009, the Lesotho College of Education introduced an Advanced Diploma in Special Education for both primary and secondary teachers, with six lecturers. This was a response to the scarcity of training for SEN among teachers in special schools as well as in mainstream schools which practise inclusion.

Special education received mention in the *Education Sector Strategic Plan*, along with other 'special programmes' and was given a budget of M2.4 million (about US$300,000) for the financial year 2006-07 (Ministry of Education and Training, 2005, p. 116). But this figure is an aspiration rather than a reality, occurring in the context of a funding gap of 82% in that year for the special programmes collectively. Before 2008, none of the international development partners of the education sector had shown interest in any major intervention for the benefit of SEN pupils other than orphans. Since 2008, however, international development partners, such as UNICEF, the Global Fund, the Sentebale trust and the Norwegian Association for the Disabled, have shown more interest in SEN. Some assistance has been given to special schools and mainstream schools that include children with SEN through the Special Education Unit and even directly to schools where applicable. This increased activity shows a closer attention to EFA Goals 2 and 6.

Work has now started on a revision of the official policy on special education, which was formulated as long ago as 1989-90 and is extremely brief. A comprehensive and relevant policy statement would encourage both the government of Lesotho and international development partners to support the much needed strengthening and expansion of the staffing for special and inclusive education, both at national and district levels.

Developments in Uganda: progress towards the educational MDGs

Uganda has received considerable acclaim for its rapid progress towards UPE and gender equality in access to primary education. The government of Uganda abolished tuition fees in public primary education for up to four children per family in 1997 and extended this to all children in 2002. The Ministry of Education and Sports (2004, p. 4) reports that between 1996 and 2004, the number of primary school teachers increased by 55% and the number of classrooms by about 74%. The national GER for primary education is reported as 125% in 1999, 117% in 2006 (UNESCO, 2008, p. 307) and 116% in 2008 (Ministry of Education and Sports, 2009). These GERs suggest that over-age enrolment has declined somewhat, but, as in most of sub-Saharan Africa, it remains a major issue. It combines with a fairly high grade-repetition rate (repeaters being 10% of the enrolment in 2008) to put pressure on available resources and to contribute to a low survival rate for the primary cycle (see Okuni, 2003).

The fact that the official statistics have repeatedly shown some NERs above 100% suggests that the population projections used are unreliable. The GERs, as well as the NERs, are probably overestimated. Nevertheless, they are of interest for comparisons by gender and by region (see Table I). For 2008, for example, NERs of 109% and 103% are reported for the eastern and northern regions. Okuni (2003) complains of the same problem in earlier years.

The gender parity indices associated with the above primary GERs are 0.92 for 1999, 1.01 for 2006 and 0.95 for 2008. As Table I also shows, the gender differences in primary GER across the regions of Uganda in 2008 are generally small. This applies even in the north, where there has traditionally been more resistance to girls' enrolment. At the secondary level, however, girls have a marked disadvantage, within a generally low level of participation. In the northern regions, boarding facilities for girls are considered essential by many parents for security reasons. Women are also severely underrepresented in secondary-level teaching (at 25% in 2008).

Uganda's impressive progress towards the educational MDGs helped until about 2009 to maintain its status as one of the most favoured client nations in the eyes of international development agencies. For instance, Calderisi (2007, p. 209), a former World Bank officer, lists Uganda as one of four or five African countries that 'are serious about reducing poverty' and deserving of direct foreign aid. This diplomatic achievement in itself may have been useful for Uganda. But, as in Lesotho, there are issues about the status of subsectors other than primary education and about how the government of Uganda will cope with the repercussions of UPE in those subsectors. It is also questionable, as in Lesotho, whether gender disparities at the primary level have deserved the amount of attention they have received vis-à-vis regional disparities. As Table I shows, Uganda has important regional differences in the primary GER, reflecting inequalities both in participation and in the proportion of over-age pupils.

Region	GER (%) for primary-level pupils			
	Male	Female	All	Gender parity index
Central	101.7	101.7	101.7	1.00
Eastern	131.4	124.9	128.1	0.95
North-eastern	83.2	81.5	84.1	0.98
Northern	134.2	117.9	125.9	0.88
South-western	107.6	103.2	105.4	0.96
Western	120.1	114.5	117.2	0.95
All regions	118.8	112.5	115.7	0.95
Standard deviation (n = 6)	17.80	14.07	15.17	

Region	GER (%) for secondary-level pupils			
	Male	Female	All	Gender parity index
Central	39.2	38.3	38.7	10.98
Eastern	31.9	22.5	27.0	0.71
North-eastern	19.1	14.9	17.0	0.78
Northern	22.5	12.3	17.3	0.55
South-western	23.7	18.1	20.8	0.76
Western	33.0	28.6	30.7	0.87
All regions	30.7	24.7	27.6	0.80
Standard deviation (n = 6)	6.99	8.83	7.80	

Table I. Uganda's gross enrolment rate in primary and secondary education by region and by gender in 2008. (Analysis of data from Ministry of Education and Sports, 2009.)

Early Childhood Education

In this chapter, the term 'early childhood education' refers to the pre-primary level only, but some Ugandan documents use it with reference to the lower primary grades as well. Uganda's situation with regard to pre-primary childcare and education, focusing on the three-to-five age group, is fairly typical of low-income countries in tropical Africa. The awareness of and demand for institutionalised services is strong in urban and peri-urban areas, but weak in rural areas. The national GER for this level of education in 2008 was estimated as 5.6% only, with little difference between the sexes (Ministry of Education and Sports, 2009, p. 11). The service providers include both an elite element of relatively expensive nursery schools and a mass element of community-based and home-based early childhood development (ECD) centres and day-care centres. The training of ECD teachers and nurses is also provided by private or charitable organisations, with the exception of the Grade II and diploma programmes for teachers at Kyambogo University. The government of Uganda defines its own role, for the three-to-five age group, as one of guidance on management and curriculum, advocacy, coordination, regulation and monitoring (see Ministry of Education and Sports, 2007).

In the context of Uganda's official commitment to the EFA goals, an NGO report (Uganda Child Rights NGO Network, 2006) took the government of Uganda to task for its neglect of early childhood education. The report points to the poor quality of learning environments and hygiene, the acute shortage of qualified teachers, the very low pay of teachers, the use of some materials and methods intended for older children and the lack of inspection in many centres.

Partly as a result of this report, the Ministry of Education and Sports did publish a comprehensive policy for ECD in October 2007 (Ministry of Education and Sports, 2007). While this policy document has well-considered objectives and uses attractive language about the holistic development of children and the value of 'public-private partnerships', it refrains from any suggestion that the government of Uganda will contribute anything to the pay of ECD teachers or nurses, even if they are suitably trained and qualified. A strategy for providing investment support or credit facilities for the managing bodies is also lacking in the document, beyond an exhortation to local governments to make 'supporting budgetary provisions'. As in Lesotho, the neo-liberal assumption that the management of early childhood education should be left to the market apparently persists in the government of Uganda and among some of its development partners. As elsewhere, UNICEF has shown more interest than other agencies and has provided financial and technical support for the pilot community-based ECD centres spread over 34 districts. But there were signs that local governments and communities would not manage to maintain these centres after the start-up period (Pennells, 2005).

Restricted public involvement has also adversely affected the training situation. The ECD training at Kyambogo University effectively serves the nursery schools rather than the mass element in provision. Pennells (2005) points to the need for greater recognition and coordination of the other training programmes that are more suited to the less costly ECD centres, and for the training of ECD nurses as well as teachers. In 2008 about half of the teachers at this level were uncertified (Ministry of Education and Sports, 2009, p. 16).

Quality in Primary Education

In a country of Uganda's size, poverty and diversity, it has been very challenging to improve or even maintain the quality of school inputs in the context of an FPE policy. There is no doubt that the government of Uganda has made determined efforts in the training and recruitment of teachers, the provision of material resources and the structure and content of the curriculum. It is much harder to judge how successful these efforts have been and whether they have been helped or hindered by the policy context of UPE. One advantage for the government of Uganda has been a high level of cooperation among major aid donors within the framework of an education sector investment plan started in 1998 (Higgins & Rwanyange, 2005, p. 12; Penny et al, 2008, pp. 269-271). The main donor group, while operating through a sector-wide approach, has been closely consulted on policy and implementation.

In the period 1998-2002, the number of primary school teachers increased by 41% and the national pupil-teacher ratio was reduced from 64:1 to 52:1 (Okuni, 2003). In 2008, however, the national ratio was still high at 50:1, with major regional variations (Ministry of Education and Sports, 2009, p. 43). Although the proportion of trained teachers was raised to 77% by 2002, it was somewhat lower in 2008. Those with A level qualifications or below and no teaching certificate were 30% of the total, with a further 2% of 'unknown' status (Ministry of Education and Sports, 2009, Table P17). As in Lesotho, there is considerable use of untrained school leavers. Responses to a poverty survey of 2002 indicated support for UPE but concern about large classes and the poor quality of teaching and management (Higgins & Rwanyange, 2005, p. 14). Since then, the government of Uganda has been seeking to address the human resource problems, particularly through in-service training based in outreach departments at the teacher colleges. It has also made notable progress in the area of textbook supply through the introduction of a more competitive and transparent tendering process (Penny et al, 2008, pp. 274-275).

The SACMEQ II monitoring of Grade 6 pupils' reading and mathematics achievement showed Uganda's position to be average among the SACMEQ countries, with means of 482.4 for reading and 506.3 for mathematics (Byamugisha & Ssenabulya, 2005). The position of Lesotho was considerably worse, with means of 451.5 for reading and 447.3 for mathematics. What is of more concern is that 25.5% of those tested in Uganda were placed in the 'illiterate' categories and 38.8% in the 'innumerate' categories (Byamugisha & Ssenabulya, 2005, pp. 163, 166). Findings such as these partly account for the efforts of the government of Uganda to reform the primary school curriculum. The two main strands of reform at present, initiated in 2007, are the introduction of local languages as the media of instruction at the lower primary level and that of a thematic curricular organisation at the same level. The dilemma for such reform initiatives is that they require additional learning materials, teacher training and supervision in a situation where resources are already stretched. It is too early to say whether they will help to improve learning outcomes in the context of UPE. A conference paper by a head teacher (Kisembo, 2008) makes sympathetic but critical comments.

Provision for Special Educational Needs

We shall now consider how far Uganda has focused on the educational needs of 'children in difficult circumstances'. In this area, Uganda, unlike Lesotho, has developed a strong framework of administration and policy. The Ministry of Education and Sports established a 'fully fledged' department (headed by a commissioner) that was responsible for special needs education and career guidance and counselling in 1999 (Ministry of Education and Sports, 2003) and has now progressed to having separate departments in these two areas. Under a 'Policy Framework for Educationally Disadvantaged Children', approved in 2002 (Ministry of Education and Sports, 2003, pp. 3-4), attention has been given both to groups of children disadvantaged by living conditions or neglect and to the main group of those with disabilities and learning difficulties. The main issues relate to the implementation of this policy in the context of UPE.

An important initiative to promote the inclusion of the main SEN group in regular education began before UPE, in 1992, with support from the Danish International Development Agency (DANIDA). The main focus was on establishing educational assessment and resource service centres at district level, which would provide systematic assessment of SEN, help schools to provide appropriate support and collaborate with health specialists and social workers. In keeping with the ideas of the Salamanca Declaration (UNESCO, 1994), DANIDA emphasised the goal of mainstreaming in regular classrooms, although some use was made of special classes (Dyssegaard, 2004). The Uganda National Institute for Special Education, also with support from DANIDA, provided both full-time and part-time training for teachers and auxiliary staff, intended both for special and for inclusive classrooms. In 2003, the Institute subsequently became the Faculty of Special Needs and Rehabilitation within Kyambogo University (Okwaput, 2006).

With the start of the UPE programme in 1997, the responsibilities of the educational assessment and resource service centres were enlarged to include orphaned, HIV-positive and traumatised children. Because of this and the large classes and pressure on resources, the conditions for implementation became even more difficult. Nevertheless, by the end of DANIDA's partnership in 2003, there were centres in 45 districts (out of a total of 80). DANIDA representatives admitted the difficulties of moving towards inclusive schooling, but felt that attitudes to SEN were improving and that teachers were responding well to training (Dyssegaard, 2004, pp. 36-37). At the school level, a network of SEN coordinators was started, each serving a cluster of schools. Available accounts do not make clear how far the existing special schools were involved, if at all, in the new system for SEN. But the Ministry of Education and Sports (2003) records that, in 2002, it provided subventions to 92 special schools and units, with a total enrolment of 2100 pupils.

The actual scale of SEN provision and the scope of opportunities for pupils are matters for concern. The Ministry of Education and Sports' (2009) statistics show that there were, in 2008, 183,537 'disabled pupils' in primary education and 11,145 in secondary education. (The production of these statistics, showing six categories of disability, is, in itself, commendable.) Against this background, the 2002 enrolment in special schools and units looks very small if we assume that, for many disabled pupils, there is no suitable support available in regular classrooms. The small training output for SEN from Kyambogo University was also noted at the time (Okwaput, 2006).

In spite of the above limitations, the government of Uganda and its partners have developed some well-conceived alternative education programmes, outside the regular primary curriculum, for other disadvantaged groups of children. Among these, Alternative Basic Education for Karamoja, Basic Education for Urban Poverty Areas and (for out-of-school children) Complementary Opportunities for Primary Education are notable (Commonwealth Secretariat, 2003, p. 11; Mulyalya, n.d.). The government of Uganda has also responded in flexible ways to problems caused by guerrilla activity in the north, paying hardship allowances to teachers in the affected areas and moving some entire schools to safer, temporary locations.

Conclusion

These examples of recent educational development show the importance, for national governments and their development partners, of moving away from a narrow focus on the crude targets of achieving UPE or 'gender parity' in enrolment by a certain date. The real task is to chart a coherent course for the whole education sector, an art which many African countries seem to have lost since the 1960s. The existence on paper of a sector strategic plan does not guarantee that this will happen, but the relatively high degree of cooperation achieved recently between the government and a group of donors, both in Lesotho and in Uganda, is an advantage. The educational goals agreed at the Dakar Forum have long-term value and are consistent with a balanced approach to planning.

Of those who attend formal primary education where the MDG targets are the main focus of policy, many, according to Lewin & Akyeampong (2009, p. 143) 'fail to achieve minimum levels of competence in basic numeracy and literacy after six or more years of schooling and many are over age for their grade'. Lewin & Akyeampong (2009) consider that, although progress in respect of enrolment has been rapid, it is still of an uneven, degrading quality and, by accommodating all, has generated costs that become 'unsustainable without reform' and mask 'much silent exclusion'. In this chapter, we have similarly noted the tendency for issues of quality in primary education to be sidelined. We also argue that the links between primary education and other subsectors at the base of the education pyramid have been undervalued. Special needs education is not, of course, limited, in principle, to the lowest academic levels, but is, in practice, available mainly at the primary level in Lesotho and Uganda.

A balanced approach to national planning is especially important for these subsectors at the base of the pyramid – early childhood, primary and special needs education – as they are, arguably, the subsectors least amenable to a market approach to service provision. While there is a long tradition of market provision of early childhood care and education – loosely regulated, if at all, in many countries – the arguments for public support to poorer households at this level are just as strong as at the primary level. Those households which have the most to gain from the service tend to be those which can least afford to pay for it. Public subsidies and credit facilities (in addition to the regulation and curricular guidance so far provided) could go a long way to reinforcing the efforts of local communities in providing this important service.

In the SEN subsector, the situation is, in some respects, analogous. There has been a traditional reliance on NGOs and charitable bodies to provide special schools and to identify disabilities, but without some public intervention those services are inaccessible to many who need them. Market incentives alone are not likely to produce inclusive provision for children with disabilities or SEN in regular schools, but such provision can greatly improve the social and economic opportunities of the children in the long run, as well as the general learning environment of schools.

We argue that a balanced and inclusive approach to policy and planning in the education sector – reflected in the *Dakar Framework* but 'trimmed down' by the MDGs – is necessary in order to tackle the cycle of poverty in sub-Saharan Africa.

Note

[1] An earlier version of this chapter was presented at the 10th UK Forum for International Education and Training international conference on

Education and Development, New College, Oxford, 15-17 September 2009.

References

Akyeampong, K. (2009) Revisiting Free Compulsory Universal Basic Education (FCUBE) in Ghana, *Comparative Education*, 45(2), 151-175. http://dx.doi.org/10.1080/03050060902920534

Baine, D. (1991) Methods for Instructing Students with Handicaps Integrated into Regular Education Classrooms in Developing Countries, *Psychology and Developing Societies*, 3(2), 157-169. http://dx.doi.org/10.1177/097133369100300202

Bruns, B., Mingat, A. & Rakotomalala, R. (2003) *A Chance for Every Child.* Washington, DC: World Bank.

Byamugisha, A. & Ssenabulya, F. (2005) *The SACMEQ II Project in Uganda: a study of the conditions of schooling and the quality of education.* Harare: Southern and Eastern Africa Consortium for Monitoring Educational Quality.

Calderisi, R. (2007) *The Trouble with Africa: why foreign aid isn't working.* New Haven, CT: Yale University Press.

Cammack, P. (2006) UN Imperialism: unleashing entrepreneurship in the developing world, in C. Mooers (Ed.) *The New Imperialists: ideologies of empire*, pp. 229-260. Oxford: Oneworld.

Commonwealth Secretariat (2003) *Access, Inclusion and Achievement. Closing the Gap: synthesis of country reports, presented at the 15th Conference of Commonwealth Education Ministers, Edinburgh, 27-30 October.* London: Commonwealth Secretariat.

Dyssegaard, B. (2004) Inclusive Education: experiences in Uganda, in Commonwealth Secretariat (Ed.) *Access, Inclusion and Achievement: closing the gap*, pp. 34-38. London: Commonwealth Secretariat.

Gay, J. & Hall, D. (2000) *Poverty and Livelihoods in Lesotho: more than a mapping exercise.* Maseru: Sechaba Consultants.

Higgins, L. & Rwanyange, R. (2005) Ownership in the Education Reform Process in Uganda, *Compare*, 35(1), 7-26. http://dx.doi.org/10.1080/03057920500033464

Kholowa, F. & Rose, P. (2007) Parental or Policy Maker Misunderstandings? Contextual Dilemmas of Pre-Schooling for Poverty Reduction in Malawi, *International Journal of Educational Development*, 27(4), 458-472. http://dx.doi.org/10.1016/j.ijedudev.2006.10.007

King, K. (2009) Education, Skills, Sustainability and Growth: complex relations, *International Journal of Educational Development*, 29(2), 175-181. http://dx.doi.org/10.1016/j.ijedudev.2008.09.012

Kisembo, A. (2008) Thematic Curriculum and Local Languages Policy: achievements and challenges. Paper presented at the Annual Regional Assembly on the Education and Sports Sector, Western Region, Mbarara, Uganda, 16-17 October.

Lesotho College of Education (2006) *Needs Analysis for Improvement of the Teaching of Sesotho, English and Mathematics in Lesotho Primary Schools: final report.* Maseru: Ministry of Education and Training.

Lesotho College of Education (2007) *Education Policies, Programmes and Legislation in Lesotho Relating to Disadvantaged Children and Children with Disabilities: final report.* Maseru: Special Education Unit, Ministry of Education and Training.

Lewin, K.M. (2005) Planning Post-Primary Education: taking targets to task, *International Journal of Educational Development*, 25(4), 408-422. http://dx.doi.org/10.1016/j.ijedudev.2005.04.004

Lewin, K.M. (2007) Diversity in Convergence: access to education for all, *Compare*, 37(5), 577-599. http://dx.doi.org/10.1080/03057920701582434

Lewin, K.M. (2008) *Strategies for Sustainable Financing of Secondary Education in Sub-Saharan Africa.* Washington, DC: World Bank. http://dx.doi.org/10.1596/978-0-8213-7115-2

Lewin, K.M. & Akyeampong, K. (2009) Education in Sub-Saharan Africa: researching access, transitions and equity, *Comparative Education*, 45(2), 141-143. http://dx.doi.org/10.1080/03050060902920468

Ministry of Education and Sports (2003) Department of Special Needs Education/Career Guidance and Counselling in Uganda – as at 31st January 2003. Unpublished report.

Ministry of Education and Sports (MOES) (2004) Uganda – Second ESSP (Planning and Budgeting). Unpublished report.

Ministry of Education and Sports (MOES) (2007) *The Early Childhood Development (ECD) Policy.* Kampala: Department of Pre-Primary and Primary Education, MOES.

Ministry of Education and Sports (MOES) (2009) *Uganda Educational Statistics Abstract, Volume 1, 2008.* Kampala: MOES. http://www.education.go.ug/emis-statistics/statistics-abstarct.html

Ministry of Education and Training (MOET) (2005) *Education Sector Strategic Plan 2005-2015.* Maseru: MOET.

Mitchell, D. (2008) *What Really Works in Special and Inclusive Education.* London: Routledge.

Mothibeli, A. & Maema, M. (2005) *The SACMEQ II Project in Lesotho: a study of the conditions of schools and the quality of education.* Harare: Southern and Eastern Africa Consortium for Monitoring Educational Quality.

Mulyalya, C. (n.d.) *Case Study of the Impact of UPE on the Quality of Basic Education in Uganda (Draft Report).* Kampala: Ministry of Education and Sports.

Mwaura, P., Sylva, K. & Malmberg, L. (2008) Evaluating the Madrasa Preschool Programme in East Africa: a quasi-experimental study, *International Journal of Early Years Education*, 16(3), 237-255. http://dx.doi.org/10.1080/09669760802357121

Okuni, A. (2003) EFA Policies, Strategies and Reforms in Uganda: assessment of the current potential for sustainable progress towards achieving the EFA goals by 2015. Unpublished paper prepared for the 2003 EFA Global Monitoring Report.

Okwaput, K. (2006) Teacher Training in Uganda, *EENET Newsletter*, 10. http://www.eenet.org.uk/resources/eenet_newsletter/news10/page8.php

Palmer, R., Wedgwood, R. & Hayman, R. (2007) *Educating Out of Poverty? A Synthesis Report on Ghana, India, Kenya, Rwanda, Tanzania and South Africa.* London: Department for International Development.

Pennells, J. (2005) Uganda: ECD situational analysis and needs assessment. Briefing Report to Ka Tutandike Trust, United Kingdom. http://www.katutandike.org/early-childhood-development

Penny, A., Ward, M., Read, T. & Bines, H. (2008) Education Sector Reform: the Ugandan experience, *International Journal of Educational Development*, 28(3), 268-285. http://dx.doi.org/10.1016/j.ijedudev.2007.04.004

Robertson, S., Novelli, M., Dale, R., Tikly, L., Dachi, H. & Alphonce, N. (2007) *Globalisation, Education and Development: ideas, actors and dynamics.* London: Department for International Development.

Taiwo, A. & Tyolo, J. (2002) The Effect of Preschool Education on Academic Performance in Primary School: a case study of grade one pupils in Botswana, *International Journal of Educational Development*, 22(2), 169-180. http://dx.doi.org/10.1016/S0738-0593(01)00020-7

Uganda Child Rights NGO Network (UCRNN) (2006) *Hope amidst Obstacles: the state of nursery education in Uganda.* Kamwokya: UCRNN.

UNESCO (1994) *The Salamanca Statement on Principles, Policy and Practice in Special Needs Education.* Paris: UNESCO.

UNESCO (2000) *The Dakar Framework for Action. Education for All: meeting our collective commitments.* Paris: UNESCO.

UNESCO (2008) *Global Monitoring Report 2009. Statistical Tables 2009: final longer version.* Paris: UNESCO & Oxford University Press. http://www.unesco.org/new/en/education/themes/leading-the-international-agenda/efareport/statistics/statistical-tables

United Nations (UN) (2000) *United Nations Millennium Declaration.* New York: UN.

Urwick, J. (2011) 'Free Primary Education' in Lesotho and the Disadvantages of the Highlands, *International Journal of Educational Development*, 31(3), 234-243. http://dx.doi.org/10.1016/j.ijedudev.2010.07.004

World Bank (2005) *Building on Free Primary Education, Primary and Secondary Education in Lesotho: a country status report.* Washington, DC: World Bank.

CHAPTER 5

A Critical Overview of Education for Sustainable Development with Particular Focus upon the Development of Quality Teacher Education in Sub-Saharan Africa

DAVID STEPHENS

SUMMARY We are now halfway through the United Nations Decade of Education for Sustainable Development (2005-14) and it seems an appropriate moment to stand back and critically review progress to date and the major challenges facing educationists in turning UN rhetoric into reality. The first part of the chapter examines global efforts to introduce Education for Sustainable Development (ESD) into schools and colleges, and in particular the role ESD can play in developing quality teacher education in sub-Saharan Africa. The main thrust of the argument is that without a well-informed and trained teaching force ESD will face severe problems in becoming mainstreamed in the learning of children. The importance of context also lies at efforts to introduce ESD into teacher education, and with that in mind the second part of the chapter moves from the global to the local by evaluating an ESD teacher education project in Madagascar, an island with much at stake in terms of sustainable development. The chapter concludes with a discussion of lessons that can be learned from this evaluation more generally in sub-Saharan Africa and elsewhere.

Introduction

Our biggest challenge in this new century is to take an idea
that sounds abstract – sustainable development – and turn it ...
into a daily reality for all the world's people. (Annan, 2001)

> Education for sustainable development is about the learning needed to maintain and improve our quality of life and the quality of life of generations to come. It is about equipping individuals, communities, groups, businesses and government to live and act sustainably; as well as giving them an understanding of the environmental, social and economic issues involved. It is about preparing for the world in which we will live in the next century, and making sure we are not found wanting. (Department for Environment, Transport and the Regions, 1999, p. 30)

Sustainable development, and more specifically education for sustainable development (ESD), is now part of a global educational discourse. At every turn, teachers and students are exhorted to develop a 'green' lifestyle and to mainstream sustainability, a little like the calls for the promotion and embedding of gender equality in the 1980s.

A quick search of the Internet reveals 10,600,000 items for 'education for sustainable development', reflecting an alarming proliferation of inter-government initiatives, international networks, round tables and such like. ESD has become a mantra of hope, essentially a call for change in the way we educate our children and ourselves with the express purposes of ensuring a sustainable future. Within ESD, it is clear that if the education sector is to come close to achieving and sustaining such a change, it will fall to teacher education to provide the necessary cadre of appropriately trained personnel through pre and in-service training.

We are now about halfway through the United Nations Decade of Education for Sustainable Development (DESD; 2005-14) and it is worthwhile to stand back for a moment and critically review progress to date and to look at the journey ahead. The purpose of this chapter, therefore, is to provide a brief critical overview of ESD and to discuss the challenges and possibilities ESD has for the development and sustainability of *quality* teacher education in sub-Saharan Africa. Particular attention will be paid to issues of culture, context and indigenous knowledge in the development of such ESD and teacher education.

Given the importance of context within ESD – for example, 'think global/act local' – the chapter will attempt to critique the more general issues and practices promoted by organisations such as UNESCO through evaluation of one ESD teacher education project in Madagascar. The chapter will conclude with lessons learned from the case study and suggestions for ways forward.

ESD and Teacher Education

Let us start briefly by reviewing some of the major developments in ESD with a particular eye towards the relationship generally between schools and teacher education.

The notion of sustainable development was coined more than 20 years ago when the Brundtland Commission famously connoted that such development 'meets the needs of the present without compromising the ability of future generations to meet their own needs' (World Commission on Environment and Development, 1987, p. 43). Since then, there has been much debate about both the extent to which the environment and climate are at risk and the relative strengths of the remedial action that would be required to meet future generations' needs.

The aim of sustainable development was endorsed by 149 countries, including the United Kingdom, at the United Nations Conference on Environment and Development in 1992. This conference agreed on Agenda 21 (United Nations, 1993), a global action plan for sustainable development that required governments to draw up their own agendas in consultation with business and civil society. The European Union, the United Kingdom government, the Scottish Executive, the Welsh Assembly and local authorities such as Nottinghamshire subsequently produced agendas or strategies for sustainable development. At the 2002 Earth Summit in Johannesburg, the emphasis was on the implementation of such agendas as part of the United Nations Millennium Development Goals (MDGs). Agenda 21 suggests the content, process and tools of sustainable development (see Table I).

What is not in question is the potential that education may have in the future realisation of a vision of sustainability that links economic well-being with respect for cultural diversity, the earth and its resources (UNESCO, 2007). UNESCO suggests that ESD as quality education is characterised by six features: it is interdisciplinary and holistic; values-driven; encourages critical thinking and problem solving; uses a wide range of methods, media and activities; fosters participatory decision making; and addresses local as well as global issues using the language(s) which learners most commonly use. There are eight key action themes for the DESD – overcoming poverty, gender equality, health promotion, the environment, rural development, cultural diversity, peace and human security, and sustainable urbanisation – and the DESD website [1] outlines these, gives visibility to related local, national and international ESD initiatives, and offers dissemination tools (Huckle, 2006). The overall goal of the DESD, led by UNESCO, is therefore:

> to integrate values, activities and principles that are inherently
> linked to sustainable development into all forms of education
> and learning and help usher in a change in attitudes,

behaviours, and values to ensure a more sustainable future in social, environmental and economic terms. (UNESCO, 2007, p. 5)

The four thrusts of ESD are improving access to quality basic education; reorienting existing education programmes; developing public understanding and awareness; and providing training (Little & Green, 2009, p. 172).

Content	Process	Tools
Reduce use of resources and production of waste; increase resource efficiency; reuse; recycle.	Active planning and management.	Education; information; awareness-raising.
	Consultation; participation; empowerment.	Capacity-building; institutional know-how; confidence; experience.
Conserve fragile ecosystems.	Decisions at most local level possible; local government pivotal.	
Social equity (between and within countries and across generations).	Partnerships and collaborations between all sectors.	Regulations and enforcement.
Quality of life (broader than standard of living).		Market management; taxes; levies; subsidies.
Respect for traditional knowledge, ways of life, diversity.		Public investment.

Table I. Content, process and tools of sustainable development.
Source: UNCED, 1993.

The Quality of Teacher Education in Africa

Before we examine the efforts to reorient teacher education and training towards the goals of ESD – which is much easier to say than do – it is worth remembering the parlous state of much of teacher education, particularly in Africa where it has languished as the Cinderella of education development.

In the late 1990s, I co-directed a large research project, funded by the UK Department for International Development, exploring teacher education in five national contexts, four of which were in sub-Saharan Africa. The conclusions of the Multi-Site Teacher Education Research (MUSTER) project are clear:

The Millennium Development Goals (MDG) relating to education cannot be met unless the supply of teachers is adequate to keep pupil-teacher ratios within reasonable limits, and the quality of their training is sufficient to result in minimum acceptable levels of pupil achievement. The costs of existing methods of training are such that simple expansion of existing capacity is often not financially viable. Improvements in efficiency and effectiveness are needed that can lower costs and expand output within sustainable budgets. It may also be necessary to consider alternatives to two or three years' full-time, pre-career training. Traditional teacher education programmes are heavily 'front-loaded' with most investment at the beginning of a teaching career. Their unit costs can exceed those of university education and may be 50 or more times the annual cost of a primary school place. If the average length of teacher careers is declining, as it is in some cases as a result of HIV/AIDS, and if the numbers which have to be trained are much larger than current capacity, teacher education programmes with lower costs are needed. The alternative is to revise MDG targets for universalising access and achieving gender equity in primary schooling. (Lewin & Stuart, 2003, p. ix)

A major tension – or conundrum – therefore, is to balance the adequate numbers of teachers being trained cost-effectively with an increased quality of training that prepares the new teacher for the challenges raised by the MDGs. This is the context within which demands are being made upon the teacher education sector, not only to raise the quality of its graduates in terms of the traditional criteria of what makes a good teacher, but additionally to innovate with the introduction of ESD.

Part of the problem is that teacher education, far from being innovative, is actually often reactionary and authoritarian. In 2010, I and a colleague had the privilege to evaluate a number of teacher education projects in four sub-Saharan national contexts (Harber & Stephens, 2010). Though we found numerous examples of good practice, we also encountered a subsector that belied the notion of the preparation of teachers as being in any sense liberal and progressive. As we say in our report:

In many countries, including those in Africa, teacher education is a part of the problem of poor quality in education rather than the solution. This is because teacher education tends to perpetuate traditional, unreflective and teacher-centred pedagogy rather than challenge it. Some thirty years ago Bartholomew put forward the idea of the 'myth of the liberal college' – that is a myth that there is a contradiction between the liberal, progressive and democratic college or university on the one hand and the traditional, conservative and authoritarian school on the other. (Harber & Stephens, 2010)

This myth suggests that student teachers are exposed to the more radical, democratic forms of teaching and learning during their courses in higher education with a high emphasis on learner participation, but are rapidly re-socialised into more authoritarian understandings and practices during their teaching practice and their subsequent employment in education. Rather than there being a contradiction between the two – in terms of power over what is taught and learned, how and when, let alone the contradiction between 'do as I say and do as I do' – it is argued that, in reality, teacher education is often an authoritarian and reproductive preparation for teaching in schools. But, as I have said, this is not to deny the examples of good practice that can be found in different parts of the continent. The case study of such practice from Madagascar will be presented and discussed later.

Teachers have long been identified as a major target audience for environmental education. The Belgrade Charter (1975), for example, and Recommendations 17 and 18 from the 1977 Tbilisi Intergovernmental Conference on Environmental Education (UNESCO, 1978) specifically refer to pre-service teacher education and in-service teacher education, and call for teacher education to include environmental education (Gough, 2009).

These early recommendations were framed around the belief that all teachers need 'to understand the importance of environmental emphasis in their teaching' and so 'environmental sciences and environmental education [need to] be included in curricula for pre-service teacher education' and 'the necessary steps [need to be taken] to make in-service training of teachers in environmental education available for all who need it' (UNESCO, 1978, pp. 35-36). Within this context, environmental education was seen as preparing

> the individual for life through an understanding of the major
> problems of the contemporary world, and the provision of
> skills and attributes needed to play a productive role towards
> improving life and protecting the environment with due regard
> given to ethical values. (UNESCO, 1978, p. 24)

Twenty years on, there was a noticeable shift from 'environmental education' to 'education for sustainable development'. In 1998, UNESCO established a chair at York University in Toronto, Canada, with the specific responsibility to 'reorient' teacher education internationally in order to address issues of sustainability. An international network of 30 teacher education institutions in 28 countries was established and guidelines produced. Reporting in 2005, a number of institutions reported success in 'weaving sustainability themes into their own classroom curricula', with new courses and modules developed for their own students. The challenges related mostly to trying to advocate change beyond 'their own sphere of direct control' (UNESCO, 2005, p. 59).

Despite all this activity, an evaluation of these programmes revealed evidence that ESD has not yet become an integral part of most teacher education programmes. Indeed, one analysis of the international efforts to promote ESD within teacher education states that: 'there has been no teacher education initiative that has strategically set out to mainstream sustainability into the core of teacher education programs'. I have written elsewhere (Stephens, 2007) of the need to develop teacher education in such a way as to embed it within frameworks that take appropriate account of the broader issues of quality, culture and context, and specifically the relationship between Western and indigenous knowledge systems. Let us pause for a moment and examine how these issues or questions impact upon the development of ESD within teacher education.

ESD and Teacher Education: questions of quality, culture, context and indigenous knowledge

Questions of Quality

In the late 1980s, with a colleague Hugh Hawes, I spent a significant period of time researching, writing and teaching about issues of quality in sub-Saharan Africa. In our study (Hawes & Stephens, 1990), we devoted a chapter to the centrality of teacher education to efforts to raise the standard of teaching and learning in the continent's classrooms. Our conclusion was simple: teachers in training needed to learn less about theories of education (often outdated and imported from the West) and more about the pedagogic processes of classroom instruction and learning. We also made the case for new teachers to be exposed to models of good practice, again rooted in the situation of the classroom and grounded in the realities of such environments often constrained by a lack of resources, large enrolments and subject to increasing waves of innovation and change.

It was also clear to us that in order for a new teacher fresh out of teacher college to thrive – and to continue to learn the craft of teaching – they would need to be well supported *in situ*. In other words, there needs to be a clear link between pre- and in-service education. These questions or issues were not particularly new in the 1980s and from the Save the Children evaluation conducted in four sub-Saharan African countries in 2010 (Harber & Stephens, 2010). What has changed over the past 30 years has been recognition of the pre- and in-service relationship, coupled with clear evidence of the pressing need for ESD to be central to teacher education. And there is some evidence of models of good practice. The Madagascar case study reported here is one such example.

Culture, Context and Indigenous Knowledge

If teacher education is to promote sustainable environmental education, then some thought needs to be given to the sidelining of indigenous and exogenous models of development, and the promotion – even if unintentionally – of Western notions of what constitutes ESD or, come to that, teacher education.

By its very definition, environmental education is related to the context and cultures of the communities it seeks to develop. Much of the debate about sustainable development is, however, Western, with Western knowledge and science playing a hegemonic role in development efforts in the South, and indigenous and local solutions being characterised as inefficient, old-fashioned and unscientific (Breidlid, 2009). As Sillitoe (2000, p. 5) puts it: 'The discrediting of existing knowledge and techniques (invariably subsistence-oriented and often environmentally well-adjusted and sustainable), and their replacement with scientifically informed and controlled technology, furthers outside hegemony'.

Recently, however, there has been somewhat of a resurgence of interest in indigenous knowledge and what has been called the 'integration of knowledge systems' (Odora Hoppers, 2002). What characterises such 'integration' is a holistic view of social and economic development, giving as much priority in environmental matters to the spiritual as well as the physical. Indigenous knowledge is not only the transmission of knowledge, but also of skills from one generation to another, characterised by oral transmission and learning through experience and repetitive practice (Sillitoe, 2000, p. 4). As my Norwegian colleague Anders Breidlid notes:

> The lack of respect for local or indigenous knowledge and the assumption by many Western scientists about the superiority of Western epistemology and scientific discourse is a serious obstacle to sustainable development in light of their apparent failure to meet human development needs and, at the same time, to protect nature and the eco-system. In some scientific circles in the West there is, however, a growing realisation that the South may have something to teach the West, and that indigenous knowledge may increase our scientific understanding of natural phenomena which may be crucial for sustainable development. (Breidlid, 2009, p. 142)

There are therefore two major challenges facing the worthy folk of the large development agencies and ministries of education who desire to turn the rhetoric of Brundtland into a reality. First, that education, and more specifically teacher education, in sub-Saharan Africa is still beset by a number of systemic and cultural problems, ranging from high levels of poverty and the impact of the HIV/AIDS crisis to deeply entrenched cultural understandings of how to teach and the role of the school or teacher college in community and national development. Second, that ESD, like many other well-intentioned exports from the West (and one can remember distance learning, participatory rural appraisal and child-centred learning), is in danger, ironically, of failing to make its mark because it has not been adequately configured culturally in the light of indigenous understandings, needs and resources.

But, as I intimated earlier, there are models of good practice to be found in the African continent. One of these is in Madagascar and it is to this that we now turn.

The Madagascar Case Study

I have argued for the importance of culture and context. Let me briefly describe the environmental and educational contexts of the island of Madagascar.

The Malagasy Environmental Context

Madagascar is located off the coast of Africa and is the fourth largest island in the world – it is sometimes referred to as an 'island continent'. It formed when it broke away from the African continent over 100 million years ago, taking with it many of the species found on the mainland. Being isolated, over time these populations began to diverge from their mainland ancestors. Populations on the island also diverged as climatic changes – warmer and cooler, wetter and dryer periods – isolated forest areas from one another.

The country has a variety of climatic zones, including both tropical and temperate, with 85% of the plants and animals on the island found nowhere else in the world. There is both internal and external pressure to preserve this extraordinary ecosystem.

In April 2008, more than 100 scientists completed an acre-by-acre inventory of over 2300 living plant and animal species found only on the island. It is believed that 106 of the 250 bird species and 233 of the 245 reptile species are endemic to the island, while nearly 90% of the flowering plant species are also unique to the island; in fact, Madagascar has more orchid species than the entire continent of Africa. It is also well known for its variety of amphibian species. There are, for example, approximately 230 species of frog living on the island, nearly all of which are endemic.

In 1988, Madagascar became one of the first African countries to develop a national environmental plan calling for measures to reduce poverty, develop sustainable land management practices, and set aside land in parks and reserves. Most of the population, who are rural poor, are employed in subsistence agriculture, and traditional methods of slash-and-burn farming have already led to a loss of 80% of the country's original forest cover. International conservation organisations have become active in conservation efforts within the country. The World Bank and the World Wildlife Fund negotiated a debt for nature swap in which the World Wildlife Fund purchased US$5 million of the country's foreign debt at a discounted rate in exchange for government support for local conservation projects. Additional conservation investment has come from the Critical Ecosystem Partnership Fund, a joint project of Conservation International, the Global Environment Facility and the World Bank. As of April 2007, the government of Madagascar set aside 15 new protected areas, bringing the total number up to 60. The government's National Association for the Management of Protected Areas in Madagascar has introduced a new park management system to conserve wildlife using sustainable development programmes that can also provide direct benefits to the local people (Environmental Literacy Council, 2008).

The Malagasy Education Context

Two-thirds of Madagascar's population live below the poverty line, and as many as 890,000 children aged 6 to 10 years are out of school. Also, 50 of the 111 school districts have primary completion rates of less than 45%. The dropout rates are therefore still very high. Only 30% of children continue until the age of 10 years in the old system. Even though the repetition rate is lower, it is still high and reduces considerably the effectiveness of school. In 2006-07, the net enrolment rate at primary level was 85%, but only 53% completed primary school. The private education sector is important in Madagascar, catering for 24% of the students at primary level and 45% at secondary level.

As seen elsewhere on the African continent, a weakness in the education system is the lack of qualified teachers in the schools. Both the training and engagement of teachers have been exposed to reductions due to economic constraints and demands from structural adjustment programmes. There are many challenges to face. However, the government is determined to improve the education system. In 2003, the Ministry of Education developed an Education for All (EFA) plan, which was revised in 2005. During the past 10 years, an important partnership has been developed with different partners of EFA. Madagascar entered the Education for All – Fast Track Initiative in early 2005, following a policy decision in 2003 to abolish primary education fees and provide support for community-recruited teachers and children's school supplies. In 2007, the government updated its poverty-reduction strategy with the Madagascar Action Plan 2007-12 (MAP), which is in line with the MDGs.

One of the commitments of the MAP is the transformation of education, which includes the decision to extend the primary cycle from five to seven years, and to restructure the junior and senior secondary cycles respectively to three and two years. Madagascar wishes to extend the provision of basic education to 10 years in line with tendencies in sub-Saharan Africa and other countries. The EFA plan was therefore revised in 2005 and a new generation of reforms was elaborated. This new plan is more ambitious and detailed compared to the earlier plan.

The reform includes strategies to improve quality, access and equity, developing institutional and implementation capacity. The strategy to improve quality includes, for example, curriculum reform with strategies for the procurement, development and production of learning resources, teacher guides and support material for teachers, and the competency-based approach (CBA), which was already introduced earlier. Another characteristic of the reform is the introduction of the Malagasy language as the language of instruction for the first five years of primary school.

The government is working in partnership with a strong and active non-governmental organisation (NGO) sector to establish and develop a sustainable education programme that will not only raise the quality of ESD at school level, but also centrally involve the teacher training colleges. The most important of these programmes is the ProVert or 'green education' programme.

The ProVert or 'Green Education' Programme[2]

The NGO at the heart of this initiative is the Malagasy Lutheran Church. It has developed a holistic programme for green education that combines theoretical learning with practical life skills in a modern pedagogical conception, and tries to reconcile economic development with sustainable use of natural resources and protection of the environment. The programme is closely connected with the government's efforts for good governance. The programme was initiated in 2007, reviewed in 2008 and is funded, largely by the Norwegian aid programme, until 2012. In general terms, the programme aims to contribute to an improvement of the living conditions of the Malagasy people and, with locally based sustainable development processes and a special focus on education, environment and human rights, promote the achievement of the MDGs. It is based on a Christian conception of Man and focuses on the protection of human dignity, the rights and the needs of the child, civil society and good government, the empowerment of women and the special promotion of marginalised groups and areas.

Figure 1 illustrates the three reciprocal areas of the programme: a relevant and human education; a rich and intact environment; and a democratic and fair society. It is perhaps worth noting that as much as capacity building lies at the centre of the programme (the capacity of the learners, teachers, institutions and community), so do human rights – namely the right of the child to receive an education that is relevant, efficient and of value, both to him- or herself as an individual and to the society to which he or she belongs. It is also worth reiterating that since 2007, the government has been committed to children learning for the first five years of their primary education in the mother tongue.

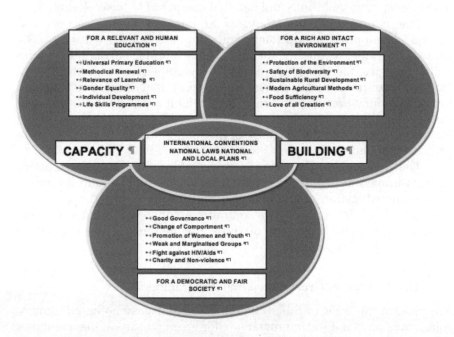

Figure 1. Green Education Programme in FLM. Source: Antsirabe: ProVert.

At the school and college levels, the green education programme, in tandem with the government's own efforts, has at least two specific and reciprocal objectives. The first concerns its impact on the Malagasy education system. By integrating green elements into the subjects taught at school, the national curriculum is very likely to include these elements when it is eventually revised. This should apply to the curricula for primary education as well as secondary education, and not least the teacher training curricula. Secondly, if the green programme is taught in a comprehensive and coherent manner, the outcome is likely to benefit the Malagasy environment – it will be better taken care of and the soil and resources will be more effectively managed for the benefit of local people. People will have more and better food to eat as a consequence of the programme. Education therefore becomes the primary vehicle to meet such priorities.

The programme document details a number of specific objectives which correspond to the MDGs: for example, 'to contribute to the elimination of gender and geographical disparity in all education' (MDG 2, Target 4 [ProVert, 2006, p. 20]). The *general objectives* of the programme are:

- to promote collective action to achieve a change of comportment and standard of living;
- to ensure that the development activities are based on international conventions, national laws and national and local plans;
- to show Christian charity through diaconal activities and efforts to assist weak groups and poor and marginalised persons, and through a special responsibility for God's creation.

In terms of *educational objectives*, the green education programme aims to provide children with the means by which they can engage in those processes of change that will bring about the realisation of their rights and prepare them for an active part in society and change. These rights to be heard, for freedom of expression, for information and association, create a new type of social paradigm between adults and children, i.e.:

- to contribute to achieving universal primary education by 2015;
- to ensure that the learning needs of the young and adults are met through equitable access to appropriate learning and life skills programmes;
- to promote the relevance of learning materials and methodological renewal and improvement;
- to contribute to the elimination of gender and geographical disparity in all education.

The *environmental* objectives are an integral part of the educational work. These include:

- to work for the protection of the environment, conservation of biodiversity and the reversal of the loss of environmental resources;
- to promote environmental sustainability and sustainable development;
- to integrate the principles of the protection of the environment and sustainable development into the education programmes.

Finally, the *social* objectives include:

- to stimulate the idea of the dignity of man, promote gender equality and empower women and youth;
- to fight for democracy, the importance of countering oppression and corruption, and to support equality, tolerance, transparency and justice;
- to promote the protection of life and well-being.

Improving Teacher Education and Pedagogy: evidence from the field[3]

So, how far has the programme translated the heady rhetoric of its aims and objectives into visible educational improvements on the ground? This was the question that preoccupied me as we sped – somewhat too fast – out of the capital Antananarivo towards the south-west of the island where we were to visit a number of teacher colleges and their satellite primary schools.

As I looked out of the window, I also saw the environmental and educational challenges facing the nation: mile upon mile of relatively newly planted rice paddies where once ancient forests had stood. After an eight-hour journey, we arrived at our first teacher college. The principal of the college wanted to make it clear from the start that ProVert is seeking to introduce both new content and new pedagogy into primary and teacher education institutions. They are also working hard to build effective linkages between the training that occurs at preschool teacher education level (in the college and on teaching practice) and the daily life – and needs – of the teacher once embarked upon his or her teaching career. And the colleges are transforming themselves into educational institutions in which environmental education is, if not yet central or mainstreamed, at least taken more seriously. Teacher education curricula are being rewritten to embrace ESD, colleges are establishing farms as both laboratories for learning and a source of income, and some efforts are being made to reform pedagogy.

A major plank of ProVert is to establish effective and inspiring pedagogic improvements at both school and teacher college level. Many of the teacher colleges involved carry out both pre- and in-service training with a cluster of primary and secondary schools in the surrounding community. The initiatives are closely connected to national efforts to improve pedagogy and teacher education generally.

With this in mind, the Ministry of Education, with the support of UNICEF and international consultants, has developed, piloted, adjusted and implemented a competency-based approach (CBA) to teacher education for all public primary and most private schools. The decision of the government to extend primary education from five to seven years means the development of a CBA for these grades will be integrated into the planned revised curricula for the sixth and seventh years. The ProVert colleges visited showed a good understanding of the CBA and had participated in national and local workshops.[4]

At one project primary school, we observed the director of the school using the CBA approach. He clearly understood the relationship between the transmission of theoretical knowledge in an applied way and in, giving the pupils the opportunity to practise what he had taught. The Malagasy language was used to explain the lesson concepts and emphasis was put upon the learning *processes* involved. The lesson was, however, very teacher-centred with no pair- or group-work activities. Importantly, a disproportionate amount of lesson time was devoted to teaching and much less to practice and the monitoring of learning outcomes. The content of the lesson was admirably about environmental issues and practices, but it was delivered in a very traditional way. Thinking back to our discussion about the importance of indigenous knowledge, there appears to be a tension between respect for indigenous content and a recognisable need to move indigenous or traditional pedagogy away from chalk 'n' talk methods.

At a second school – more isolated and in a poorer community – 140 pupils were being taught by two teachers. Here, the school director occasionally grouped pupils, had tried to integrate environmental issues into the curriculum, and had made good progress in developing a school garden. But we saw few teaching and learning resources, which may well have contributed to only 10 out of 18 pupils passing their primary leaving examination. However, at this school and others visited, the directors showed commitment to the educational reforms and the CBA, and had clearly benefited from participation in in-service training programmes provided by the local teacher training colleges. Links were being consolidated between the colleges and the schools.

In terms of pedagogy, there is clearly still more that needs to be done in this part of Africa in demonstrating to teachers and teacher educators what characterises a green education pedagogy – i.e. the application of a CBA to a curriculum focusing upon the integration of green issues, inclusion and gender equality.

One teacher training college visited appeared very much aware of the role it played and the contribution it could make to pedagogic improvement across the whole ProVert programme. It was well supported by the NGO and there was clearly a great deal of political and professional will to support pedagogic change both within the NGO leadership and within the college management. The college was looking to develop its own strategic plan, which would have at its heart two concerns: first, careful planning and monitoring of its new training programme, particularly with regard to integrating ProVert principles into the whole programme, and, second, the 'outreach' work of the college in relation to supporting ProVert (and non-ProVert) schools and colleges.

From an intensive round of visits to schools and colleges on the island, it was clear that the green education programme is now well established and is moving into a consolidation phase, with increased attention being paid to the clarification and dissemination of its pedagogy. As with many development projects, what began as a relatively small pilot programme is now being considered for scaling up nationally. Equally important is the recognition that Madagascar could use its own indigenous models of good practice to carry its educational reforms to the next level. Concern, however, was raised at the risk of losing the ability to tailor environmental education to meet local and specific needs. It was suggested that one way forward would be to hold a national workshop on ways to integrate CBA principles into environmental education lessons generally. Supporting teacher guides could result from such a workshop, which would include practical ways to teach – for example, from whole-class to group work, an understanding of lesson aims in relation to learning outcomes, the use of effective resources currently being developed, appropriate assessment techniques and realistic ways to extend the work from the classroom to the school compound and community.

If we think back to the raft of noble words uttered by the international community with regard to ESD, there is a paucity of advice concerning the pedagogical reforms that will be needed to deliver the content of ESD. I suspect this may have something to do with those employed as advisers and consultants at the international level – they often have little experience or qualification of actually teaching in African classrooms.

It is clear that innovations of this kind require competent and dedicated leadership at ministry and NGO level, in teacher colleges and at school level. ProVert will need leadership at the national level to oversee understanding of the pedagogic principles that underpin ProVert, and the successful application of these in the partner institutions.

Conclusion: lessons to be learned for ESD and teacher education from Madagascar

Madagascar offers the global community a number of lessons to be learned:

1. ESD at school and college level involves a holistic approach to development, embracing educational, environmental and social objectives working together in tandem. The green education programme has at its core four key components directly related to the MDGs: namely, the mainstreaming of environmental education at school and college level; the centrality of gender in education; efforts to improve the inclusion of all children; and pedagogic reform to deliver more relevant and efficient learning and training.

2. Good ESD has to address the endemic quality issues that have bedevilled the education system of sub-Saharan Africa for decades: relevance, efficiency and effectiveness; a balance between theory and practice, i.e. using the institutions' farms both to link theory and practice and to support the college or school financially; effective means of pupil assessment and teacher evaluation; and strong school-community links.

3. Good teacher education and effective high-quality classroom learning require *less* of a focus upon content and that *more* attention be paid to pedagogy.
4. There is a synergy between the initiator and driver of the programme – in this case an NGO – and the government's willingness to radically overhaul the education system, particularly at the primary level. The 2007 Madagascar Ministry of Education reforms involving a change in the language of instruction for the first five years and a shift towards a new pedagogy are reciprocally reinforced by the objectives and practices of the programme.
5. Recognition should be given to the potential to bridge the gap between classroom knowledge and the reality which makes up the daily lives of the children involved. Good ESD needs to be locally relevant and culturally appropriate. By starting small and in a number of different island sites, however, the programme is characterised by a respect for difference. A challenge, should it be scaled up nationally, will be to maintain this respect. ESD, in other words, is not 'one size fits all', but must be created to account for regional and local differences.
6. For ESD to be effective at the teacher education level, account must be taken of the situation of the schools in which trainee teachers and graduating teachers begin their teaching careers. Teachers, like flowers, need good soil in which to grow and plenty of tender, loving care to flourish.

Notes

[1] http://www.unesco.org/new/en.../education-for-sustainable-development/

[2] The evidence for this case study is taken from an evaluation of the ProVert green education programme carried out in November 2008 by myself and a team of consultants for the Norwegian government (Stephens et al, 2008).

[3] Evidence for this section is drawn from my field visit to evaluate the green education programme in November 2007. The visit consisted of 10 days, during which time six primary schools, three teacher colleges and government officials at the local and national level were consulted. The evaluation was carried out on behalf of the Norwegian Agency for Development Cooperation, the major donor supporting the programme.

[4] By the end of 2007, 1957 teacher trainers and 78,700 teachers (including private schools) had been trained in the CBA (Razafindrabe & Van der Zwan, 2008).

David Stephens

References

Annan, K. (2001) Secretary General Calls for Break in Political Stalemate over Environmental Issues. United Nations Press Release, SG/SM/7739, ENV/DEV/561, 14 March.
http://www.un.org/News/Press/docs/2001/sgsm7739.doc.htm

Belgrade Charter (1975) http://portal.unesco.org/education/en/ev./php

Breidlid, A. (2009) Culture, Indigenous Knowledge Systems and Sustainable Development: a view of education in an African context, *International Journal of Educational Development*, 29(2), 140-148.
http://dx.doi.org/10.1016/j.ijedudev.2008.09.009

Department for Environment, Transport and the Regions (DETR) (1999) *Sustainable Development Education Panel: first annual report*. London: DETR.

Environmental Literacy Council (2008) Madagascar.
http://www.enviroliteracy.org/article.php/499.html

Gough, A. (2009) 4th World Teachers' Day in Thailand and the 12th UNESCO-APEID International Conference on Quality Innovations for Teaching and Learning, Thailand, 4-26 March.

Harber, C. & Stephens, D. (2010) *From Shouters to Supporters: quality education project – final evaluation report*. Oslo: Save the Children, Norway.

Hawes, H. & Stephens, D. (1990) *Questions of Quality: primary education and development*. Harlow: Longman.

Huckle, J. (2006) *Education for Sustainable Development: a briefing paper for the Training and Development Agency for Schools*. London: Training and Development Agency for Schools.

Lewin, K.M. & Stuart, J.S. (2003) *Researching Teacher Education: new perspectives on practice, performance and policy*. DfID Educational Paper No. 49a. London: Department for International Development.

Little, A. & Green, A. (2009) Successful Globalisation, Education and Sustainable Development, *International Journal of Educational Development*, 29(2), 166-174. http://dx.doi.org/10.1016/j.ijedudev.2008.09.011

Odora Hoppers, C.A. (Ed.) (2002) *Indigenous Knowledge and the Integration of Knowledge Systems in the Third World*. Claremont: New Africa Books.

Razafindrabe, N.H. & Zwan, L. van der (2008) *End-Review of Norway's Support to UNICEF's Programme in Madagascar (2005-2007) and Appraisal of UNICEF's Proposal for a New Education Programme 2008-2011*. Norad Collected Reviews 14/2008. Oslo: Norwegian Agency for Development Cooperation.

Sillitoe, P. (2000) Let Them Eat Cake: indigenous knowledge, science and the 'poorest of the poor', *Anthropology Today*, 16(6), 3-7.
http://dx.doi.org/10.1111/1467-8322.00031

Stephens, D. (2007) *Culture in Education and Development: principles, practice and policy*. Oxford: Symposium Books.

Stephens, D., Nielssen, H. & Rajaonah, R. (2008) *ProVert: an integrated green education programme for Madagascar.* Mid-Term Review. Antananarivo: Norwegian Agency for Development Cooperation.

UNESCO (1978) *Intergovernmental Conference on Environmental Education, Tbilisi (USSR), 14-26 October 1977. Final Report.* Paris: UNESCO.

UNESCO (2005) *Guidelines and Recommendations for Reorienting Teacher Education to Address Sustainability.* Education for Sustainable Development in Action, Technical Paper No. 2. Paris: Section for Education for Sustainable Development, UNESCO.

UNESCO (2007) *Good Practices in Teacher Education Institutions.* Education for Sustainable Development in Action, Good Practices No. 1. Paris: Section for Education for Sustainable Development, UNESCO.

United Nations Conference on Environment and Development (UNCED) (1993) *United Nations Conference on Environment and Development, Rio de Janeiro. Volume 1, Agenda 21.* New York: United Nations.

World Commission on Environment and Development (1987) *Our Common Future.* New York: United Nations.

CHAPTER 6

Building Capacity for Educational Research in Sub-Saharan Africa: opportunities, constraints and lessons in the context of Mozambique, Tanzania and Uganda

**PEADAR CREMIN,
MARY GORETTI NAKABUGO
& EIMEAR BARRETT**

SUMMARY This chapter offers insights into the manner in which institutional culture, strategy, supports and structures can nurture the building of capacity for educational research. The particular opportunities and challenges to developing an enabling research environment in the sub-Saharan African university context, at both the individual and institutional level, are considered. Evidence is drawn from research undertaken within a programme of strategic cooperation, funded by Irish Aid, which forged a formal partnership between Irish and African institutions and academics in the period 2007 to 2011. The chapter focuses on issues involved in building capacity for educational research in universities in Mozambique, Tanzania and Uganda, arguing that such research in higher education institutions is critical to the achievement of Education for All and the Millennium Development Goals.

Introduction: building capacity for educational research

At the outset, it will be helpful to discuss what we mean by building capacity for research. Trostle (1992, p. 1321) has defined research capacity building (RCB) as 'a process of individual, institutional and inter-institutional development which leads to higher levels of skills and greater ability to perform useful research'. While it is easy to define building research capacity as the ongoing improvement of the individual or the institution's capacity to conduct research, the factors on the ground which may militate against this happening need to be taken into account. It is our view that the capacity to engage in research is something that can be grown and nurtured, whether at the individual or institutional level.

To a considerable extent, the 'doing' of research contributes to building capacity for further and higher-level research. Each discrete piece of research has the possibility of involving greater and deeper levels of research, whether that is based on a deeper familiarity with different modes of research (quantitative or qualitative) or on different support tools (data analysis, SPSS, etc.). It also seems reasonable to suggest that beginning researchers need to be encouraged, supported, mentored and exposed to critical audiences, whether through conference presentations or publications of different types (general research publications, peer-reviewed publications), if they are to grow in capacity and confidence.

No matter how talented, researchers need an enabling institutional environment in which to flourish. Similarly, the best research system in the world will not produce good research without talented, skilled and motivated researchers. It is worth considering the possibility that centres of educational research may suffer from the fact that many of those who work in the field of education have come from other fields (such as those of psychology, sociology, history, and so on) or have considered themselves primarily as teachers rather than researchers. As such, their primary interest may not always have been in education or in educational research. Relatively few commence their careers by setting out to be educational researchers. Consequently, in order to excel in educational research they need to make a critical conversion as they shift focus.

At the institutional level, the establishment and nurturing of a research culture can be very challenging, requiring both time and resources. This is particularly true in the field of educational research, which does not always attract the kinds or levels of funding that may be the norm in fields such as scientific, technological or health research. Long-term and sustainable research is likely to flourish in a context of greater career certainty and the likelihood of ongoing funding for the field in which one specialises. It is reasonable to suggest that funding in the field of educational research is largely sporadic and opportunistic, often depending on the skill of a researcher in preparing a research bid more than on the capability of the researcher as researcher.

In the context of sub-Saharan Africa and the multiple pressures on its educational sector, there are very real constraints which need to be considered when we attempt to promote the building of research capacity.

Review of Literature on Research Capacity Building in the South

A first perspective which emerges from the literature on RCB in developing countries is the overwhelming agreement that there is a serious deficit in this area, most especially when the more developed countries are compared to their developing peers. While writing in relation to health, it is likely that the comment made by Nchinda also carries some currency when applied to education:

> the industrialized countries have the largest number of highly trained scientists working in well-equipped laboratories and having at their disposal financial resources to carry out good quality work. A research tradition has become established in the scientific community of these countries. The same cannot be said for developing countries. The latter countries lack the appropriate self-sustained research capacities both in the numbers and quality of trained researchers and appropriate institutional capacities for high-level research.
> (Nchinda, 2002, p. 1701)

Sawyerr (2004, p. 213) offers a similar analysis of the problems in educational research capacity, arguing that 'in most African countries, conditions for research have been severely compromised as manifest by the generally poor remuneration, heavy teaching loads, inability to maintain faculty and inadequate infrastructure'. As long ago as 1999, Samoff (1999, p. 250) spoke of the 'troubled state of education research in Africa today', identifying 'the very limited research capabilities within most African countries'. The problems arising from this weakness in research capacity are multifaceted. Among other challenges, they expose African countries and their universities to the 'intellectual erosion of their programs of study, losing their critical ability to assess claims to knowledge, and becoming dependent on the outside supply of knowledge' (Zakri, 2006).

A great number of the studies and research conducted in Africa are conducted by external bodies and agencies, with governments having little more than nominal involvement, control or ownership. Samoff (1999, p. 250) points out that most research on education development in Africa has been funded and undertaken by donor agencies and foreign consultants (sometimes with assistantship of African counterparts). The findings and policy recommendations from such donor-driven studies have usually lacked national relevance, control and ownership. Samoff has argued that 'where there is little effective and genuine partnership in initiating and managing education sector studies, there is even less national ownership of their results' (p. 253). This leads to the creation of what Samoff identifies as two separate research tracks (internal and external) and to the fact that 'only infrequently do internally initiated and externally commissioned studies even mention each other' (p. 250). Furthermore, most donors retain the rights to the research for which they have paid, which, as a consequence, is very often not put into the public domain:

> those who are responsible for guiding and managing Africa's
> education systems do not regard these as their studies,
> developed for their benefit, and useful in their daily work.
> Those who operate Africa's education systems, from principals
> and headmasters to teachers, have even less sense of
> ownership. Students, parents and communities have none at
> all. (Samoff, 1999, p. 253)

There are very real risks when any society depends on others for knowledge generation. Developing countries cannot rely on external bodies or agencies to prioritise their specific needs. These countries must grow their own capacity for research; must increase the numbers of home-grown researchers; must follow their own research agendas; must improve on an ongoing basis the quality of the research done; and must ensure that all of this is done in a sustainable way. As happens in the developed world, it is important that African universities should become powerhouses of research production, as well as being the primary producers of skilled researchers who may go on to work for government and other agencies. In the words of Sawyerr (2004, p. 217): 'the strength of African Universities and research institutions is a key condition for its development and their weakness is an index of, as well as a contributor to, its poverty'. The connections between research at third level and poverty reduction in sub-Saharan Africa might, at first glance, appear tenuous. However, every society, especially in the context of an increasingly knowledge-based economy, needs to have its own knowledge-generating sources, compiling data, conducting analysis, making proposals to government and other key stakeholders in that society, and ultimately showing how research can be applied at a grass-roots level to bring about significant change, most especially in relation to poverty alleviation.

Weakness in research capability is but part of the malaise of the African university sector in general. A decline in per-unit costs (from US$6800 in 1980 to US$1200 in 2002) amid rapidly rising enrolments; insufficient numbers of qualified academic staff in higher education institutions as the result of brain drain, retirements and HIV/AIDS, as well as low internal and external efficiency; and poor governance have all been factors contributing to a crisis in the sector and in public confidence in the quality of education offered by the university sector (Materu, 2007, p. xiv).

Another consequence of the paucity of research conducted at and through African universities has been the emergence of a poor publishing culture. Most of the research done by African scholars has remained inaccessible to the global community because it is rarely published. Weak publication records mean that few African universities merit inclusion in world university rankings, which focus on research quality and output. This, in turn, reduces the profile of the universities and has implications for their standing and status both nationally and internationally:

> according to the 2005 Shanghai Jiao Tong University
> worldwide rankings, only 5 African HEIs [higher education
> institutions] appear in the top 500 (4 from South Africa and 1
> from Egypt). This compares poorly not only with developed
> countries but also with other developing regions like the
> Asia/Pacific region which listed 92 universities in the top 500.
> Even if the population factor is taken into account, this is still
> a dismal comparison. A likely explanation could be the
> limited availability of published and internationally
> comparable data on African HEIs since these global rankings
> are based on publicly available information on academic and
> research performance ... Thus, for African HEIs to improve
> their international standing, quality improvement has to go
> beyond quality assurance within institutions and by national
> agencies to include strategies to ensure that academic and
> research outputs are published in internationally recognized
> media. (Materu, 2007, p. 7)

A similar situation applies to other university rankings. For example, the *Times Higher Education* World University Rankings for 2009 show a single African university (the University of Cape Town at number 146) in the top 200. The *Times Higher Education* ranking for 2010/2011 lists two African universities (Cape Town and Alexandria).

The perception of poor quality has impacted most strongly on the traditional state-supported universities, leading to rapid growth in many countries of private universities, many of which are profit-led. It is now estimated that in sub-Saharan Africa, there are 'about 740 million people, some 200 public universities, a fast increasing number of private higher education institutions and the lowest tertiary gross enrolment ratio in the world (about 5 percent)'. It is likely that there are as many as 100 private universities in Africa at this stage, most of which have been opened since 2000 (Materu, 2007, p. xiii).

This brief review of the literature clearly indicates that addressing current weaknesses and, in particular, the lack of research capacity –

both institutional and individual – in many African universities ought to be a key priority for those who are concerned about poverty alleviation, whether at government level or within international development agencies.

Building Research Capacity in Partnership

The Irish-African Partnership for Research Capacity Building (IAPRCB) commenced in 2008 with support from the development arm of the Irish government, Irish Aid. The concept for this partnership built on an exploratory visit by representatives of the Irish university sector to Uganda in 2005. The Universities Ireland delegation was conscious that (according to the visit's terms of reference) any future cooperation between Irish and Ugandan higher education institutions should be based on 'a commitment to enhancing sustainability, local ownership and leadership, and consistency with national policies and programmes' (Pollack et al, 2005, p. 2) in Uganda. Two of the three general recommendations emerging from this visit touch upon the issue of RCB, using a partnership model:

* Funding should be identified (higher education authority, Department of Foreign Affairs, Department for International Development, Atlantic Philanthropies, the European Union or other) to sustain long-term partnerships between higher education institutions in Ireland and their counterparts in Uganda and other Irish Aid priority countries in sub-Saharan Africa. These would enable strategic placements (long and short term) of senior staff, staff exchanges, pre- and post-retirement placements, joint research initiatives, student mobility, and the mentoring and training of trainers and researchers as a means of building capacity, solidarity and mutual understanding.
* In the context of the above, Universities Ireland should seek a long-term partnership between the higher education sector, North and South, in Ireland (including universities, colleges of education, institutes of technology, and further and higher education colleges) and the Irish Aid Division of the Department of Foreign Affairs through which the higher education sector in Ireland would build the capacity to respond to the needs identified and prioritised by partners in sub-Saharan Africa. This may require the establishment of a separate higher education development partnership fund.

In the event, the Irish government, in December 2006, announced a 'Programme of Strategic Cooperation between Irish Aid and Higher Education and Research Institutes, 2007-2011', with a budget of €12.5 million. In July 2007, it was announced that over €7 million in funding was being awarded to higher education and research institutes in Ireland for research into development issues. One of the funded projects was the Irish-African Partnership for Research Capacity Building. The IAPRCB is a partnership of the nine universities in Ireland together with four African universities, with the overall aim of building research capacity for poverty reduction.[1] The programme's underlying rationale is to collaboratively strengthen research capacity in the service of the global development imperative of poverty reduction (and associated challenges such as livelihood security, environmental protection and disaster risk reduction), in particular in sub-Saharan Africa.

From the outset, the IAPRCB set out to identify the scope for development research in the partner African and Irish institutions. The IAPRCB's particular focus on RCB derives from the 'greater recognition of the potential of the higher education and research sectors in developing countries to contribute to achieving the Millennium Development Goals (MDGs)' (Irish Aid, 2007, p. 2). As a corollary of this, there is a need to ensure that development-related research is being adequately supported, both in terms of personnel with appropriate knowledge and skills as well as in terms of appropriate infrastructure. An initial goal of the IAPRCB was to establish targeted capacity-building programmes in the context of real issues and priorities for Africa.

A first step towards identifying the need for, and potential of, partnership in building capacity for research involved a survey of stakeholders' views. This stakeholder consultation sought to establish a baseline understanding of research capacity for international development in the Irish universities, as well as research capacity in general in the four participating African universities. The consultation sought to elicit the views of administrators and researchers within all 13 universities on the opportunities and constraints to RCB at both institutional and individual levels, together with their views on priority research themes and on partnerships within health and education, both within partner universities and elsewhere. In this chapter, the focus is on three African universities (in Mozambique, Tanzania and Uganda).

Methodology of the Stakeholder Consultation

The objective of the stakeholder consultation was to elicit stakeholders' views and experiences in several key areas:

- Individual capacity development, including the highs and lows of the individual's research career and the factors contributing to this.
- Institutional research capacity development, the setting of research strategies and institutional incentives for engaging in research.
- Opportunities and barriers to engaging in international development research within the partner universities and possible ways of overcoming these barriers.

The field research took place between June and September 2008. During the process, the two project researchers visited all 13 institutions and spent three to four days in each location. In total, over 300 academics and administrators were consulted. This number included 69 African colleagues, all active in the field of education, who participated in education-specific group interviews and workshops conducted as part of the research. These colleagues came from Eduardo Mondlane University in Mozambique (12), the University of Dar es Salaam in Tanzania (15) and Makerere University in Uganda (42).

During some of the group interviews and workshops, the researchers employed an exercise whereby participants were asked to plot perceived levels of research capacity against their research career during the last 10 years. This allowed for an evaluation of the factors perceived to be responsible for low or high levels of capacity and the factors that represented turning points from low to high levels, or vice versa. Group discussions were also used to explore factors associated with institutional capacity building. Transcripts were analysed for emerging themes and trends and organised under two main headings: opportunities and constraints to RCB.

General Overview of the Three Focus Universities

All three universities are the oldest and largest public higher education institutions in their respective countries. They occupy a unique position in those countries as they are the only universities that provide all-round education, covering most of the academic disciplines. Their outputs in terms of human capital development can be seen in all areas of society. The vast majority of graduates working in the education sector, the health sector, in government and in the private sector are products of these universities.

Makerere University, the oldest of the three, was established in 1922 as a technical college. To date, it has evolved into one of the leading universities in sub-Saharan Africa. Its mission is 'to provide quality teaching, carry out research and offer professional services to meet the changing needs of society by utilising world-wide and internally generated human resources, information and technology to enhance the University's leading position in Uganda and beyond' (Makerere University, 2007, p. 9).

The University of Dar es Salaam was founded in 1961 to serve three core functions: (1) to transmit, through teaching, knowledge from one generation to another and to meet the high-level human resource needs of the Tanzanian society; (2) to produce knowledge through research; and (3) to provide services to the community that address the country's existing and future problems, through consultancy and outreach programmes (University of Dar es Salaam, 2008a). The mission of the university positions it at the centre of the country's economic development in 'the unrelenting pursuit of scholarly and strategic research, education, training and public service directed at the attainment of equitable and sustainable socio-economic development of Tanzania and the rest of Africa' (University of Dar es Salaam, 2008b, p. 3).

Eduardo Mondlane University was established in 1962 and served the needs of the Portuguese colonial regime. The development of research capacity in Mozambique faced an acute crisis following the mass exodus of the Portuguese in the aftermath of the country's independence in 1975. The dearth of university graduates and the illiteracy rates (about 90% at the time) made building research capacity in this context an uphill task (Alberts et al, 2003). While the situation has improved following the return to peace in 1992, Mozambique, and Eduardo Mondlane University in particular, still has a long way to go in addressing the deficit in the capacity for research.

Table I summarises some of the key facts in relation to the three universities. While all three universities have, as their core function, to contribute to the sustainable development of their respective countries, their impact has remained minimal over the years. This is due to a number of factors, including constrained funding and resources (both physical and human), and teaching and research that are often detached from societal needs.

University	Year founded	Undergraduate students	Postgraduate students	Total students	Academic staff
Eduardo Mondlane University	1962	15,681	605	16,286	1255
University of Dar es Salaam	1961	17,098	2552	19,650	1045
Makerere University	1922	34,968	1910	36,878	1714

Table I. Background information on the three universities as of 2008-09.[2]

Table I shows the discrepancy between the number of undergraduate and postgraduate students at the three universities, looked at across all faculties. Based on this data, the percentage of postgraduate students ranges from 3.7% at Eduardo Mondlane University to 13% at the University of Dar es Salaam. This indicates that postgraduates make up a very small proportion of the student body. Table I also suggests that a very large proportion of the time of academic staff will be spent in meeting the needs of the undergraduate student body, rather than in directing postgraduate research.

Staffing of the Three Focus Universities

All three universities have strikingly similar patterns in relation to the proportion of staff at senior ranks (senior lecturer to professor) as compared to the number at lower levels (teaching assistant to lecturer; see Table II).

	Eduardo Mondlane University	University of Dar es Salaam	Makerere University
Professor	9	80	52
Associate Professor	48	131	82
Senior Lecturer	146	277	193
Lecturer	575	234	394
Assistant Lecturer	477	399	376
Teaching Assistant	–	346	285
Totals	1255	1467	1382

Table II. Staffing at different ranks in the three universities as of 2007-08.

This pattern is partly a consequence of the lack of research capacity and, more especially, the weakness in research output. Staff in the three universities are promoted mainly on the basis of research productivity and number of internationally recognised peer-reviewed publications. The fewer number of staff at senior ranks could be described as an indicator of low research productivity. It also highlights the necessity for building research capacity in the three universities. The fact that these three universities are arguably the strongest in their respective states indicates how big a problem research capacity is across the university sector in these countries and in sub-Saharan Africa generally.

Developing the human resources for research is even more problematic in teacher education faculties or schools, where there are significantly fewer staff occupying the senior ranks, where the gender gap is high and where there are many unfilled positions. Many faculties or schools have to depend on part-time staff or suffer from the fact that the small number of full-time staff are too overloaded to engage in any meaningful research. Detailed data on staffing in all the three universities' schools of education was not easily accessible. However, Makerere University, the oldest and largest of the three, where out of the 112 established academic staff posts only 76 are filled and, of these, only 12 are at a senior rank (Table III), serves to illustrate this bleak picture.

The pattern in Table III shows the extent to which lower-level posts (from lecturer level down) have been filled, while the more senior posts remain unfilled. This situation has cost benefits to the university as the greatest savings are to be made by keeping these senior posts fallow. To be fair to the universities, it must also be noted that, on many occasions, when such senior posts are advertised, there is a paucity of properly qualified candidates capable of filling the posts in question. There is a further difficulty in that the concentration of staff at the lower ranks means that many, sometimes even the majority, are either on contract or on probation. In the current research, many staff on such temporary employment terms reported that they had missed out on opportunities that would build their individual research capacity. In part, this is because staff on contract or probation do not qualify for PhD study leave, and can neither benefit from in-house research grants nor participate as principal investigators in donor-funded research bids.

Position	Established academic posts	Filled positions	Number of males	Number of females
Professor	8	1	1	–
Associate Professor	13	1	1	–
Senior Lecturer	22	10	8	2
Lecturer	33	33	20	13
Assistant Lecturer	24	19	12	7
Teaching Assistant	12	12	10	2
Totals	112	76	52	24
Student population	Undergraduates: 5100		Postgraduates: 320	

Table III. Research capacity in Makerere University's
School of Education as of 2009.

The current situation has the consequence that the senior staffing layer, which might be expected to engage most thoroughly with research, both as active researchers and as people directing research, remains under-filled. The mentorship, modelling and strategic direction that might come from the professorial levels are absent. Clearly, the data in Table III, although limited, gives a clear picture of the multifaceted reasons for weaknesses in research capacity and the many challenges that will need to be addressed in programmes of RCB.

Constraints to Research Capacity Building

In this section, we consider the particular needs of research in the field of teacher education in Mozambique, Tanzania and Uganda, setting out the perceived individual constraints to, as well as the opportunities for, RCB. Many of the constraints and opportunities cited by the interviewees during the field research were of a generic nature, and were applicable to almost any discipline and geographical location. These generic factors included, among others, the lack of funding opportunities and research infrastructure, workloads, the presence or lack of mentorship, opportunities for postgraduate training, gender barriers, low salaries, and enabling or disabling institutional support. For the purposes of this chapter, we focus the discussion on those that specifically relate to teacher education.

Most of the researchers consulted felt that their research careers had evolved from a low point (in the past 10 years) because they had been employed primarily to teach and train student teachers and not necessarily to do research. Those who engaged in research did so individually rather than as a professional requirement. Because research was not a major requirement for their initial university employment, many individuals started their academic career as 'novice researchers' with a very limited history or capacity for research. A reduced institutional focus on research in teacher education also meant that there was little, if any, funding or any other support available from within the universities to encourage individuals to undertake research. Most available support was for undergraduate teaching.

Even when the institutional research landscape has changed and there is a requirement that staff must be research-productive, some individuals have found themselves having to do research on a part-time basis. This occurs when individuals have had to pursue their advanced research degrees whilst already working full-time in academic positions. Since doctorates were not a requirement to be recruited as an academic, in the first instance, many have now had to engage with the changing job requirements. To take paid leave would allow a researcher to retain a basic salary but with the loss of all other emoluments, such as transport, housing, etc. Furthermore, where many university teachers engage in supplementary teaching in other institutions or in providing private tuition, these income streams would either be curtailed or become impossible due to lack of time. In short, few university staff can afford the luxury of dedicating themselves to full-time study and research, except where a full scholarship to support this is made available.

Currently, the major barrier to individual RCB, reported in the teacher education institutions included in this study, is the lack of time to engage in research due to heavy teaching loads, compounded by several other job responsibilities including supervision of students on school practice, meetings and programme management. Due to the lack of staff at senior ranks, as highlighted in the preceding section, in some instances early career research staff have been required to take on administrative responsibilities, acting as heads of units/departments before establishing themselves as researchers within their disciplines. It was also noted that a culture of mentorship and peer support is absent from most departments, where there are few senior staff and many more junior staff. In many instances, those interviewed spoke of a 'generation gap', with many upcoming researchers struggling on their own. Some research-active educationalists from institutions in the current study reported that they had been involved with local communities in action-based research in areas such as literacy, inclusion and access. However, they felt that this type of action-based research was given limited recognition compared with more theoretical research that results in 'scholarly' publications.

While the lack of funding for educational research is a widespread phenomenon globally (see, for example, Rees et al, 2007), the situation is even worse in cash-strapped countries such as Mozambique, Tanzania and Uganda, where there is limited support from government or university sources and where much of the available funding is targeted towards undergraduate training. While the research funding environment has improved over the years with new funding streams coming from institutions such as the Swedish International Development Cooperation Agency, the Swedish Agency for Research Cooperation with Developing Countries, the United Kingdom's Department for International Development, the Norwegian Agency for Development Cooperation and the Japan International Cooperation Agency, among others, there is still a widespread lack of funding for research in the schools of education included in the current study. This prompts a number of staff members to take on any funded research assignments that come up, or what some termed 'engagement in opportunity-based research', even when they do not have the specialist knowledge of the discipline. In the longer term, this means that people lack the opportunity to build research capacity within their own education specialisations, publishing becomes difficult and many have resorted to becoming generalists.

Although the lack of supportive research infrastructure and conducive research environments was highlighted by staff across faculties, it was perceived to be more acute in the schools of education because they have such difficulty in attracting external funding to supplement the meagre resources and supports that the universities provide. By way of contrast, they report that their counterparts in science-based disciplines, such as health and engineering, are able to secure funding, procure supplementary research equipment and hire additional research staff from the various donor-supported research grants that they attract. In interviews conducted for the current research, stakeholders in the schools of education mentioned issues such as their inability to avail themselves of the services of research assistants, the lack of office space and, in some instances, the problem of poorly equipped libraries.

While gender inequity is cited as a major problem in higher education globally, in the context of RCB in sub-Saharan Africa, some disciples are more prone to gender challenges than others. Pritchard (2007) claimed that gender inequality is a ubiquitous problem in higher education, characterised by under-representation of women in senior management and over-representation in low-level and temporary positions. In a study entitled 'Gender Equity in Commonwealth Higher Education', Morley (2005) stated that the dominant gender issues included access to education, especially higher education, the absence of women in senior academic and management positions, the gendered division of labour and gender violence. Capacity-building programmes have been in existence in the African partner institutions, including the three focus institutions, for up to 30 years in some cases. These initiatives have included fellowships for postgraduate study such as Master's or PhD programmes. Historically, women have encountered barriers to accessing such programmes. Those interviewed as part of this study reported that the first barrier is the requirement that a fellowship, or a portion of it (in the case of sandwich programmes), be completed abroad, meaning that women would have to leave their homes and families. Certain fellowships place a restriction on the age of application, normally 35 years of age, and this also presents a major barrier to women who return to work after raising families. Female academics in professional disciplines such as teaching, where research funding is very much constrained, are much more affected when compared to the science-based disciplines, where, sometimes, there are dedicated scholarships for female academics, irrespective of age, to try and increase the number of women in science disciplines.

In summary, it is clear from the current research that there is a range of constraints to nurturing research capability in schools of education in sub-Saharan Africa. Some constraints arise from the personal circumstances of the researchers, others are institutionally generated, while others still arise from gender inequities. The lack of money, together with the absence of institutional research traditions, suggests that this will continue unless a very concerted effort is made to establish new norms and new supports.

Opportunities for Research Capacity Building

Those interviewed identified opportunities within the three institutions that portray some positive trends in RCB. For example, the wider demand for research at third level and the global emphasis on higher education and its contribution to sustainable development has compelled institutions in Africa to nurture environments that encourage individuals to engage in research. As such, there are now in place more strategic approaches to RCB within the universities, from which all disciplines, including teacher education, have benefited. For example, there are now formal structures that have been created at the different levels to facilitate RCB. At the higher levels, there are deputy vice-chancellors, vice-rectors or directors in charge of research, while at the faculty level there are now positions of deputy deans of research. The responsibilities of these officials include, among others, coordinating research funding schemes as well as capacity-building programmes for staff and graduate students.

Individual researchers have also had to take personal responsibility to look out for research opportunities and to exploit them. This includes networking with other educational researchers at the national, regional and international level. Several of those who had pursued their advanced degrees elsewhere, or had worked abroad, reported having been able to utilise their international contacts to develop their research capacity in the form of resource sharing, joint publications and joint research-bid writing.

Finally, in all three institutions and their associated schools of education, initiatives are in place for individuals to complete postgraduate study on the job, either at Master's or PhD level. Staff who register for postgraduate studies within their local university may be given fee waivers, while those who are able to secure scholarships to study abroad are granted study leave.

Overall, while there is still a concentration of researchers in science-based areas, efforts are now being made to build up a critical mass in areas not traditionally associated with research, such as teacher education. This means that efforts are being made to emphasise the importance of building a research culture as well as highlighting the importance of a PhD in a research career.

Conclusions

When the core focus of development activity in sub-Saharan Africa is on poverty reduction (and associated challenges such as livelihood and food security, environmental protection and disaster risk reduction), it is imperative that education, at whatever level, should be part of the toolkit which addresses poverty alleviation. This gives rise to questions about the kinds of education which might need to be prioritised (scientific, mathematical, literacy, etc.) if expenditure on educational provision is appropriately targeted so that poverty reduction is maximised. There is a growing acceptance that the research conducted in higher education institutions is critical to such prioritisation and to achieving the Education for All and Millennium Development Goals.

The current research has helped to substantiate the deficits which exist with regard to building research capability in education faculties in sub-Saharan Africa. It highlights the perceived impediments to building a research path in the field of education. The relative scarcity of funding for educational research was frequently cited as a barrier among those interviewed. The belief that action-based research at community level, even in fields as critical as literacy, access and inclusion, is undervalued as well as underfunded may have implications for the achievement of the Millennium Development Goals. Further research may be required to test whether this belief is grounded in reality or not. The extent to which there is a dependency on non-African funding for core resourcing of

African research is clearly an issue, as is the question of ownership, where outside agencies have funded research but without finding ways of ensuring that the findings and outcomes are embraced locally and have local application.

The research further highlights the need to consider RCB at three different levels – namely, the individual, the institutional and the inter-institutional (or partnership) levels. None of these levels of RCB can be seen as self-sufficient and all must be advanced at the same time to maximise overall capability. A partnership model offering African researchers an opportunity to engage in north-south research partnerships, from which they will gain mentoring, support and possible financial resourcing, remains an attractive model and is an integral element in the current IAPRCB project.

Notes

[1] The Irish universities are the four University Colleges of the National University of Ireland (University College Cork, University College Dublin, the National University of Ireland, Galway and the National University of Ireland, Maynooth), Trinity College Dublin, Dublin City University, the University of Limerick/Mary Immaculate College (where the education research component of this project was based and coordinated), Queen's University Belfast and the University of Ulster. The four African universities are Makerere University (Uganda), the University of Dar es Salaam (Tanzania), the University of Malawi and Eduardo Mondlane University (Mozambique).

[2] For the facts and figures for the University of Dar es Salaam, see http://www.udsm.ac.tz/about_us/facts.php; for Makerere University, see http://mak.ac.ug/index.php?option=com_content&task=view&id=319&Itemid=301; and for Eduardo Mondlane University, the facts and figures are from the University International Office.

References

Alberts, Thomas, Abegaz, Berhanu, Coughlin, Peter, et al (2003) *Sida's Support to the University Eduardo Mondlane, Mozambique.* Sida Evaluation 03/35. Stockholm: Sida.

Irish Aid (2007) *Programme of Strategic Cooperation between Irish Aid and Higher Education and Research Institutes 2007-2011.* Dublin: Department of Foreign Affairs.

Makerere University (2007) *Makerere University Quality Assurance Policy Framework.* Kampala: Makerere University.

Materu, P. (2007) Higher Education Quality Assurance in Sub-Saharan Africa: status, challenges, opportunities, and promising practices. Working Paper

No. 124. Washington, DC: Africa Region Human Development Department, World Bank.

Morley, M. (2005) Gender Equity in Commonwealth Higher Education, *Women's Studies International Forum*, 28(2/3), 209-221. http://dx.doi.org/10.1016/j.wsif.2005.04.008

Nchinda, T.C. (2002) Research Capacity Strengthening in the South, *Social Science and Medicine*, 54(11), 1677-1711. http://dx.doi.org/10.1016/S0277-9536(01)00338-0

Pollak, A., Cremin, P., Grimson, J. & Bennett, W.N. (2005) Report on Universities Ireland Visit to Uganda 19-26 November 2005. Dublin: Unpublished.

Pritchard, R. (2007) Gender Inequality in British and German Universities, *Compare*, 37(5), 651-669. http://dx.doi.org/10.1080/03057920701582582

Rees, G., Baron, S., Boyask, R. & Taylor, C. (2007) Research-Capacity Building, Professional Learning and the Social Practices of Educational Research, *British Educational Research Journal*, 33(5), 761-779. http://dx.doi.org/10.1080/01411920701582447

Samoff, J. (1999) Education Sector Analysis in Africa: limited national control and even less national ownership, *International Journal of Educational Development*, 19(4), 249-272. http://dx.doi.org/10.1016/S0738-0593(99)00028-0

Sawyerr, A. (2004) African Universities and the Challenge of Research Capacity Development, *Journal of Higher Education in Africa*, 2(1), 213-242.

Trostle, J. (1992) Research Capacity Building in International Health: definition, evaluations, and strategies for success, *Social Science and Medicine*, 35(11), 1321-1324. http://dx.doi.org/10.1016/0277-9536(92)90035-O

University of Dar es Salaam (UDSM) (2008a) *University of Dar es Salaam Research Policy and Operational Procedures*, 2nd edn. Dar es Salaam: UDSM.

University of Dar es Salaam (UDSM) (2008b) *University of Dar es Salaam Research Programmes 2009-18: strengthening research capacity for poverty reduction and sustainable development.* Dar es Salaam: UDSM.

Zakri, A.H. (2006) Research Universities in the 21st Century: global challenges and local implications. Global Keynote Scenario at UNESCO Forum on Higher Education, Research and Knowledge, Colloquium on Research and Higher Education Policy, Paris, 29 November-1 December.

CHAPTER 7

Towards a Holistic Understanding of Special Educational Needs

JACQUI O'RIORDAN, JAMES URWICK
STELLA LONG & MARIA CAMPBELL

SUMMARY This chapter provides an overview of the current policies and practices relating to the inclusive education of children with special educational needs in Lesotho. It draws on research undertaken in Lesotho in 2009 that was carried out through the collaboration of a team of researchers working in various higher education institutions in Ireland and in the Lesotho College of Education. The research process was facilitated by the Centre for Global Development through Education, Limerick, Ireland and funded by Irish Aid. While special education policy initiatives in Lesotho date back to 1989, their development in practice has not reached policy expectations, in the context of limited resources and the absence of clear guidelines for assessment. This chapter details the range and types of formal and informal identification, assessment and more general SEN capacity within Lesotho, and draws on international debates and discussions on inclusive education as well as on current developments on classification. As such, it identifies key strategies for the development of an SEN framework in Lesotho that incorporates a broad range of key stakeholders.

Introduction

A national initiative to provide for special educational needs (SEN) in Lesotho began with a brief statement of policy in 1989 (Ministry of Education and Training, 1989) and the establishment of the Special Education Unit, within the Ministry of Education and Training, in 1991. The policy statement set out goals of including children with SEN in the regular school system and of using resource centres both to assess their needs and to prepare them for mainstreaming. A complete primary education and some vocational training were to be provided for such children. A team of 'itinerant teachers' was to be formed based at district level, in order to assist classroom teachers with SEN issues. Initial teacher training at the National Teacher Training College – reconstituted as the Lesotho College of Education (LCE) since 2002 – was to include an introduction to special education on its initial teacher education certificate programme.

Efforts to introduce 'inclusive schooling' in line with the above policy began in the 1990s with apparent success, but in the long run had very limited achievements. Following a feasibility study (Mariga & Phachaka, 1993), a pilot scheme of mainstreaming was completed in 10 primary schools in 1993-96 (Khatleli et al, 1995) and, thereafter, increasing numbers of primary schools were designated to practise inclusion. However, the effectiveness of this programme was constrained by a lack of resources to match its ambitious goals; a problem which was intensified by the launching of the Free Primary Education (FPE) programme in 2000 and the rapidly growing numbers of orphaned children needing special support as a result of the AIDS pandemic (Urwick & Elliott, 2010, pp. 143-144). A team of itinerant teachers was established in the 1990s at district level, but has remained extremely small (comprising less than five teachers by late 2011) in relation to national needs. The number of special schools is limited to five, almost the same as in the 1990s, and their capacity to function as resource centres is very limited. The official policy of 1989 seeks to maximise inclusion, but provides no guidelines for identification or assessment of SEN. It does not define the role of special schools or explain how 'resource centres' are to be related to them; neither does it outline any provision for SEN in early childhood, secondary or tertiary education (Urwick & Elliott, 2010, p. 142). A more comprehensive policy has yet to be officially published.

In this situation, the identification and assessment of disabilities and SEN in children has been largely haphazard and uncoordinated, depending on the initiatives of, for instance, individual parents, teachers, school principals, health workers and non-governmental organisation (NGO) workers. The limited statistical evidence available suggests that a large proportion of children of school age with severe or moderate levels of disability are either out of school or not receiving special educational support (Lesotho College of Education, 2007, pp. 7-10). Among children with moderate to mild levels of disability, incorrect identification or non-identification of the impairment by teachers is common. This leads to cases of inappropriate special school placement, as well as contributing to widespread casual inclusion in regular classrooms with no meaningful support. The LCE's 2007 report on the educational provision for disadvantaged children reached the general conclusion that, while there was a positive disposition to assist children with SEN, the task required much improvement in organisation, setting of priorities and allocation of resources (Lesotho College of Education, 2007, p. 26).

The capacity to identify, assess and provide for SEN depends partly on training. An introductory course on special education, with a broad treatment of SEN issues, has been included in the full-time teacher training programmes at the LCE since 2003, but until recently no specialised training or qualification in SEN was available in Lesotho. The LCE, however, took an initiative to remedy the situation and in 2009 launched a programme for an Advanced Diploma in Special Education (ADSE), open to qualified teachers. Both the LCE and the National University of Lesotho are also planning to start degree programmes in the field. The existence of the ADSE training considerably increases the potential for improved staffing both of the itinerant teachers' cadre and of the special schools. This is the context in which the Centre for Global Development through Education (CGDE) carried out research on capacity for identification, assessment and support of SEN in Lesotho (CGDE, 2011). This chapter reviews professional issues, movements and practices that influenced this work and then discusses the major findings.

A Brief Review of Literature and SEN Debates

Over the past 20 years, one important influence on provision for SEN has been international agreements about goals and rights in the care of children, the provision of education and the treatment of people with disabilities. The United Nations (UN) Convention on the Rights of the Child (United Nations, 1989), the Jomtien Declaration (UNESCO, 1990), the Salamanca Statement (UNESCO, 1994), the Dakar Framework for Action (UNESCO, 2000) and the UN Convention on the Rights of Persons with Disabilities (United Nations, 2006) have been of particular importance, being endorsed by a large proportion of governments around the world. The Convention on the Rights of the Child asserts the right of disabled children to provision for their educational, health and other needs in order to maximise their 'social integration and individual development' (United Nations, 1989, p. 8). Both this convention and the Jomtien Declaration base the right to education on the principle of equality of opportunity; a focus on rights for learners with special needs has been encouraged by the designation of basic education itself as a right in the Jomtien and Dakar agreements. The recent Convention on the Rights of Persons with Disabilities goes further in requiring signatories to provide all necessary support, including specialised teachers, for an 'effective education' (United Nations, 2006, p. 17). The government of Lesotho is a party to all these agreements.

The Inclusive Schooling Movement

The Salamanca Statement (UNESCO, 1994) goes beyond the requirement that provision for children with SEN should be made within national educational systems to assert that 'regular schools' with an 'inclusive orientation' should be used for the purpose, that such schools are appropriate for 'building an inclusive society' and that they 'provide an effective education to the majority of children'. This element reflects another powerful influence on policy in developing countries: the international movement for 'inclusive schooling'. Part of the background to this movement is that various high-income countries have gradually, over several decades, 'mainstreamed' increasing proportions of children with SEN – i.e. included them in regular schools and, to some extent, regular classes and curricula.

The change has coincided with the recognition, through research, of a wider range of SEN, which has increased the complexity of the demand on schools. Some advocates (for example, Peters, 2007) associate inclusive schooling with a 'social model' of disability, in which the latter is defined as a socially constructed form of discrimination, and, in contrast, associate special schools with a 'medical model', in which disability is regarded as a problem of the individual requiring intervention (see the discussion by Lindsay, 2003, pp. 5-6). The dangers of labelling and social discrimination are emphasised.

International agreements relating to SEN and the inclusive schooling movement have presented great challenges for the governments of low-income countries. Before 1990, such countries, including Lesotho, tended to have a large proportion of children with disabilities out of school altogether and a small proportion in special schools that were not well staffed or equipped. Nevertheless, influenced by foreign consultants and by the Salamanca Statement, some educational leaders in these countries uncritically accepted the case for total mainstreaming. In Lesotho, this. resulted in the mainstreaming initiative of the 1990s as mentioned, and different researchers are in agreement that the achievements of the inclusion policy on the ground have been very limited (Lesotho College of Education, 2007; Johnstone & Chapman, 2009). As Urwick & Elliott (2010) explain, it is very difficult to implement inclusive schooling in such a context. Eleweke & Rodda (2002) note that, by 1999, some 18 developing countries had started pilot mainstreaming projects, but with very limited coverage. They comment on the general inadequacy of specific facilities, learning materials, teacher training, support personnel and funding structures for effective support to students with SEN in regular schools. The same problems are reported from East and Central Africa by Charema (2005).

The problem goes much further than this, however. Urwick & Elliott (2010, p. 140) point out that the pedagogic, administrative and policy environments of 'regular schooling' in low-income countries, at a time of rapid expansion, pose great problems for any serious programme of mainstreaming. The context of large classes, scarce learning materials and restrictive pedagogy, as studied in Lesotho by Moloi et al (2008), is not a promising one for students needing adapted curricula, special materials or individual educational plans. As the recent Education for All Global Monitoring Report warns: 'integrating children with disabilities into poorly resourced, overcrowded schools ... is not a prescription for inclusive education' (UNESCO, 2010, p. 202).

The Needs-Based, Pragmatic Approach

Another school of thought is one which is based on the principle of meeting the varied needs of individual children as effectively as possible, but is pragmatic about the institutional means of doing so (see, for example, Kavale & Mostert, 2003; Lindsay, 2003). This approach is consistent with the Warnock Report in the United Kingdom (Warnock Committee, 1978) and with the UN Convention on the Rights of the Child. For many children with disabilities, mainstreaming is a responsible choice, but even in high-income countries this is not always the case and, of course, varying degrees of separation – separate activity in the regular classroom, 'pull-out' periods and special classes as well as special schools – are often used in practice. The professionals concerned tend to concur that the issues are not straightforward and that flexibility is needed in order to meet individual needs (Norwich, 2008).

With particular reference to Lesotho, Urwick & Elliott (2010) make the case for a needs-based, pragmatic approach in low-income countries, where the average school lacks the resources and skills to cater for a wide range of SEN, especially severe impairments. Two strategies within this approach are of particular importance for this study. One is the development of a multi-track system of support, with categories of regular schools, in limited number, that are adequately equipped and staffed for the inclusion of students with various types of special needs. This kind of strategy is illustrated by South Africa's initiative to develop a network of 'full-service schools' (Department of Education, Republic of South Africa, 2001, pp. 22-23) and there has been a similar initiative in Laos (UNESCO, 2010, p. 202). The second strategy is to strengthen the existing special schools (which are few but of vital importance in Lesotho) and give them additional functions as assessment and resource centres for SEN as far as possible. With reference to South Africa, Hall & Engelbrecht (1999, pp. 232-233) draw attention to the potential of special schools both to contribute to the support services (including assessment) for SEN in regular schools and to provide venues for practical teacher training in SEN. UNESCO (2010, p. 203) reports a similar strategy in Ethiopia, and Reena (2000), in the Indian context, expresses a similar view about the role of special schools. In Lesotho itself, the beginnings of such a strategy already exist in the links formed between the special schools and neighbouring primary schools, to which visually and hearing-impaired students transfer after suitable preparation. These strategies build on existing resources and seek to establish viable structures, rather than hoping for a rapid 'transformation' of all schools.

Issues of Cost and Financial Support

Research on the effectiveness of inclusive schooling often neglects comparative financial costs, which are all the more important in low-income countries. For reasons of cost as well as scarcity, some concentration of students with severe or moderate impairments around specialist personnel, equipment and facilities is essential in low-income countries (Urwick & Elliott, 2010, p. 141) and also elsewhere to some extent (Lindsay, 2003, p. 10). It is for similar reasons that the authorities in some low-income countries maintain separate post-primary schools for technical and vocational education. In mentioning this, we do not overlook the financial and social implications of grouping students with disabilities in selected regular schools, with enhanced support, or in special schools. The costs of available options in a local context need to be studied carefully, along with the professional arguments. A somewhat more straightforward task is to ensure that children with physical and sensory impairments are provided with assistive devices which, in many cases, enable them to be mainstreamed effectively. A report on a recent pilot project in Lesotho (Special Education Unit, Ministry of Education and Training & Lesotho College of Education, 2008) gives some indicative costs for identification, assessment and appliances in such cases.

For support to families that are affected by disabilities, advocates of inclusive schooling tend to place faith in community-based rehabilitation as a policy (see, for example, Eleweke & Rodda, 2002, p. 121). In this they follow the lead of the Salamanca Statement (UNESCO, 1994, pp. 18-19). There are examples which suggest that the active support of the local community and of NGOs can improve opportunities for children with disabilities to gain access to education and benefit from it (see Save the Children UK, 2008; UNESCO, 2010, p. 202). However, a note of caution is warranted here: the prevalence of poverty in developing countries and the links between impairment and poverty (UNESCO, 2010, p. 181) imply that the local capacity to provide support may be lacking where it is most needed. Such interventions could be organised in partnership with communities and combined with a realistic encouragement of community-based rehabilitation.

The Role of a Classification System

Classification systems are used in many countries (Farrell, 2010, p. 52) to identify different types of learners and, in turn, to provide additional supports and services based on an identified category of disability (Norwich, 1999; McLaughlin et al, 2006). Such systems of classification are considered as essential by Florian et al (2006) and Norwich (2007) in order to ensure equal opportunities in the allocation of support services. Despite the value of classifications in special education, the literature notes the difficulties that exist in finding a 'systematic, coherent and evidence-based position about classification that commands wide support' (Norwich, 2007, p. 55). Current thinking on categorisation lies in determining the level of difficulty a child has in learning (McLaughlin et al, 2006, p. 56). A national framework for the identification and categorisation of children with disabilities in Lesotho is so far lacking and the development of such a framework needs to be given careful consideration.

Examples of Levels of Intervention

As the mainstreaming of pupils with SEN has increased, the governments of some high- and middle-income countries have distinguished officially between different levels of intervention for such pupils, rather than focusing on alternative school or classroom settings. Placement issues in the latter, narrower sense do continue to be important, however, within the framework of levels of intervention. This section outlines some examples of officially defined levels of intervention from Ireland, England and South Africa. The focus is on ideas that are relevant to the context of Lesotho.

Official policy in the Republic of Ireland distinguishes between three 'stages' of intervention (Department of Education and Science, Republic of Ireland, 2003, Appendix 1). Stage One involves screening and extra help by regular teachers (by the class teacher at the primary or pre-primary level), whereas Stage Two involves fuller assessment and the use of a 'learning plan' with the help of a special teacher based within the school. Stage Three involves assessment by one or more outside specialists at the request of the school, leading to a formal individual educational plan and any necessary use of additional resources from outside the school.

The three Irish 'stages' bear some resemblance to the three levels of intervention designated for individual pupils in England [1]: School Action, School Action Plus and the statutory Statement of SEN (see Department for Education and Skills, 2001). School Action uses the normal resources of a regular school, but provides some 'interventions that are *additional to* or *different from* those provided as part of the school's usual differentiated curriculum offer and strategies' (Department for Education and Skills, 2001, p. 52; original emphasis). School Action Plus may use extra resources allocated to the schools for SEN in general. Both levels require an individual educational plan. In pre-primary education, there are equivalent levels of intervention known as Early Action and Early Action Plus.

In the case of the Free State Province of South Africa, five levels of intervention are distinguished, the criteria being: (a) the extent to which the pupil can take part in the regular curriculum; (b) the amount of additional support needed; and (c) the need for assistance from outside the school. Outside support begins at Level Four, while Level Five may require a 'specialised learning programme'.[2]

Examples of Support Structures and Personnel

Some other features of the official structures for SEN in these three countries may be mentioned. Both the Irish and the English regulations require the involvement of parents and of regular class teachers in the assessment of SEN and in planning, at all levels of intervention. For the organisation of support at the school level, Irish schools are expected to have a 'special education support team', usually including at least one 'resource teacher' (Carey, 2005, pp. 189-190). In England, the school is required to have a SENCO (SEN coordinator), who tends to be the deputy head teacher in the case of primary schools, or a SEN team. Considerable use is made, in England, of 'learning support assistants', with in-service training, to assist pupils with SEN and there is some positive evidence of their effectiveness (Lindsay, 2007). Coordination above the school level is provided, in Ireland, by SENOs (special educational needs organisers) serving clusters of schools (Carey, 2005, pp. 189-190) and, in England, by SEN advisers based in the local education authorities. In South Africa, there is a policy of establishing both 'institutional-level support teams' for SEN in schools and district support teams providing a 'full range of education support services' (Department of Education, Republic of South Africa, 2001, p. 29).

For specialist consultation outside the school, both Irish and English regulations emphasise that educational psychologists (a special cadre within the education sector) are available and the latter often play a leading role in Stage Three assessments or statutory statements. The possible involvement of paediatricians, speech and language therapists, audiologists and other relevant health and social service professionals is also mentioned (Department for Education and Skills, 2001, pp. 76-77; Department of Education and Science, Republic of Ireland, 2003, Appendix 1). In a context such as Lesotho, however, where educational psychologists and paediatricians are almost totally lacking, it is appropriate for SEN specialists to coordinate assessments of SEN both at the school level and in early childhood.

Issues of School Placement

Irish and English policy documents place the emphasis on intervention within regular schools, but some placements in special schools do, in fact, occur within the context of Stage Three in Ireland and the statutory statement in England. In Ireland, the National Council for Special Education, established in 2004, has the authority to designate a particular school for a child and may do so at the request of parents (Republic of Ireland, 2004, p. 15). In practice, a special school is only designated after careful consideration and in the light of a Stage Three assessment. In South Africa, where regular schools have far fewer resources for SEN, there is a policy of giving the special schools a major outreach role as 'resource centres', as well as improving their quality (Department of Education, Republic of South Africa, 2001, p. 47).

Irish and English national policy documents also say little about the important issue of differentiation among regular schools for SEN purposes. In practice, however, local education authorities in England may designate certain schools to be 'additionally resourced' for SEN – an example is the provision of additional staff for the hearing-impaired. They may also 'federate' a special school with regular schools near it, to facilitate some sharing of staff and transfers of pupils.[3] South Africa, which has hitherto depended heavily on special schools, has an interim objective of establishing at least one 'full-service' school in every district, able to include pupils with a wide range of SEN (Department of Education, Republic of South Africa, 2001, p. 23). These examples show that Lesotho's designation of certain primary schools to practise inclusion is a strategy that is widely used, but suggests that the links between certain designated schools and special schools could be made more explicit in Lesotho's policy. Clarity about the actual roles of schools helps to provide a setting for placement decisions which are concerned not only with choices between special and regular schools, but also with the extent to which special settings are to be used for particular children within regular schools.

Physical Adjustments to Promote Mainstreaming

Physical adjustments – notably, the provision of assistive devices to children with physical and sensory impairments and the design of 'disability-friendly' school buildings – can enable more children to be mainstreamed successfully. The pilot project of 2008 (Special Education Unit, Ministry of Education and Training & Lesotho College of Education, 2008) shows the importance of initiatives by the education sector, in collaboration with the health sector, both to identify such impairments and to ensure that vision and hearing aids and other assistive devices are provided. In addition, the poor accessibility of classrooms and school toilets to children with physical disabilities is a

137

problem in low-income countries generally (Peters, 2003, p. 37), and Lesotho in particular (Lesotho College of Education, 2007, pp. 22-23).

The CGDE Research Design

This enhanced understanding and critique of SEN identification, assessment and support informed the research, coordinated by CGDE, that was conducted by the authors, together with colleagues from the LCE, in 2009-10. The research broadly followed an interpretive framework. The main source of data was 75 interviews, with a wide variety of informants, held in Lesotho during April 2009, following discussions and the development of questionnaire templates. A limited number of geographical areas were targeted in order to elucidate the types of strengths and weaknesses representative of lowland and highland areas and of urban and rural centres. These areas were within the Leribe, Berea, Maseru and Quthing Districts. The aim was to explore SEN capacity and understanding within each of the identified sectors. The interviews varied in time from ten minutes to over two hours. Six of the interviews were conducted in Sesotho and all the others in English. The research was informed by a holistic view of education, which sees the child as central and looks at how the institution of education, its formal elements and more informal connections, can come together to serve the best interests of the child. Therefore, in conceptualising the capacity mapping exercise, the research from its outset incorporated formal educational settings: pre-primary, primary, special and secondary schools. Importantly, it also included attention to relevant administrative and medical units at national and district level, international agencies, national NGOs, community-based groups and households having children with disabilities. For the purpose of data analysis, 'template analysis' (King, 2004, p. 118) was used, which is also referred to as 'thematic analysis' (Van Manen, 1998).

Background to Key Policy Indications and Challenges Identified

As indicated already, the scope of the mapping exercise was broad, encompassing a range of sectors and levels of enquiry, from ministerial, national and international NGO levels, to local education districts, schools, families and communities. We now forefront findings related to relevant policy developments, capacities and challenges posed in order to highlight potential SEN directions in Lesotho and to offer a flavour of the wider SEN contexts in which teacher educators, teachers, children, their families and communities live and operate. It is important to note at this juncture that the government of Lesotho became a signatory to the UN Convention on the Rights of Persons with Disabilities in December 2008. The convention affirms that persons with disabilities have a right to access an inclusive and quality primary and secondary education on an equal basis with other people in the communities in which they live (United Nations, 2006, Article 24).

State responsibility in this area lies with two key ministries: the Ministry of Education and Training (MOET) and the Ministry of Health and Welfare (MOHSW). Among the interviews undertaken were included those with senior officers and decision makers both in the MOET and MOHSW. Within the MOET, these were the Principal Secretary, the Chief Education Officer, Primary and the Inspector, Special Education. Within the MOHSW, they were the Director of Social Welfare and the Chief Rehabilitation Officer.

SEN Support Systems: role and capacity within various ministries, bureaucratic structure and personnel

The findings indicated that established responsibilities and practices within MOET and MOHSW contributed to some extent to a willingness to develop capacity to provide for SEN and to cooperate across sectors in this task. Both ministries had units and officers with specific responsibilities for disabled and vulnerable children. However, the inadequacy of funding, personnel and facilities for these units was very obvious, especially at MOET.

The MOET has also developed the Education Sector Strategic Plan 2005-15, one of the aims of which is to increase access to education for children with SEN by 2015 and 'to accelerate inclusion/integration of children with SEN/disabilities from 4.8% to 20% by 2009 and to 40% by 2015', but these ambitious targets were accompanied by large funding gaps in the Plan (MOET, 2005, pp. 106, 115). The plan states that the MOET will facilitate the establishment of three assessment centres for SEN in the country and that the MOHSW will provide rehabilitation services to the children who are already under the care of the MOET. These more structural developments indicate movement on developing structural frameworks and an existing capacity for cooperation across the departments.

With regard to personnel, the MOET has a much greater capacity than the MOHSW for contact with the population. In 2006, it employed about 15,000 teachers, while the health workers were one-tenth of that figure and the number of social workers is extremely small – less than 35 nationally. Furthermore, in general, there was a willingness among staff to cooperate. All the senior officers of the MOET and MOHSW who were interviewed showed a positive attitude to collaboration between these ministries. It was reported that they had already agreed in principle to work together on children's issues. The Principal Secretary of the MOET felt that the Ministry of Local Government also had a part to play, probably because the district councils are responsible for the new District Child Protection Teams.

Challenges Regarding Collaborative Approaches

A potential difficulty for collaboration is the relatively low rank of the head of the Special Education Unit – inspector only. This office seems not to have parity with that of the Chief Rehabilitation Officer in the MOHSW. Such issues raise concerns related to the authority of key decision makers and stakeholders, thus limiting the potential of effective cooperation and collaboration. The representatives of the education and health ministries supported the use of collaborative assessment teams that would include both education and health specialists, and social workers where possible. They accepted the need for some private medical practitioners to be involved where public specialists are not available and for them to be paid accordingly. This willingness needs to be envisioned as a first step in opening assessment routes for more children to have SEN assessments. However, it needs to be in the context of difficulties in the formation of assessment teams that lie in the small numbers of available specialists, their existing commitments, and the inadequate provision of vehicles and equipment. Funding is, therefore, a critical issue for the assessment process and access to key medical, educational and psychological staff.

Challenges Posed by Limited Funding

Throughout each of the sectors, the lack of funding and the bureaucracy associated with accessing the available funding constituted a substantial challenge. The MOET leadership recognised their obligations in promoting the rights of children with disabilities, but found it difficult to support these within the current level of funding in the education sector. However, the senior officers of both the MOET and MOHSW who were interviewed were receptive to the idea of seeking external funding for a limited period in order to establish a proposed system for identification and assessment of SEN. Interviews undertaken with international NGOs suggest that international agencies and NGOs have the potential to play an important part in helping to seek and source such funding.

Funding for physical facilities planned for the Department of Special Education at the LCE is also an important issue, as this department provides the main recruitment pool for itinerant teachers and school-based SEN teachers. According to information available to us, the LCE has not been receiving the necessary capital budget allocations for action on the facilities plan that was completed in 2008, but the MOET is now showing some willingness to consider the issue. Lack of funding posed a key challenge at all levels – that is, from the ministries, to training and recruitment, to the lack of funding to provide basic resources within the classroom.

Capacity to Access Support from External Sources such as NGOs

The research demonstrated that NGOs – both national and international – have the capacity to help in the development of the SEN structure and in obtaining additional funding for this purpose. There are many national and international NGOs involved directly or indirectly with support for disability issues in Lesotho. The Rehabilitation Unit of the MOHSW has quarterly meetings with the NGOs representing the disabled. The Department of Social Welfare has an orphans and vulnerable children coordinator and thinks that children with disabilities can benefit from the framework of assistance to orphans and vulnerable children. The Special Education Unit has also worked with the disabled people's NGOs over a long period, especially in relation to special schools. The unit's representative was a key member of the steering committee of a disability project which was managed by Skillshare International since 2006, with funding from the European Union and Tribal Group.

However, issues remain relating to the coordination of state and NGO involvement, reaching out to community-based NGOs, and sometimes the differing priorities and policy directions of particular NGOs. For instance, the National Association of the Deaf in Lesotho opposes the use of hearing aids, instead emphasising the promotion of sign language as a way forward for the deaf community. Locally based community groups often have little or no communication or information on national and international NGOs, a challenge often exacerbated by the difficulties in accessing rural and highland areas. Such difficulties pose challenges on the ground in developing inclusive, holistic and needs-based educational supports for children with disabilities.

Capacity to Identify and Assess

The MOET sees the need to ensure that teacher training has an identification and assessment component so that the teachers produced by the LCE and by the National University of Lesotho have basic skills in identification and assessment. This element of training is established at the LCE, but it needs to be expanded. Furthermore, the Rehabilitation Unit of the MOHSW has developed a curriculum to start training auxiliary social welfare officers. There is agreement from the European Union to pay the salaries of the first 10 officers trained under the programme.

However, the area of capacity for identification and assessment is beset with challenges, including insufficient training capacity for teachers' initial identification of specific SEN, especially in areas such as autism and attention deficit hyperactivity disorder, which sometimes results in teachers' misidentification of these impairments. In practice, this role mainly lies with class teachers, the majority of whom have little or no training in this area. Some exceptions to this were found in relation to the role of health professionals, itinerant teachers and some social welfare officers. In particular, the existing occupational therapists, audiologists, opticians and psychiatrists in Lesotho have important contributions to make to screening and assessment for SEN.

Capacity for Placement and Provision of SEN

There was general agreement that the capacity for placement and provision fell far short of the needs. This was due to a number of factors, including the choice of educational setting, support at secondary level, the workloads of support teachers and ambiguity around the role of special schools. The choice of educational placement option depends on the type and degree of the difficulty a child has and potentially includes inclusive educational settings, special educational programmes – mostly in special schools or centres – and vocational training centres for some older students.

Our interviews indicated that the MOET is aware of the lack of support for SEN at the secondary level. For more effective mainstreaming (i.e. inclusion in regular schools), the MOET administration advocates a more diversified curriculum, provision of special learning materials, provision of assistive devices, making physical facilities more accessible to pupils with physical disabilities, and good linkage with parents and local communities. However, the current workload of the itinerant teachers is too great in view of the large number of designated inclusive schools in each district. The 2007 LCE report pointed out that there were too many schools for the actual number of itinerant teachers (less than one per district) to handle, yet the list is now even longer. As stated earlier, the role of special schools is not defined in the existing policy document but the previous Inspector, Special Education saw special schools as having three functions: (1) to prepare some children with disabilities for mainstreaming; (2) to provide outreach services to regular schools; and (3) to educate children for whom mainstreaming is not practicable. This kind of multi-purpose approach is supported by Urwick & Elliot (2010) – it is important to build on existing resources.

Other challenges identified included the absence of national guidelines for school placement decisions relating to SEN; little hope of funding to provide the required educational materials for SEN programmes in the country; variances in management skills across schools; and shortages of language and support personnel.

Upskilling Personnel and Training for
Identification, Assessment and Support for SEN

A key finding of our study was the need to increase the scope and numbers of personnel in receipt of upskilling and more specific training in identification and support for SEN, including continuing professional development, through accredited programmes where possible, in order to ensure a continuum and develop coherence in support for children and their families. Currently, training is offered at the LCE at Advanced Diploma level, where the teachers acquire basic skills in identification, assessment and management of various categories of special needs. With regard to teachers who have completed the Advanced Diploma in Special Education at the LCE, the Chief Education Officer, Primary at the MOET thought that under the new teachers' career structure, the MOET would be able to pay increments to teachers for work in areas of special needs, as well as work in difficult locations. Such teachers, if duly identified and assigned duties, would be useful as members of assessment teams in addition to their teaching and mentoring activities.

The officers of the Department of Social Welfare also seemed ready to commit social workers to help streamline assessment procedures in each district. They indicated that the new district child protection committees are potentially useful for support to assessment teams, but it remains to be seen how well they function. On the issue of the provision of trained personnel for the identification and assessment of SEN, there are various challenges, including a shortage of specialists. A challenge is also presenting in coordination at national and local levels.

Concluding Comments

The findings confirm that there is public recognition in Lesotho of special education as an area of service provision and of the importance of including children with SEN in the educational system. This is evident not only in the commitment of the government of Lesotho to international agreements, but also in the attitudes and statements of senior government officials and of educators with relevant responsibilities. There is potential to develop capacity at bureaucratic, structural and personnel levels among key decision-making institutions and personnel. However, challenges to establishing structures centre around issues related to mobilising funding and resources for the provision of services that would match the recognition given in principle.

Previous research (see, for example, Lesotho College of Education, 2007) suggests that in the recent past, the structural weaknesses of the special education subsector, and of services for children with disabilities more generally, have made it less likely that the necessary resources would be mobilised. The specialised training for SEN recently started at the LCE is a hopeful development, but is only one of several interlocking structures that need to be established. Although an effective response to SEN depends heavily on the public services, it also requires the support of families, local communities, NGOs and donor agencies. The significance of this policy context to teacher educators and teachers is obvious, framing, as it does, the challenges that are faced in developing SEN supports within and outside of the classroom.

Notes

[1] The policy applies to England only, in the context of devolved responsibility for education in other parts of the United Kingdom.

[2] Official memorandum of the Department of Education, Free State Province, South Africa.

[3] Information provided by Gateshead Local Education Authority, County Durham, United Kingdom.

References

Carey, D.J. (2005) *The Essential Guide to Special Education in Ireland*. Dublin: Primary ABC.

Centre for Global Development through Education (2011) *Identification, Assessment and Inclusion for Learners with Special Educational Needs: towards a national system for Lesotho*. Limerick: Mary Immaculate College.

Charema, J. (2005) From Special Schools to Inclusive Education: the way forward for developing countries south of the Sahara. Paper presented at International Special Education Congress, Glasgow, 1-4 August. http://www.isec2005.org/isec/abstracts/papers_c/charema_j.shtml

Department for Education and Skills (DfES) (2001) *Special Educational Needs Code of Practice*. London: DfES.

Department of Education, Republic of South Africa (2001) *Education White Paper 6. Special Needs Education: building an inclusive education and training system*. Pretoria: Department of Education.

Department of Education and Science, Republic of Ireland (2003) *Allocation of Resources for Pupils with Special Educational Needs in National Schools (Circular 24/03)*. Dublin: Department of Education and Science.

Eleweke, C.J. & Rodda, M. (2002) The Challenge of Enhancing Inclusive Education in Developing Countries, *International Journal of Inclusive Education*, 6(2), 113-126. http://dx.doi.org/10.1080/13603110110067190

Farrell, M. (2010) *Debating Special Education*. London: Routledge.

Florian, L., Hollenweger, J., Simeonsson, R.J., Wedell, K., Riddell, S., Terzi, L. & Holland, A. (2006) Cross-Cultural Perspectives on the Classification of Children with Disabilities, Part I: issues in the classification of children with disabilities, *Journal of Special Education*, 40(1), 36-45. http://dx.doi.org/10.1177/00224669060400010401

Hall, R. & Engelbrecht, P. (1999) The Possible Role of Special Schools in Inclusive Education, *South African Journal of Education*, 19(3), 230-234.

Johnstone, C.J. & Chapman, D.W. (2009) Contributions and Constraints to the Implementation of Inclusive Education in Lesotho, *International Journal of Disability, Development and Education*, 56(2), 131-148. http://dx.doi.org/10.1080/10349120902868582

Kavale, K.A. & Mostert, M.P. (2003) River of Ideology, Islands of Evidence, *Exceptionality*, 11(4), 191-208. http://dx.doi.org/10.1207/S15327035EX1104_1

Khatleli, M., Mariga, L., Phachaka, L. & Stubbs, S. (1995) Schools for All: national planning in Lesotho, in B. O'Toole & R. McConkey (Eds) *Innovations in Developing Countries for People with Disabilities*, pp. 135-160. Chorley: Lisieux Hall.

King, N. (2004) Using Templates in the Thematic Analysis of Text, in C. Cassel & G. Symon (Eds) *Essential Guide to Qualitative Methods in Organizational Research*. London: Sage.

Lesotho College of Education (2007) *Education Policies, Programmes and Legislation in Lesotho Relating to Disadvantaged Children and Children with Disabilities: final report*. Maseru: Special Education Unit, Ministry of Education and Training.

Lindsay, G. (2003) Inclusive Education: a critical perspective, *British Journal of Special Education*, 30(1), 3-12. http://dx.doi.org/10.1111/1467-8527.00275

Lindsay, G. (2007) Educational Psychology and the Effectiveness of Inclusive Education/Mainstreaming, *British Journal of Educational Psychology*, 77(1), 1-24. http://dx.doi.org/10.1348/000709906X156881

Mariga, L. & Phachaka, L. (1993) *Integrating Children with Special Needs into Regular Primary Schools in Lesotho: report of a feasibility study*. Maseru: Ministry of Education and Training.

McLaughlin, M.J., Dyson, A., Nagle, K., Thurlow, M., Rouse, M., Hardman, M., Norwich, B., Burke, P.J. & Perlin, M. (2006) Cross-Cultural Perspectives on the Classification of Children with Disabilities, Part II: implementing classification systems in schools, *Journal of Special Education*, 40(1), 46-58. http://dx.doi.org/10.1177/00224669060400010501

Ministry of Education and Training (MOET) (1989) *Clarification of Lesotho's Educational Policies, Part II: operations plan*. Maseru: MOET.

Ministry of Education and Training (MOET) (2005) *Education Sector Strategic Plan 2005-2015*. Maseru: MOET.

Moloi, F.N., Morobe, N. & Urwick, J. (2008) Free but Inaccessible Primary Education: a critique of the pedagogy of English and mathematics in Lesotho, *International Journal of Educational Development*, 28(5), 612-621. http://dx.doi.org/10.1016/j.ijedudev.2007.12.003

Norwich, B. (1999) The Connotation of Special Education Labels for Professionals in the Field, *British Journal of Special Education*, 26(4), 179-183.

Norwich, B. (2007) Categories of Special Educational Needs, in L. Florian (Ed.) *The Sage Handbook of Special Education*. London: Sage.

Norwich, B. (2008) Dilemmas of Difference, Inclusion and Disability: international perspectives on placement, *European Journal of Special Education*, 23(4), 287-304. http://dx.doi.org/10.1080/08856250802387166

Peters, S.J. (2003) *Inclusive Education: achieving education for all by including those with disabilities and special educational needs*. Washington, DC: World Bank.

Peters, S.J. (2007) A Historical Analysis of International Inclusive Education Policy and Individuals with Disabilities, *Journal of Disability Policy Studies*, 18(2), 98-108. http://dx.doi.org/10.1177/10442073070180020601

Reena, S. (2000) Facilitating Inclusive Education: the changing role of special education centres. Paper presented at International Special Education Congress, University of Manchester, 24-28 July.

Republic of Ireland (2004) *Education for Persons with Special Educational Needs Act 2004*. Dublin: Houses of the Oireachtas.

Save the Children UK (2008) *Making Schools Inclusive: how change can happen*. London: Save the Children.

Special Education Unit, Ministry of Education and Training & Lesotho College of Education (2008) *Pilot Scheme for Provision of Assistive Devices to Children with Impairments in Primary and Secondary Schools: fund-raising proposal*. Maseru: Lesotho College of Education.

UNESCO (1990) *World Declaration on Education for All and Framework for Action to Meet Basic Learning Needs*. Paris: UNESCO.

UNESCO (1994) *The Salamanca Statement on Principles, Policy and Practice in Special Needs Education*. Paris: UNESCO.

UNESCO (2000) *The Dakar Framework for Action*. Paris: UNESCO.

UNESCO (2010) *EFA Global Monitoring Report 2010. Reaching the Marginalized*. Paris: UNESCO & Oxford University Press.

United Nations (UN) (1989) *Convention on the Rights of the Child*. New York: UN.

United Nations (UN) (2006) *Convention on the Rights of Persons with Disabilities*. New York: UN.

Urwick, J. & Elliott, J. (2010) International Orthodoxy versus National Realities: inclusive schooling and the education of children with disabilities in Lesotho, *Comparative Education*, 46(2), 137-150. http://dx.doi.org/10.1080/03050061003775421

Van Manen, M. (1998) *Researching Lived Experience: human science for an action sensitive pedagogy*. London: Althouse Press.

Warnock Committee (1978) *Special Educational Needs: report of the Committee of Enquiry into the Education of Handicapped Children and Young People*. London: Her Majesty's Stationery Office.

CHAPTER 8

The Teaching and Learning of Mathematics in Ugandan Secondary Schools: poised for change?

PAUL CONWAY, ELIZABETH OLDHAM, JAMES URWICK, SARAH KISA, JUSTINE OTTALA & ANNE MUGWERA

SUMMARY In the context of the increased faith by governments in the reform of mathematics and science teaching as the basis for economic development, this chapter examines pedagogy of mathematics in Ugandan secondary schools. The study involved data collection in 16 secondary schools based on a purposive sample in four different regions of Uganda. Focusing on the classroom learning environment, key findings are presented under four headings: (i) pedagogy, (ii) teachers' attitudes to participatory learning, (iii) teachers' needs for continuing professional development, and (iv) the restrictive influence of national examinations on teaching. The authors then consider the findings and recommendations in light of current developments in mathematics education reform.

Introduction

This chapter focuses on the pedagogy of mathematics in Ugandan secondary schools, using this as a lens through which the needs of Ugandan mathematics teachers with regard to teacher education can be viewed. The chapter is based on an empirical research study funded by Irish Aid and administered through the Centre for Global Development through Education (CGDE) between 2008 and 2010; it involved academics in both Uganda and Ireland. The study focused on teacher effectiveness in both mathematics and the sciences, and was influenced by two major factors. One was the relatively poor results experienced in these subjects in the Uganda Certificate of Education (UCE)

147

examinations. The other was the introduction by the Ugandan Ministry of Education and Sports (MOES) in 2007 of a new in-career development programme for teachers of secondary mathematics and science (the Secondary Science and Mathematics Teachers' [SESEMAT] programme) and the desire of the MOES to monitor the effects of this programme.

A focus on pedagogy, whatever the subject, throws light on the quality of teaching undertaken in classrooms – for the purpose of this chapter, mathematics classrooms in Ugandan secondary schools. Recent scholarship in teaching and teacher education has highlighted teaching quality as one of the most important school-level factors influencing student learning (Darling-Hammond & Bransford, 2005; Moreno, 2005; Organisation for Economic Co-operation and Development, 2005; Schwille & Dembelé, 2007).

The chapter is organised into four sections. First, we highlight the international and national debates on mathematics teaching and learning that informed the research questions and the policy recommendations emerging from this study. Secondly, we describe the study design and implementation. Thirdly, with a focus on the classroom learning environment – in particular, the approaches to pedagogy in the context of the prevailing resource constraints – we note key findings under four headings concerned with: (1) pedagogy; (2) teachers' attitudes to participatory learning; (3) teachers' need for continuing professional development; and (4) the restrictive influence of national examinations on teaching. Finally, we consider the findings and recommendations in the light of developments in mathematics education in some other sub-Saharan countries.

The Pedagogy of Secondary Mathematics in Uganda: international and national contexts

International Developments

It has become something of a convention for politicians, academics and journalists around the world periodically to raise the alarm about the poor results of school mathematics, often in conjunction with science. In some well-known instances, these cries of alarm have been related to technological and military competition between the richer countries and have, because of that context, led to curriculum reform. The formation of the Neglect of Science Committee and its influence on a new school certificate in England, 1916-17, is one example (Dzama & Osborne, 1999, p. 395); the post-Sputnik campaign leading to the National Defense Education Act of 1958 in the USA is another (Kliebard, 1987, pp. 264-268). More recently, such cries of alarm are often occasioned by the results of international studies of achievement or by national 'league tables' of school results. A journalist advocating the adoption of 'national standards' in the USA, for example, complains that, in the 2006

Programme for International Student Assessment (PISA) of achievement at age 15 in 30 countries of the Organisation for Economic Co-operation and Development (OECD), the Americans 'came a dismal 21st in science and 25th in maths' ('Improving Education', 2009). Another journalist uses national assessment results in England to complain that over a quarter of the children entering secondary education cannot 'do basic arithmetic' (Brown, 2009).

Similar concerns are voiced in developing countries. Just over a decade ago, a special issue of the *Journal of Research in Science Teaching* began with the assertion that the quality of science education in the developing world had 'seen a steady decline' for some time (Gray, 1999, p. 261). There is nothing unusual, therefore, about the current concern of the government of Uganda about poor results in mathematics and science. The belief that these two subjects form skills needed for national survival in a rapidly changing and competitive world is not a new one, but may have been intensified by 'globalisation' in the past two decades (Stromquist & Monkman, 2000, p. 13). The subjects also have an aura of being especially challenging for learners. In particular, in the context of the current wave of globalisation, governments worldwide and transnational policy bodies (such as the World Bank and OECD) are paying increasing attention to the potential economic leverage from enhanced human capital in terms of graduates' knowledge and skills in mathematics, science and reading literacy especially (consider the OECD's PISA). However, it has been argued that this approach is founded on naive beliefs in neo-liberal models of economic growth (see, for example, Suarez-Orozco & Qin-Hilliard, 2004).

While many leaders and scholars agree that achievement in mathematics and science is not satisfactory, they differ greatly about the causes of the problem. In the context of developing countries, some researchers (for example, Fuller & Heyneman, 1989) place the emphasis on the neglect of key resources, while others focus on inadequate teacher knowledge (Darling-Hammond & Bransford, 2005; Moreno, 2005; UNESCO, 2005). A third group points to the general context of poor planning and unsustainable policies of expansion (Walberg, 1991; Lewin, 2008) and a fourth group argues that science curricula in Africa are not well adapted to the context (Gray, 1999).

Of particular relevance for this chapter is Moreno's (2005) review of research on teacher education in developing and transition countries, which draws on the globally influential teacher knowledge framework of Shulman (1987). This framework highlights three types of knowledge: subject content knowledge; general knowledge about teaching and learning; and, finally, pedagogical content knowledge. Crucially, teacher education has been shown to play an important part in all three types, but especially the second and third. While the wider study from which this chapter is drawn includes consideration of resources and the broader labour market dynamics of teacher availability, retention and employment patterns, this chapter focuses on issues of pedagogy and teachers' knowledge.

Government Policy

Sharing the general belief in the importance of mathematics and science for national development, the government of Uganda has developed policies to promote the learning of science. These policies are incorporated in its strategic plan for the education sector (Ministry of Education and Sports, 2008a). The main policies are ones of prioritising science subjects within the lower secondary school curriculum and encouraging specialisation in science at the upper secondary and undergraduate levels. From 2005, biology, chemistry and physics were made compulsory subjects throughout the lower secondary level, in the belief that this would enhance the development of productive and marketable skills and promote scientific literacy.

This curricular emphasis puts increased demands on the teaching of mathematics because of its important role in the natural sciences. The government therefore treats advancement in mathematics as both a problem and a priority. In so doing, it is typical within Africa: Ottevanger et al (2007), in a study of education in science, mathematics and information and communications technology in 10 countries of sub-Saharan Africa, show the increased elevation of all these subjects in curriculum policy.

The SESEMAT Training Programme

The MOES states in the science teachers guidelines that 'self-reliance' and globalisation require quality science, mathematics and technological education. However, it is widely acknowledged that some classroom practices are far below the national expectations. Baseline surveys indicated weaknesses in classroom practices, relating both to content and to methodology. This realisation served as a basis for the SESEMAT in-service training programme which was introduced by the MOES with technical assistance from the Japanese International Cooperation Agency in 2005.

The objectives of the SESEMAT training programme, as spelt out in the teachers guidelines, are: (1) to analyse the current teaching, learning and practices in science and mathematics; (2) to bring about a shift from teacher-centred to learner-centred teaching and learning (not precisely defined); (3) to create an active, motivating and supportive learning environment; (4) to help teachers to use appropriately the relevant materials and local resources that are available; and (5) to promote appropriate lesson-development strategies.

However, the SESEMAT objectives are not matched by strategies that would address those administrative and environmental factors in the educational system, the school and the classroom that actually constrain the teaching of science and mathematics. The situation has been exacerbated by subsequent policy developments. In 2007, the introduction of the Universal Secondary Education (USE) programme had a profound effect on the number of students attending secondary schools, with all the participating schools almost doubling their student intake and greatly increasing the student-teacher ratio (Ministry of Education and Sports, 2008b). Teachers are now even more constrained than heretofore by large class sizes, inadequate laboratory facilities, and lack of teaching and learning materials. In such conditions, it is very challenging to implement the intended teaching methods.

The Curriculum and Examination Context

Before describing the study on which this chapter is based, it is appropriate here to outline the structure of the Ugandan education system and the arrangements that are in place for curriculum and assessment. With regard to structure, primary education covers seven grades and secondary education spans six grades (S1 to S6), with four years being given to lower secondary education and two years to upper secondary education. Students take the UCE (Uganda Certificate of Education) examinations in S4 and the UACE (Uganda Advanced Certificate of Education) examinations in S6. The examinations are often referred to as O level and A level respectively.

There are two sets of national syllabi. The 'teaching syllabi' are authorised by the National Curriculum Development Centre (NCDC); the 'examination syllabi', on which the O level and A level examinations are based, are authorised by the Uganda National Examinations Board (UNEB). The two sets of syllabi differ to some extent in their emphasis. In the case of mathematics, the goals and objectives of the UNEB syllabus have a much more academic emphasis than those of the NCDC syllabus: five of the six objectives focus on mastery of skills, concepts and relationships. In the modules of the UNEB syllabus, only the scope of the content is described; there is no indication of the kinds of contexts in which problems are to be solved. The preamble of the NCDC mathematics syllabus demands that there should be linkage with other subjects, but leaves the modalities to teachers and does not specify occupational linkages. Moreover, for syllabi that are to be followed by all students – no differentiation in content being specified for students of different abilities or levels of attainment – the content for lower secondary education can be seen as rather ambitious. For example, it includes work on abstract algebraic structures (vectors and matrices) that reflect the 'modern mathematics' of the 1960s. These topics do not appear in the assessment frameworks reported by the Trends in International Mathematics and Science Study (TIMSS) for Grade 8 students (Mullis et al, 2008), indicating that the topics were not important in the syllabi of many participating systems at this level. Even for the 2008 TIMSS Advanced study, carried out with students in the final year of secondary schooling and taking advanced mathematics courses, matrices are not mentioned in the assessment frameworks and the material on vectors is rather basic (Mullis et al, 2009). Thus, at most, limited importance is accorded to these topics – even for students taking pre-university mathematics courses – at any rate in the rather small set of countries participating in that study. Overall, this does not mean that such topics are necessarily inappropriate for the curriculum at lower secondary level, but it does suggest that their inclusion may not be essential.

In short, our wider study found the mathematics syllabi to be both ambitious in the scope of content and lacking in guidance to teachers about how to contextualise the content. This description is consistent with comments recently made about the teaching of statistics, within school mathematics, in Uganda (Opolot-Okurut et al, 2008).

Study Design and Implementation

Research Questions and Study Design

The study described in this chapter was intended, among other things, to examine the implementation of the intended curricula and the extent to which the desired move towards more learner-centred methods was being achieved – for example, in order to facilitate constructivist learning. The objectives of the project were framed in terms of six questions, of which the following three are the focus of this chapter:

1. What are the teaching methods used in secondary mathematics and what are the learning opportunities for students?
2. What is the role of assessment in the teaching and learning of secondary mathematics?
3. How relevant is the secondary mathematics curriculum to students and national goals and needs?

In order to address these questions, the research used a qualitative approach, studying in depth 16 examples of mathematics classes and 16 examples of science classes. Through the use of a range of research tools, the study aimed to capture the complex role of the teacher, students, schools and other variables in contributing to the quality of mathematics and science education in Ugandan secondary schools. The study focused particularly on the effectiveness of the teacher, the role of the curriculum and the role of assessment.

The design specified that four research teams would be set up, each having three research participants: two Ugandan academics and one Irish academic. The purpose of this composition was to facilitate capacity building between the partners and to generate a synergy between the Irish and Ugandan academics. The teams were also selected so as to provide expertise both in mathematics and in science education. Each team was to visit one of the four regions (North, East, West and Central) of Uganda. The four regions were selected to provide a representative geographical spread of the schools and to capture the cultural differences among the regions.

The general approach to data collection was: (a) to observe examples of teaching in a purposive sample of secondary schools; (b) to record relevant experiences and perceptions of the teachers concerned, as expressed in interviews; and (c) to explore the school and managerial context through interviews with the head teachers of the schools concerned. The design therefore entailed each of the teams visiting four schools in its region. Purposive sampling was used in each region to identify a cluster of four schools that represented as far as possible both government and private ownership, single-sex and co-educational enrolments, and rural and urban locations. Team members would observe at least one mathematics and one science lesson for classes in the second or third year (S2 or S3) of the lower secondary cycle in each school; they would interview the teachers of the classes observed, and also hold a focus group discussion with selected students from each of these classes; and they would interview the head teacher.

Instruments, Data Collection and Context

The instruments included a lesson observation schedule, a semi-structured interview schedule for the teachers observed, a semi-structured interview schedule for the head teacher and a schedule for the focus group discussion with the students. Apart from the lesson observation schedule, all the instruments began with brief introductory questions, before which the researcher had to explain to the subject(s) the purpose of the research.

The instruments were designed with the participation of all the researchers. Each of the four research teams then visited one school in Kampala (Central Region) to conduct a pilot study. While in the school, the team together observed a mathematics lesson and a science lesson, interviewed the teachers and head teacher, and conducted the student focus group discussions. This provided an opportunity for not only checking the validity of the instruments, but also sharing experiences on how to use them during the research. The outcomes of the pilot study were shared at a meeting of all researchers and were used to update the instruments. The updated instruments were then used in the main study.

It can be noted here that, as intended in the study design, the four teams encountered a wide range of school environments. Some of the schools they visited were well resourced, with good library and laboratory facilities and some Internet connectivity. However, in many schools, resources were very limited. Large and poorly lit classrooms were typically equipped with one blackboard, often with a poor surface that made legibility difficult even for the students near the front of the room. Mathematics classes of between 60 and 140 students were observed. Topics addressed in the classes included vectors and matrices, as discussed earlier. Textbooks were not readily available and calculators were rarely evident.

The study was carried out in accordance with the ethical guidelines of the ASA and conformed to the requirements of the Uganda National Council for Science and Technology. Permission was sought from the identified district education authorities and schools, and letters were written to the schools to inform them of the purpose and timing of the forthcoming visits. The selected head teachers, teachers and students were willing to participate and all participants in the research were guaranteed anonymity and confidentiality.

Analysis

After the data collection was completed, the teams met again in Kampala to report their initial responses. The full team systematically addressed the items on the teacher interview protocol and recorded preliminary findings. Forty-three sub-themes were identified at that meeting and later consolidated into ten overarching themes. An amalgamation of a subset of these themes forms the basis for the findings we present in this chapter. The focus here is on pedagogy, teacher experiences and aspirations, and curriculum and examinations, as lenses through which teacher education issues can be viewed.

The analysis and interpretation of the data are influenced by the literature discussed earlier in this chapter. This discussion encompasses not only theoretical issues and previous research findings, but also relevant perspectives on policy.

Findings

Four sets of findings are reported in this section. They are based on the recorded observations of 16 mathematics lessons (one from each school visited) and the associated teacher interviews.

The Dominance of Teacher-Led Expository Pedagogy

This part of the findings draws on the data in the lesson observation schedules. In particular, it summarises the information from two questions: one on the 'dominant pedagogy' and one on the way in which the lesson developed after its introductory phase. They are discussed in turn.

For the question on the dominant pedagogy, observers were asked to supply a free response. The space for this was followed by a list of suggested categories (exposition, problem solving or investigations, teacher-led discussions, student discussion in groups, individual seat work/practice), but a space was also provided for observers to supply other classifications. During analysis, the responses were categorised under headings that covered the responses and also suited both mathematics and science. Thus, in Table I:

- 'Lecture' is used to include general teacher talk or exposition involving little or no interaction with students.
- 'Teacher-led demonstration' [1] is used to cover the cases in which the teacher worked stage by stage – perhaps with limited student participation – through a mathematical example, showing the students how to execute the procedure.
- 'Individual work' typically involves students working through mathematical examples, writing in their notebooks or on sheets of paper, in general without interacting with their neighbours or the teacher.

Type of pedagogy (from more to less didactic)	Frequency
Lecture	1
Teacher-led demonstration	2
Lecture and teacher-led demonstration	2
Lecture and whole-class discussion	2
Lecture and individual work	1
Teacher-led demonstration and whole-class discussion	1
Teacher-led demonstration and individual work	3
Question-and-answer method and teacher-led demonstration	1
Review of homework	1
Group work	1
Total	15*

*There is one case of missing data.

Table I. Dominant pedagogies observed,
with frequency of corresponding lessons.

In Table I, the various dominant pedagogies are listed, in a sequence that progresses, approximately, from the most didactic to the most interactive. Most of the categories have more than one element and the order in which these are given corresponds as far as possible to the sequence that teachers used. For example, in 'lecture and whole-class discussion', the lecture element took place largely prior to the discussion.

Since lessons often began in lecture mode, it is of interest to examine the way in which they were developed after the introductory phase. The question that addressed this in the observation schedule gave a list of suggestions, including 'question-and-answer method', and again allowed for free responses to be written in. Responses were coded so as to match the categories in Table I, with additions where necessary. The results are shown in Table II.

Type of pedagogy (from more to less didactic)	Frequency
Teacher-led demonstration	2
Lecture and teacher-led demonstration	1
Lecture and whole-class discussion	1
Lecture and individual work	1
Teacher-led demonstration and whole-class discussion	1
Question-and-answer method	4
Question-and-answer method and lecture	3
Question-and-answer method and whole-class discussion	1
Question-and-answer method and group work	1
Review of homework	1
Total	16

Table II. Types of lesson development observed,
with frequency of corresponding lessons.

As the frequencies show, there was a dominant pattern of expository, whole-class teaching. However, this generalisation must be qualified in two ways. Firstly, in a majority of the cases the expository element was seen to be combined with some other element that involved a greater degree of student participation (for example, whole-class discussion or individual work). Secondly, in the 'lesson development' phase of the lesson, the question-and-answer method was seen to be part of the approach in nine cases and as the main approach in four cases (see Table II). In spite of this, the question-and-answer method was not considered by the observers to be part of the dominant pedagogy, except in one case.

An overview of comments relating to the general effectiveness of the lessons observed indicates that they varied greatly in this regard and that effectiveness was less related to the types of method used than to such factors as the teacher's level of preparation, commitment, interactive skill and allocation of time to the various activities. The more traditional, teacher-dominated lessons included some that engaged students very effectively, as well as others that were not very stimulating. Equally, lessons involving seat work as a major component included some which were rather poorly organised and so of limited usefulness, as well as some which were very effective in promoting learning.

Overall, it can be said that a variety of teaching methods is in use, but executed with very varied degrees of competence and with teacher-centred approaches predominating – hence, not reflecting the aspiration for learner-centred work that underlies current policy. From our 'snapshot' of teaching, we are not sure how far particular teachers vary their methods or avoid those in which they are less skilled.

Teachers' Attitudes to Greater Learner
Activity and the Perceived Constraints

This finding draws on the data from the teacher interviews. In general, teachers seemed to have a positive attitude towards participatory and active learning by students. This is an important finding and one worth noting in the context of any proposed reforms. However, favourable attitudes by teachers towards participatory and active learning methodologies need to be supported by a range of resources and learning opportunities if these aspirations are to be realised in classroom practice. We have mentioned above how limited the resources are in many schools. We have also mentioned the ambitious curriculum: the perceived need to cover this was an additional constraint on such aspirations.

Despite the large class sizes, some teachers made efforts to integrate discovery-oriented learning in small ways. As one teacher stated:

> OK, today I tried to bring in the element of expository learning
> and discovery by a mere bringing of the log tables. I thought
> these students were discovering. I told them: How can you
> read this? ... I just asked them questions and they were
> discovering this by themselves and I prefer that kind of
> teaching where they discover by themselves.

Later on in the same interview, the teacher stated that, in relation to preferred teaching methods, 'students learn best when they are investigating themselves and that's the beauty of mathematics, that it can be really learnt when people are interacting'. These remarks give some indication of teachers' openness or readiness for curriculum reforms that provide more challenging and higher-order engagement by learners in secondary mathematics. In another example, below, the teacher is well disposed towards developing student understanding of core concepts so that mathematics is more relevant and useful to students, but feels pressured to 'beat the syllabus' rather than focus on mathematics that can 'help them in the future':

> You are under pressure to beat the syllabus by time ... it's not
> like in Europe where you teach children to understand and

become better mathematicians, but maybe we have some loopholes in the education system, where we are being pressured to beat the syllabus deadlines and that hinders our work as teachers who wish to make children understand things and learn mathematics which can help them in future.

Teachers' Positive Attitudes to Continuing Professional Development and Difficulty with Core Syllabus Concepts

Teachers reported that generally they appreciated the methods being promoted in continuing professional development (CPD) initiatives such as the SESEMAT programme. In some cases, positive CPD learning opportunities encouraged teachers to initiate their own in-school CPD – a very positive move. However, teachers also reported finding the methods difficult to implement. Many difficulties appeared to stem from lack of resources and large class sizes (as indicated above), and also from concerns about preparing students for examinations (discussed below in the fourth set of findings), rather than from any lack of belief in the intrinsic value of the methods.

Moreover, there was some evidence of misunderstanding as to the basic purpose of the approaches. Both the secondary mathematics and science syllabi emphasise the importance of key higher-order thinking constructs such as problem solving (mathematics) and scientific inquiry (science). This is consonant with the aim of introducing more participatory and active approaches based on principles of individual or social constructivist learning (Conway & Sloane, 2006). It was therefore important to investigate teachers' perceptions of these concepts. One question in the interview schedule for mathematics teachers addressed the issue directly: it asked about their understanding of problem solving. Many teachers were rather vague in their responses both to this and to other core syllabus concepts, as in this example:

> *Interviewer*: There has been a lot of talk in mathematics education internationally about problem solving. What do you understand by problem solving? Is it talked about here?
> *Teacher*: Problem solving...
> *Interviewer*: Yes, it means different things to different people. So what does it mean to you in Uganda?
> *Teacher*: In Uganda, problem solving, I think it is looking into ways how we can, eh ... how we can have, ah ... modifications to really make the teaching and learning of mathematics easier to the teachers and students at the same time.

The teacher appears to be talking about problems that teachers encounter in teaching mathematics and that students experience in learning the subject – not about problem solving as a key student activity. This pattern of incomprehension (which was also noticeable in science) suggests inadequacies in the pre-service education of teachers and shows a need for CPD, such as the SESEMAT programme, to include a focus on the key concepts underpinning the syllabi, which would give more meaning to the methods advocated.

The Backwash Effect of Examinations on Curriculum Implementation

Uganda, like other African countries, has a long tradition of holding national examinations at the end of the lower secondary cycle (O level) and of the upper secondary cycle (A level). Not only this, but secondary schools hold their own examinations twice or even three times per term. Thus, examinations are likely to be an important influence on teaching.

It would be misleading to portray examinations as a purely negative influence. Their common advantages and disadvantages have been well summarised with reference to the USA by Madaus (1991). On the positive side, they help to establish standards at the national level, reward achievement clearly and relieve the individual teacher of some of the responsibility for summative assessment. But the disadvantages of examinations include encouraging a narrow focus on material that is usually tested and, in many instances, a lack of congruence between curriculum objectives and examination procedures. Preparation for examinations too often involves an emphasis on rote memorisation by students and 'drill and practice' as a teaching method (Madaus, 1991, p. 30). Similar advantages and disadvantages were earlier identified in developing countries by Brooke & Oxenham (1984).

In our wider study, 13 out of 22 teachers of mathematics and science who were interviewed (and for whom there are data for the relevant question) confirmed that they emphasised examination content in their teaching, while only four said that they did not. Both teachers and head teachers indicated that the reputations of teachers and of schools demanded such an emphasis. The prominence of examinations was a central factor in teachers' framing and enactment of their role, in terms of content selection, the rhythm of the academic year, and their sense of efficacy and identity individually and collectively. They frequently spoke of the disadvantages of such a system, typically the ones identified by Madaus, but felt compelled to focus on examinations and to emphasise the UNEB (examination) syllabus over the wider NCDC mathematics syllabus. Examinations contribute to the perceived need to 'beat the syllabus' noted earlier. If teachers focus on the transmission of knowledge and on 'drill and practice' at the expense of the real-world application of knowledge, this may be partly attributable to concern about examinations as well as wide or overloaded syllabi.

Discussion and Conclusion

As we noted earlier, the analysis and interpretation of the data are influenced by the literature cited earlier in this chapter. The following discussion encompasses not only theoretical issues and previous research findings, but also relevant perspectives on policy.

The findings highlight: (1) the current dominance of teacher-led expository teaching (an unsurprising finding given the class sizes and resource constraints); (2) teachers' general approval of more participatory and active learning for their students; (3) teacher learning and knowledge in terms of positive experiences and disposition towards past CPD, as well as limited knowledge of core concepts central to reform-minded curricula in mathematics; and (4) the backwash effect of examinations on mathematics syllabus implementation. We now consider these findings, in particular in light of developments in mathematics education in some other sub-Saharan countries.

Commenting on the challenges of promoting high-quality secondary teaching worldwide, Moreno (2005, p. iv) noted that teachers in this sector 'tend to be the hardest to attract, the most expensive to educate and the hardest to retain in schools'. Acknowledging this worldwide challenge, we ask whether the teaching of secondary school mathematics in Uganda is poised for change. We can address this question in terms of issues already discussed in this chapter – namely, pedagogy, teacher learning and openness to change, resource constraints, and the powerful backwash effect of current examination practices. These challenges are all too familiar in both developed and developing country contexts, but take on a particular dynamic in the resource-constrained setting of contemporary Ugandan secondary schools. Yet, there are a number of potential avenues worth pursuing in order to achieve curriculum reform.

At the policy level, Uganda has been attempting to study and improve the teaching of mathematics, as shown both by the SESEMAT initiative and by the selection of mathematics and science as focal areas of research in the Irish Aid-funded study from which the present chapter is drawn (CDGE, 2011). This suggests that there is a disposition at national level to consider reform. That idea seems to be matched by a favourable disposition among teachers. Their positive attitudes to CPD opportunities point to an openness and readiness – at least among the teachers we interviewed – to consider changes in curriculum content, pedagogical methods and essential changes in the examination format.

Both the prioritisation of mathematics and science and the kinds of challenges that Uganda faces in these subjects are also shared by other countries of sub-Saharan Africa, as shown by Ottevanger et al (2007). Another source for comparison is Vavrus's (2009) study of teacher education in Tanzania, which reveals a pattern of teacher-centred, transmission-oriented pedagogy very similar to that evidenced in this study. To some extent, comparative findings from the region can assist reform in Uganda.

In the study from which this chapter is drawn, however, we further differentiated teaching beyond merely stating whether it was 'teacher-centred' or not, and noted the different lesson components and lesson development patterns (Tables I and II). We think it is important to consider these components and development patterns in moving incrementally towards more active and learner-centred teaching in Uganda. For example, given the large size of classes in Uganda, it may make more sense to focus, in teacher education, on pair-work pedagogy and the use of worksheets to promote interaction, as stepping stones to more cooperative pedagogies (Cohen, 1994), rather than trying to introduce the latter in advanced forms. An overambitious approach could be counterproductive at present, owing to issues of class size, congestion and classroom management.

Too often, the global categories of 'teacher-centred' or 'learner-centred' are used and cloud important nuances within each. Specifically, in this study an important finding was that teacher-centred pedagogy comes in many guises, some of which are more likely than others to enhance participatory and active learning. For this reason, differentiating within teacher-centred approaches, both in research and in the practice of teacher education, is an important first step in advancing mathematics pedagogy.

The backwash effect of examinations is powerful in Uganda and brings with it associated problems (and some benefits), as we have noted. Past research in developing countries suggests that significant pedagogical change is unlikely to succeed unless supported by changes to the content and format of examinations (Brooke & Oxenham, 1984; Kellaghan & Greaney, 1992). With this caveat stated, we think it is important that a review of the secondary mathematics curriculum be initiated in Uganda in which aims, assumptions about learning and associated pedagogical principles and strategies, content, and modes of assessment (not only terminal examinations) are addressed in order to provide a context for mathematics education reform.

Finally, it is important to remember Moreno's (2005) observation that enhancing practice at second level faces particular challenges in terms of attracting, educating and retaining teachers. This chapter has focused on the pedagogy and assessment of mathematics and has implications for the education of teachers. Specifically, the findings show two types of teacher knowledge that need to be enhanced in order to promote participatory and active learning methods. These are both general knowledge about teaching and learning and pedagogical content knowledge that will foster a stronger problem-solving orientation among students. The initiative of the government of Uganda in establishing the SESEMAT training programme was a useful first step. The sequel, which is now needed, is to address the challenges of promoting more effective mathematics teaching even as enrolment in secondary education expands rapidly.

Note

[1] In the original analysis, the phrase 'teacher-led modelling' was chosen in preference to 'teacher-led demonstration' because the latter was reserved for practical science activities. In this chapter – focused on mathematics – 'demonstration' is employed in order to avoid confusion with the far higher-order activity known as 'mathematical modelling', in which a real-life problem is translated into mathematical terms, a mathematical solution is found and this solution is interpreted in the real-world context.

References

Brooke, N. & Oxenham, J. (1984) The Influence of Certification and Selection on Teaching and Learning, in J. Oxenham (Ed.) *Education Versus Qualifications?*, pp. 147-175. London: Allen & Unwin.

Brown, D. (2009) Doing Poorly, in Primary and Later, *Guardian Weekly*, 2 December, p. 16.

Centre for Global Development through Education (2011) Teacher Effectiveness in the Teaching of Mathematics and Science in Uganda's Secondary Schools. (A project funded by Irish Aid through the CGDE in collaboration with the Ministry of Education and Sport, Uganda.) Limerick: CGDE.

Cohen, E. (1994) *Designing Groupwork: strategies for the heterogeneous classroom*, 2nd edn. New York: Teachers College Press.

Conway, P.F. & Sloane, F.C. (2006) *International Trends in Post-Primary Mathematics Education: perspectives on learning, teaching and assessment*. Dublin: National Council for Curriculum and Assessment.

Darling-Hammond, L. & Bransford, J. (Eds) (2005) *Preparing Teachers for a Changing World: what teachers should learn and be able to do*. Washington, DC: National Academy of Education.

Dzama, E.N. & Osborne, J.F. (1999) Poor Performance in Science among African Students: an alternative explanation to the African worldview thesis, *Journal of Research in Science Teaching*, 36(3), 387-405.

Fuller, B. & Heyneman, S.P. (1989) Third World School Quality: current collapse, future potential, *Educational Researcher*, 18(2), 12-19.

Gray, B.V. (1999) Science Education in the Developing World: issues and considerations, *Journal of Research in Science Teaching*, 36(3), 255-405.

Improving Education: what to teach? (2009) *Economist*, 21 November, pp. 49-50.

Kellaghan, T. & Greaney, V. (1992) *Using Examinations to Improve Education: a study in fourteen African countries*. Washington, DC: World Bank.

Kliebard, H.M. (1987) *The Struggle for the American Curriculum 1893-1958*. New York: Routledge.

Lewin, K.M. (2008) *Strategies for Sustainable Financing of Secondary Education in Sub-Saharan Africa*. Washington, DC: World Bank. http://dx.doi.org/10.1596/978-0-8213-7115-2

Ministry of Education and Sports (MOES) (2008a) *Draft Revised Education Sector Strategic Plan 2007-2015*. Kampala: MOES. http://www.education.go.ug/MoE&S_Strategic_plan.pdf.

Ministry of Education and Sports (MOES) (2008b) *Report on the USE/BTVET Head Count, March 2008*. Kampala: MOES.

Moreno, J.M. (2005) *Learning to Teach in the Knowledge Society: final report*. Washington, DC: World Bank.

Mullis, I.V.S., Martin, M.O., Robitaille, D.F., & Foy, P. (2009) *TIMSS Advanced 2008 International Report. Findings from IEA's Study of Achievement in Advanced Mathematics and Physics in the Final Year of Secondary School*. Chestnut Hill, MA: TIMSS & PIRLS International Study Center, Boston.

Mullis, I.V.S., Martin, M.O. & Foy, P., with Olson, J.F., Preuschoff, C., Erberber, E., Arora, A. & Galia, J. (2008) *TIMSS 2007 International Mathematics Report: findings from IEA's Trends in International Mathematics and Science Study at the fourth and eighth grades*. Chestnut Hill, MA: TIMSS & PIRLS International Study Center, Boston College.

Opolot-Okurut, C., Opyene-Eluk, P. & Mwanamoiza, M. (2008) The Current Teaching of Statistics in Schools in Uganda, in C. Batanero, G. Burrill, C. Reading & A. Rossman (Eds) *Joint ICMI/IASE Study: teaching statistics in school mathematics – challenges for teaching and teacher education, Mexico 2008*. http://www.ugr.es/~icm/iase_study/Files/Topic5/T5P6_Opolot.pdf

Organisation for Economic Co-operation and Development (OECD) (2005) *Teachers Matter: attracting, retaining and developing teachers*. Paris: OECD.

Ottevanger, W., Akker, J.J.H. van den & Feiter, L. de (2007) *Developing Science, Mathematics, and ICT Education in Sub-Saharan Africa: patterns and promising practices*. Washington, DC: World Bank. http://dx.doi.org/10.1596/978-0-8213-7070-4

Schwille, J. & Dembelé, M. (2007) *Global Perspectives on Teacher Learning: improving policy and practice*. Paris: International Institute for Educational Planning.

Shulman, L.S. (1987) Knowledge and Teaching: foundations of the new reform, *Harvard Education Review*, 57(1), 1-21.

Stromquist, N.P. & Monkman, K. (2000) Defining Globalisation and Assessing Its Implications on Knowledge and Education, in N.P. Stromquist & K. Monkman (Eds) *Globalization and Education: integration and contestation across cultures*, pp. 3-25. Lanham, MD: Rowman & Littlefield.

Suarez-Orozco, M. & Qin-Hilliard, D.B. (Eds) (2004) *Globalization: culture and education in the new millennium*. Berkeley: University of California Press & Ross Institute.

UNESCO (2005) *Education for All: the quality imperative*. Paris: UNESCO.

Vavrus, F. (2009) The Cultural Politics of Constructivist Pedagogies: teacher education reform in the United Republic of Tanzania, *International Journal of Educational Development*, 29(3), 303-311. http://dx.doi.org/10.1016/j.ijedudev.2008.05.002

Walberg, H.J. (1991) Improving School Science in Advanced and Developing Countries, *Review of Educational Research*, 61(1), 25-69.

CHAPTER 9

Implementing the Thematic Curriculum in Uganda: implications for teacher education

MARTY HOLLAND, LOUISE LONG & LAURA REGAN

SUMMARY In 2007 the lower primary curriculum (Primary 1–Primary 3) in Uganda underwent a radical revision with the introduction of the Thematic Curriculum. It was the intent of the Ministry of Education and Sports in Uganda to utilise the Thematic Curriculum to raise standards in literacy and numeracy and further develop children's life-skills. This chapter presents an account of a project that involved Irish and Ugandan researchers working collaboratively to investigate how effectively teachers were implementing the Thematic Curriculum. A number of challenges to the effective delivery of the Thematic Curriculum emerged from the data. For example, the researchers observed little use of participatory methodologies and, further, teachers reported a lack of commitment to continuous assessment. In this chapter the findings from the study are discussed in the context of their implications for teacher education and should be of interest globally to policy makers, practitioners and researchers in the advancement of the quality of pupils' learning.

Introduction

Uganda has a vision to develop materially and reduce poverty so that its citizens will enjoy physical, social and economic well-being. Uganda has recognised that maximising human resource potential for prosperity is realised by placing sustained accessibility to quality education at the heart of development. From the mid 1990s, under the leadership of Museveni, Uganda initiated extensive educational reform programmes to rejuvenate the education sector, including teacher education and curriculum development. The Ugandan primary curriculum of the early twenty-first century focused on the acquisition of knowledge in specific subject areas that were taught through the medium of English and assessed by formal examinations. However, poor student engagement in the learning process and the limited repertoire of pedagogical and assessment practices utilised by teachers prevented the goal of raising educational standards from being achieved (Education Standards Agency, 2004). Moreover, such teacher-centred classrooms did not encourage spontaneity or taking initiative on the part of students, and restricted critical and creative thinking (O'Sullivan, 2004). Thus, the curriculum content and implementation were restructured for lower primary classrooms in the form of the Thematic Curriculum (TC), which, after a one-year pilot, was launched nationwide in February 2007.

In 2009, the Ministry of Education and Sports (MOES) initiated a research project in collaboration with the Centre for Global Development through Education and with the support of funding from Irish Aid that aimed to investigate how effectively teachers are implementing the TC. Researchers drawn from higher education institutes in Ireland and Uganda worked collaboratively throughout the research process. This chapter, written by three of the Irish researchers, begins with a descriptive review of the Ugandan education system and the introduction of the TC. We then move on to present the findings from the investigation into the TC. Finally, we discuss the implications of these findings for teacher education.

Background to the Introduction of the TC

It is widely accepted that education is the key to individual, communal and national prosperity. The government of Uganda recognises the importance of education as a tool for economic expansion, poverty reduction and the maintenance of democratic principles and structures in a post-colonial, post-conflict society. In recent years, the government and the MOES have taken proactive measures to raise educational standards. The *Education Strategic Investment Plan* (Ministry of Education and Sports [MOES], 1998), followed by the *Education Sector Strategic Plan 2004-2015* (MOES, 2004), has enabled Uganda to make significant progress towards achieving the education-related Millennium Development Goals and the Dakar Education for All goals. In 1997, free universal primary education was introduced for the first time, making primary education accessible to the majority of the children of the nation regardless of their families' economic circumstances. The comprehensive reform package, together with a programme of dissemination, decentralisation, awareness building and mobilisation at the local level, was effective in increasing attendance at primary school by the poor (Deininger, 2003). This resulted in an increase in primary school enrolments from 2.7 million in 1997 to over 7 million in 2007, which gives rise to pupil-teacher ratios that are among the highest in the world (Deininger, 2003). However, the expansion of class sizes in primary schools increased the urgency of the need for the government of Uganda to improve the quality of primary education.

The 2003 mid-term review by MOES identified that a problem existed with the content of the curriculum and the language of delivery. The curriculum content was not as accessible to young children as it might be. The 2000-02 primary school curriculum, which comprised four core subjects (language, mathematics, science and social studies) and eight other subjects, did not pay sufficient attention to literacy skills, numeracy skills or transferable skills, especially for Primary 1 to Primary 3 (Penny et al, 2008). High levels of early dropout and low levels of attainment marked primary education. In 2003, only 22% of pupils who started in Primary 1 completed Primary 7 (Education Standards Agency, 2004). In the same year, in one region of Uganda, only 20% of Primary 6 pupils achieved basic standards of literacy in the National Assessment of Progress in Education tests. This was compounded by the fact that children were expected to learn through the medium of English. For the majority of children in Uganda this was not their local language. There are some 43 local languages in Uganda, of which 25 can be considered to be main Ugandan languages. The majority of children do not hear or use English at home.

The Principles Underpinning the TC

In response to the challenges identified above, the MOES rolled out the TC in Primary 1 to Primary 3 classes. The TC moves away from the traditional subject-oriented approach to childhood education to embrace the treatment of concepts holistically based on themes relating to the children's own experiences, prior knowledge and needs – for example, 'Our School' and 'Our Home'. Through themes, sub-themes and constituent strands, core competencies and related skills should be rapidly developed in literacy, numeracy and life skills. Integral to the TC is the continuous assessment and monitoring of children's understanding and competencies in the core skills. Another key feature of the TC is the presentation of learning experiences in languages in which learners are already proficient (National Curriculum Development Centre, 2006a).

Language of Instruction

Recent studies illustrate the advantages for children of using African languages as the medium of learning and teaching in addition to the former colonial language. Children will learn faster and achieve more when they can use their cultural background and local knowledge to become more active participants in the learning process (Dembele, 2003).

Moreover, Tahir et al (2005) note that such a policy is also central to making the curriculum more relevant by connecting school-based learning to the children's experience, environment and culture. This strengthening of the similarity between home and school contexts also sets children at ease and is conducive to fostering nurturing and motivating learning environments (Trudell, 2005).

Clearly, implementing the use of the local language as the medium for instruction is not without its problems. For example, Penny et al (2008) acknowledge the financial implications, given that the use of too many local languages fractionalises print runs and increases the cost of essential learning materials. It also makes the supply, training and deployment of teachers more complex and expensive. Salient questions are raised for the government of Uganda and MOES about the quality of teaching and learning through the local language when enabling conditions such as reading books and appropriately trained teachers may not be in place.

Child-Centred Pedagogies

One of the most pervasive educational ideas in contemporary sub-Saharan Africa has been the introduction of a child-centred pedagogy (Anderson, 2002; O'Sullivan, 2004), which is based on the principles that knowledge is not transmitted, but is actively constructed in the mind of the learner, and learning is a process in which meaning is developed on the basis of prior knowledge and experiences determined by culture and social context (Vygotsky, 1978). The TC adopts child-centred pedagogies and considers students as the centre of the teaching and learning processes within classrooms (Altinyelken, 2010). By 'child-centred', the TC particularly refers to the following:

1. Children should have a chance to interact with each other and with the teacher during the lesson.
2. Class activities should be organised so that children learn by doing. They should be able to move around from time to time, and to use their hands.
3. Activities should be organised around a variety of learning materials, and children should be able to handle the materials.
4. Children should have an opportunity, from time to time, to have an influence on the direction that the lesson (or day) takes, allowing the lesson to reflect the interests, abilities and concerns of the children (National Curriculum Development Centre, 2006b, p. 3).

However, Chisholm & Leyendecker (2008) point out that there is a huge body of evidence from a variety of sources that the concept of child-centred education has not taken root in sub-Saharan classrooms. For example, the literature on teacher development reveals a consensus of opinion that changing pedagogic practices is difficult because of the strong social and cultural influences which have led to teachers internalising the view that, as knowledge is fixed, objective and detached from the learner, their role is to transmit this knowledge through rote-learning techniques (Fullan, 2000; O-saki & Agu, 2002; Tabulawa, 2003). Decommissioning the prevailing mindset about the nature of knowledge and reforming pedagogical practices are undoubtedly some of the major challenges for teachers and teacher educators in the effective implementation of the TC.

Preparing Teachers to Implement the TC

Before the TC was introduced across the country, it was piloted in a number of schools in various districts. Based on information from the pilot, a series of 10-day TC training workshops for all teachers from Primary 1 to Primary 3 and for head teachers was delivered across the country. Workshops on child-centred pedagogies were at the fore of these training days.

Investigating the TC

This research project aimed to support higher education in Uganda in terms of improving the quality of teacher education vis-à-vis the implementation of the TC in lower primary classes. The research team comprised representatives of the MOES, lecturers from Kyambogo University, principals of primary training colleges in Uganda and teacher educators from Ireland. There were eight Ugandan researchers and four Irish researchers. The researchers divided into four sub-teams, in which there were two Ugandan researchers and one Irish researcher. Each sub-team went to one of Uganda's four broad geographical areas: Lira (in the north of Uganda), Fort Portal (to the west of Uganda), Kampala (in central Uganda) and Soroti (to the east of Uganda). The fieldwork was conducted over four days in June 2009 in the four different regions. Four primary schools per region were randomly selected to take part in the study. In total, there were 16 case schools. Contact was first established with the head teacher of each case school by a letter that explained the nature and the purpose of the research. On the data-collection day, the head teacher introduced the researchers to the class teachers and their collaboration was sought. Confidentiality was guaranteed before the classroom observations commenced. The research methods included classroom observations in Primary 1, 2 and 3 classrooms in each school and one-to-one interviews with the relevant teachers and the head teacher. In total, 64 interviews were conducted: 16 interviews were with head teachers and 48 with class teachers. During the interviews, the head teachers' and class teacher's views were recorded. A checklist was used during the classroom observations.

All the researchers analysed the complete data set to identify emergent themes and issues by using what Robson (2002) refers to as 'coded common sense'. The entire research process benefited from the local knowledge and insights provided by the Ugandan co-researchers. Thus, in making recommendations for 'best practice' in teacher education, we were less likely to fall prey to the 'uncritical international transfer of educational policies and practices' (Crossley et al, 2005, p. 2) that proliferates in comparative research.

Key Findings from the Investigation into the TC

The majority of teachers and head teachers agreed that the TC is making a significant impact on teaching and learning in Ugandan classrooms. Class teachers and head teachers are positive about its introduction and enthusiastic about its potential. The majority of participants agreed that the TC offers new and valuable learning opportunities for children, as well as improving their competencies in literacy and numeracy.

Impact on Children

The TC is constructed around a child-centred approach and, because of this, children's participation and understanding in lessons has improved. Teachers report that children feel good about their ability to contribute to lessons in their local language. Children can relate what is being taught to their own life experiences. The central tenets of developing literacy and numeracy involve meaningful contexts, dialogue and interaction, which are now part of everyday work through the TC. Giroux (1993, p. 367) advocates that it is important to engage literacy 'not just as a skill or knowledge, but an emerging act of consciousness and resistance'. This is consistent with the comment made by a class teacher that: 'During literacy hour that is where you can talk and they can talk, you exchange ideas freely.' For all these reasons, children are much happier in school, more interested and keener to attend.

Attendance has improved as a result of the introduction of the TC and all head teachers also reported an increase in enrolments. Researchers found that teaching in the local language contributed significantly to increased pupil participation. As one head teacher commented: 'When you are using the area language that children understand, they understand better ... they even feel at home. They love the school.' Pupils are also developing communication skills through use of their local language. The use of the local language gives pupils more confidence to participate in class discussion.

The TC facilitates better understanding in numeracy, but evidence of the benefits for life skills was less apparent. The data suggest that life skills are being poorly incorporated into daily practice in the TC. In a significant minority of observed lessons, teachers failed to connect the content to the children's own life experiences.

Teacher Effectiveness

The implementation of the TC has had an impact on the pedagogical practices of teachers. Training in the TC is seen as good, but most teachers express the wish for further continuing professional development in the TC. Teachers report that planning and preparation for the TC requires much more time than for the old curriculum but they feel this is worthwhile because of the benefits they see for the children. It is clear, for example, that the learning of new skills is more effective when it is spaced over a period of time rather than when it is 'massed' into a short period of time. Yet despite this, much continuing professional development in the TC is offered in short sessions of a day or a number of days, rather than through a continuous process of engagement and re-engagement over a more extended period of time.

The majority of teachers are confident in their lesson delivery of the TC. The ability of teachers to demonstrate such competencies in classes of as many as 213 children, and with few resources at their disposal, is commendable.

Resources for the TC

The research has found that, on the whole, the TC is inadequately resourced. There is a dearth of teaching resources and textbooks in schools. Some teachers who come from other areas do not feel competent in using the local language. They, therefore, have difficulty translating the English curriculum into the local language.

The physical quality of classrooms raises major resourcing issues. In general, the classrooms observed in the research are poorly constructed, have no doors and are equipped with windows having no shutters. This makes it extremely difficult for teachers to display resources or children's work. In 41 out of 45 observations it was found that classroom displays were inadequate, and the researchers noted: 'There are no charts displayed, except when the teacher is teaching' and 'Few relevant charts, some torn and hanging on the wall'. Many researchers found 'empty classrooms' with 'none [charts] at all displayed'.

Generally, classrooms do not have storage facilities and, therefore, when resources are available, or have been created, there is nowhere safe to store them. Some schools suffer from the theft of materials which are not securely stored. Many classrooms are very poorly furnished with totally inadequate seating for children, and some have no seating at all, where children have to sit on poorly finished floors. The local environment of the schools is not adequately used as an available resource for gathering instructional materials. However, some good examples of such use in numeracy were observed with large class groups.

Teaching Methodologies

The TC promotes the use of a wide range of participatory methodologies. Unfortunately, the use of a wide range of methodologies was not evident in practice and teaching was very didactic. The use of participatory methodologies such as group work, cooperative learning, discovery learning, role play and dramatisation was not evident in lesson planning or implementation. The use of such methodologies would help to promote competencies across the TC and can assist in promoting life skills – a key component of the TC. The mitigating factors – such as large class size and lack of resources – for not using a range of methodologies are, however, acknowledged.

Assessment and Monitoring of Pupil Learning

Drawing from the teacher interviews, it is evident that teachers are not convinced about the value of continuous assessment. Overall, teachers see assessment as being mainly for administrative purposes or for informing parents of a pupil's progress at the end of term. One teacher remarked: 'The assessment is for record purposes.' Another maintained: 'We record on each of the children and at the end of the term we get an exercise book where you can record. At the end of the term you give it to the parents.' End-of-term assessments are seen as the main form of assessing pupil learning and this is partly due to parental expectations.

Teachers find it difficult to keep track of children with special educational needs, such as learning difficulties, in their classes. A number of teachers said that they had no such children in their class. The statistics on disability in Uganda are, therefore, inadequate. It would be most surprising if the percentage of children with learning disabilities in Uganda is not at least as high as the percentage in other countries (the World Health Organization [2006] estimates a 10% disability rate). It is a source of concern if these children are not being identified and this poses a serious problem for education and welfare. Many of the methodologies and strengths of the TC are particularly relevant to the needs of children with learning difficulties.

The Impact of the TC on the Wider School Community

Mixed messages were received from head teachers regarding the attitudes of parents to the TC. Substantial evidence emerged from the research indicating that many parents are not happy with their children being taught through the local language. They perceive this as being detrimental to their children's prospects in state examinations, which are in English. They see it as impacting detrimentally on their competency in English. One teacher reported: 'They complain that we use a lot of mother tongue and they want their children to speak English because this is a town.' Where this has been identified as a challenge, teachers have noted that schools have to work on parents and 'sensitise them'. Equally, parents are generally not supportive of continuous assessment. They expect, and want, end-of-term and end-of-year examinations. This is still the main way in which they measure success. A few head teachers reported that the TC had brought parents closer to the teachers and to the schools. Parents are less alienated by what is being taught and are now able to participate more fully in their children's education. This, in turn, had improved the teacher-parent relationship.

Implications for Teacher Education

This section will discuss the implications of the findings from our investigation into teacher effectiveness in the implementation of the TC for teacher education. The conclusions from this study add to an emerging body of literature on the effective practice that is improving pupil learning in Ugandan classrooms. However, the research also identified a number of challenges for teacher education in Uganda in the context of curriculum reform and pedagogical renewal, which together aim to enhance education quality. Moon (2007) acknowledges that many aspects of the problem of how to improve teacher quality and pupil achievement (UNESCO, 2005) in sub-Saharan African countries mirror those in the rest of the world. Thus, the recommendations emanating from our research should be of interest globally to education policy makers, researchers and practitioners.

In sub-Saharan Africa, there is strong agreement on the principles that underpin educational reform (Verspoor, 2006). Heneveld (2007) has articulated these principles as follows:

- Quality improvement is a process that lives or dies in the classroom through varied instructional and assessment strategies.
- Teachers are at the heart of the process.
- The school head's leadership is critical to improved learning.
- Teacher support systems are critical elements for improving school quality.

- The support of communities and civil society is often significant in improving a school's effectiveness.
- Sustained high-level political leadership and support are necessary.

We have borrowed from Heneveld's conceptualisation of educational reform to frame this discussion on how the findings from the current study, in conjunction with evidence from the literature, could influence the advancement of teacher education.

Pedagogical and Assessment Strategies

The findings from the current study are consistent with recent research studies which found that: the predominant mode of curriculum implementation is teacher-centred; classroom and assessment practices involve the recall of facts; available instructional materials are poorly utilised; and teachers make insufficient use of the local environment for instructional materials (Heneveld, 2007; Altinyelken, 2010). According to Dembele & Oviawe (2007), the failure to fully embrace child-centred pedagogies can be explained by the existence of a historically constructed 'grammar of teaching', which people learn during their school years, consolidate during pre-service training experiences and perpetuate in classroom practice. There is a paucity of critical literature on continuous assessment in Ugandan classrooms (see Heneveld, 2007). However, findings from the current study suggest that teachers may well have internalised the view that continuous assessment is burdensome and paperwork-led. We observed a general teacher profile that does not move beyond marking work to encompass engaging with students in the feedback process or using assessment information to inform future planning.

We acknowledge that the poor conditions in which teachers teach and children learn, large class sizes and inadequate resources can be disabling factors in large-scale attempts to enhance variety in pedagogical and assessment strategies. However, our awareness of these challenges from participation in the current study has helped to inform the recommendations for the advancement of enabling conditions through teacher education.

We are suggesting that the teacher education curriculum should focus more on critically examining contemporary research and scholarship on how children learn and, in particular, the pedagogies that are effective in raising achievement. The teaching methodologies implemented by teacher educators should mirror those that teachers are expected to incorporate into daily classroom life. By using activity-based approaches (for example, creating resources from the local environment for a specific curricular theme, engaging in self- and peer assessment of a cooperative learning task or collaborative problem solving based on case studies) to continuous assessment and modelling how the outcomes from an assessment task can be used to give students feedback, inform planning and provide effective remedial support, teacher education should move to a more harmonising position with the TC. Moreover, findings from the current study suggest that, for this to happen in an integrated way, teacher educators should also be advancing the teaching of life skills.

In the current educational climate, teachers are now expected to move beyond raising standards to embrace a more holistic model that promotes the physical and emotional well-being and well-becoming of students by equipping them with the general competencies, attitudes and interpersonal skills for effective functioning in life and work in the global 'information economy'. Teacher education programmes could be reconceptualised in ways that promote the advancement of the life skills (such as creativity, tolerance, problem solving, conflict resolution and teamwork) that are necessary for preparing children for the world of work (Hoppers, 1996). The introduction of psychological models and concepts such as Maslow's (1970) hierarchy of needs, emotional literacy (Goleman, 1995) and metacognition (Flavell, 1985) into teacher education programmes will advance teachers' understanding of the rationale and intended outcomes for the teaching of life skills, which should impact positively on their belief in and commitment to changing practice (Heneveld, 2007).

As the range of experiences for the promotion of life skills should be offered in the context of group work, teacher education programmes should be incorporating collaborative learning experiences, thereby enhancing teachers' understanding of group dynamics, together with group roles, stages and phases, and the need for ground rules, which serve to make learning environments safe and secure for students (Geary & McNamara, 2005). The challenge for teachers in applying the knowledge and skills gained about effective group work to large classes could be addressed by a more productive use of the two teaching staff that we observed in many classrooms in terms of co-teaching, engaging with students in meaningful dialogue and providing support for those students who have additional learning needs.

Our final point in this section is to suggest that the potentially disabling effect of limited resources could well be alleviated by the enabling exploitation of technologies. An interesting observation from the current study, which is not documented, is that the majority of teachers in the schools we visited during the research process had mobile phones. This is not surprising given that Africa has the fastest-growing telecommunications sector in the world (Minges, 2004). For Moon (2007, p. 363), such technological change offers the opportunity to 'enrich the pedagogic toolkit of teacher educators and teachers in hitherto undreamt-of ways. Information and communication tools are becoming increasingly portable, flexible and powerful and numerous studies point to the potential of these new technologies as learning tools'.

By drawing on the work that is already going on in the Eastern Cape, South Africa, and Egypt to develop primary teachers' skills in the teaching of literacy, numeracy and science through resources and communication systems derived from mobile phones and other related technologies (Leach, 2006), teacher educators should be able to advance teacher capacity and confidence in using new forms of information and communications technology (ICT) in classrooms. However, resources that utilise ICT through mobile phones need strong support rooted in local contexts and existing structures, which are closely monitored to ensure their effectiveness for teachers in differing settings (Somekh, 2001).

The successful implementation of these recommendations will undoubtedly require capacity enhancement for those who are 'entrusted with the responsibility to prepare and support teachers as they struggle to find meaning in the desired change and embrace it' (Dembele & Oviawe, 2007, p. 477); stronger links between all the institutions and organisations that are involved in advancing teacher education; and clarity of the roles and responsibilities of key stakeholders at the school, regional, national and international levels.

Connecting Teachers: connecting with communities

Teachers are members of a 'learning profession' (Darling-Hammond & Sykes, 1999), which denotes connectivity with a community of learners. Moon (2007) acknowledges the positive energising consequences when effective professional communities work collaboratively to advance practice. In view of the real and multiple pressures that teachers are experiencing, they should be given time for professional development within and across schools by working in teams and cluster groups, which could be facilitated by centre coordinating tutors. Here, teachers have the opportunity to create and share paper and electronic instructional materials that are culturally appropriate and written in the local language, and to share observations on effective classroom practice, mistakes made and lessons learned in an enabling climate that values creativity, risk-taking and cooperation. These professional development activities are cost-effective pathways to curriculum reform which provide opportunities for teachers who are secure about and experienced in the TC to share their knowledge base with other practitioners in the school setting.

The arguments for such school-based professional development are now well rehearsed (Moon, 2007). Of particular relevance to this discussion is the issue of the deployment of teachers to lower primary classrooms where they are not proficient in the vernacular and/or have limited experience of implementing the curriculum in the local language. We are suggesting that teacher educators should be identifying those teachers who wish to teach in lower primary classrooms so that they can fast-track their initial training and guide their professional development in schools that have been carefully chosen because of vernacular compatibility between teachers and learners. There should be externally evaluated rewards for effective practice and dissemination of best practice within and between schools, which will support teachers in the early stages of their professional development. As Uganda continues to invest in its technological infrastructure, consideration could be given to distance learning through well-managed online environments that support teachers, in rural and isolated areas in particular, to collaboratively develop professional knowledge, learning tools and resources. This is critical to the sustained enhancement of teacher education given the pace and scale of reform in the implementation of the TC.

At a systemic level, schools should be taking small steps to sensitise the local community on the TC, particularly in those localities where it is viewed as an initiative that sits incongruously with the traditional system of formal examinations. Involving the local community in school-based projects, for example, could help to promote sustained community engagement and concurrently alleviate uncertainties and confusion about curriculum reform. The success of the implementation of these recommendations will inevitably be predicated upon effective leadership.

The Leadership Role of Head Teachers

We are suggesting that it is critical to the success of the TC that head teachers have a vision for promoting child-centred pedagogies by walking the walk, as well as talking the talk. For example, evidence from the literature suggests that schools with better student results tend to have heads who pay more attention to teachers' preparation for teaching and the regular assessment of students (Heneveld, 2007). In the context of the current study, we are recommending that there is investment in building head teachers' capacities to mentor staff, coach teachers and identify targets that are closely linked to the ongoing professional development needs of individual teachers and their schools.

Political Leadership

Vision and sustained commitment on the part of government, educational leaders and policy makers to teacher education should contribute significantly to the effective implementation of the TC (Leach & Moon, 2002). This includes investing in curriculum documentation;

resources in local language(s), including those that utilise ICT; and teacher education and professional development. Findings from the current study point to the urgent need for investment, policy development and capacity building in inclusive education, which should help schools and teachers in Uganda achieve Education for All.

Final Reflections

The investigation into the TC is one of the few studies to inform the advancement of teacher education that has been carried out in the developing world. It was an empowering experience for local educators to share their insights from on the ground and take ownership of the recommendations that should improve the quality of education. The challenge for the Irish researchers was to remain self-aware, rational and culturally responsive to the contextual realities and capacities. We hope that the insights gained from the collaborative investigation of the TC have shed some light on what needs to change and how enhancing teacher education can help to enable those changes.

References

Altinyelken, H.K. (2010) Pedagogical Renewal in Sub-Saharan Africa: the case of Uganda, *Comparative Education*, 46(2), 151-171. http://dx.doi.org/10.1080/03050061003775454

Anderson, S. (Ed.) (2002) *School Improvement through Teacher Development: case studies of the Aga Khan Foundation Projects in East Africa.* Lisse: Swets & Zeitlinger.

Chisholm, L. & Leyendecker, R. (2008) Curriculum Reform in Post-1990s Sub-Saharan Africa, *International Journal of Educational Development*, 28, 195-205. http://dx.doi.org/10.1016/j.ijedudev.2007.04.003

Crossley, M., Chisholm, L. & Holmes, K. (2005) Educational Change and Evaluation in Eastern and Southern Africa, special issue of *Compare*, 35(1).

Darling-Hammond, L. & Sykes, G. (Eds) (1999) *Teaching as a Learning Profession.* San Francisco: Jossey-Bass.

Deininger, K. (2003) Does Cost of Schooling Affect Enrolment by the Poor? Universal Primary Education in Uganda, *Economics of Education Review*, 22, 291-305. http://dx.doi.org/10.1016/S0272-7757(02)00053-5

Dembele, M. (2003) Breaking the Mould: teacher development through pedagogical renewal, in A.M. Verspoor (Ed.) *The Challenge of Learning: improving the quality of basic education in sub-Saharan Africa.* Paris: ADEA.

Dembele, M. & Oviawe, J. (2007) Quality Education in Africa: international commitments, local challenges and responses, *International Review of Education*, 53(5/6), 477-483.

Education Standards Agency (ESA) (2004) *Report on Monitoring Learning Achievement in Lower Primary.* Kampala: ESA.

Flavell, G.H. (1985) *Cognitive Development*, 2nd edn. Englewood Cliffs, NJ: Prentice-Hall.

Fullan, M.G. (2000) The Return of Large-Scale Reform, *Journal of Educational Change*, 2(1), 5-28. http://dx.doi.org/10.1023/A:1010068703786

Geary, T. & McNamara, P. (2005) *Implementation of Social, Personal and Health Education at Junior Cycle.* Limerick: University of Limerick.

Giroux, H. (1993) Literacy and the Politics of Difference, in C. Lankshear & P. McLaren (Eds) *Critical Literacy: politics, praxis, and the postmodern*, pp. 367-377. Albany: State University of New York Press.

Goleman, D. (1995) *Emotional Intelligence.* New York: Bantam Books.

Heneveld, W. (2007) Whose Reality Counts? Local Educators as Researchers on the Quality of Primary Education, *International Review of Education*, 53(5/6), 639-663. http://dx.doi.org/10.1007/s11159-007-9059-7

Hoppers, Odora A. (1996) Development Cooperation in Education and Training at the SADC Level: challenges and possibilities. Paper prepared for UNESCO, mimeo.

Leach, J. & Moon, B. (2002) Globalisation, Digital Societies and School Reform: realising the potential of new technologies to enhance the knowledge, understanding and dignity of teachers. Paper presented at Second European Conference on Information Technologies in Education and Citizenship: a critical insight, Barcelona, 26-28 June.

Leach, J. (2006) *DEEP IMPACT: an investigation of the use of information and communication technologies for teacher education in the global south.* London: Department for International Development.

Maslow, A.H. (1970) *Motivation and Personality*, 2nd edn. New York: Harper & Row.

Minges, M. (2004) *African Telecommunication Indicators 2004.* Geneva: International Telecommunication Union.

Ministry of Education and Sports (MOES) (1998) Education Strategic Investment Plan 1998–2003, Kampala: MOES.

Ministry of Education and Sports (MOES) (2003) *Government of Uganda Mid-term Review. Final Report.* Kampala: Education Planning Department, MOES.

Ministry of Education and Sports (MOES) (2004) *Education Sector Strategic Plan 2004-2015.* Kampala: MOES.

Moon, B. (2007) School-Based Teacher Development in Sub-Saharan Africa: building a new research agenda, *Curriculum Journal*, 18(3), 355-371. http://dx.doi.org/10.1080/09585170701590007

National Curriculum Development Centre (NCDC) (2006a) *The National Primary School Curriculum for Uganda, Primary 1.* Kampala: NCDC.

National Curriculum Development Centre (NCDC) (2006b) *The National Primary School Curriculum for Uganda, Teacher's Guide, Primary 1.* Kampala: NCDC.

O'Sullivan, M. (2004) The Reconceptualisation of Learner-centred Approaches: a Namibian case-study, *International Journal of Educational Development*, 24, 585-603. http://dx.doi.org/10.1016/S0738-0593(03)00018-X

O-saki, K.M. & Agu, 1A.O. (2002) A Study of Classroom Interaction in Primary Schools in the United Republic of Tanzania, *Prospects*, XXXII, 103-116.

Penny, A., Ward, M., Read, T. & Bines, H. (2008) Education Sector Reform: the Ugandan experience, *International Journal of Educational Development*, 28, 268-285. http://dx.doi.org/10.1016/j.ijedudev.2007.04.004

Robson, C. (2002) *Real World Research: a resource for social scientists and practitioner-researchers*, 2nd edn. Oxford: Blackwell.

Somekh, B. (2001) The Role of Evaluations in Ensuring Excellence in Communications and Information Technology Initiatives, *Education, Communication and Information*, 1(1), 75-101. http://dx.doi.org/10.1080/14636310120048065

Tabulawa, R. (2003) International Aid Agencies, Learner-Centred Pedagogy and Political Democratisation: a critique, *Comparative Education,* 39(1), 7-26. http://dx.doi.org/10.1080/03050060302559

Tahir, G., Muhammad, N.D. & Muhammed, A.M. (2005) *Improving the Quality of Nomadic Education in Nigeria.* Paris: Association for the Development of Education in Africa

Trudell, B. (2005) Language Choice, Education and Community Identity, *International Journal of Educational Development*, 25, 237-251. http://dx.doi.org/10.1016/j.ijedudev.2004.08.004

UNESCO (2005*) Guidelines for Inclusion: ensuring access to education for all.* Paris: UNESCO.

Verspoor, A. (2006) Effective Schools: transforming resources into results at the classroom level. Paper presented at Association for the Development of Education in Africa 2006 Biennale on Education in Africa, Libreville, Gabon, 27-31 March.

Vygotsky, L.S. (1978) *Mind in Society: the development of higher psychological processes.* Cambridge, MA: Harvard University Press.

World Health Organisation (2006) *Country Health System Fact Sheet 2006. Uganda.* Uganda: Regional Office for Africa.

CHAPTER 10

How Much Is Enough? Investigating Mathematical Knowledge for Primary Teaching in Lesotho

DOLORES CORCORAN & ANNE DOLAN

SUMMARY There is a worldwide drive to improve standards of attainment in mathematics. It is commonly held that increased teacher knowledge of mathematics will improve student performance. However, research indicates that this relationship is far from straightforward. Different conceptions of what it means to know and use mathematics give rise to different approaches to teaching mathematics. The unique challenges presented by the education setting in Lesotho are outlined, and in this chapter, a self-audit of mathematics knowledge for teaching is introduced. This audit was administered to 22 students preparing to become primary school teachers in the Lesotho College of Education. Findings are compared with responses of student teachers in an Irish college of education. The chapter concludes with recommendations for the development of teaching that could work equally well in Lesotho as in Ireland.

Introduction

The issue of teacher quality in general and the quality of teaching mathematics in particular in sub-Saharan Africa has been highlighted in the literature (Moon, 2007). Efforts to improve teacher quality are particularly challenging in light of the low status and poor working conditions of teachers, which militates against their recruitment and retention. Teacher quality is also an important issue considering that the United Nations' Millennium Development Goals include a commitment to ensure that by 2015 all boys and girls will be able to complete a full course of primary schooling. This chapter examines the issue of mathematical knowledge of student teachers through a study which was conducted in the Lesotho College of Education. It offers a glimpse of prospective primary teachers' mathematics subject knowledge (MSK) as assessed on a mathematics self-audit instrument designed in the United Kingdom to measure student teachers' mathematical knowledge for teaching (Rowland et al, 1998). This has also been used in Ireland to investigate student teachers' MSK and their self-reported confidence in that knowledge (Corcoran, 2008). These research findings are presented as a series of snapshots, which, while temporally and contextually bound, can be compared with similar snapshots taken of student teachers in other contexts. In order to set these pictures in their unique context, the chapter provides a brief overview of Lesotho and its education system with specific reference to some of the development challenges faced there. The chapter concludes with some recommendations for teacher education which arise from this study.

The Kingdom of Lesotho

Lesotho is a small mountainous country of about two million (predominantly rural) people. The country is landlocked and completely surrounded by, and economically dependant on, South Africa. The majority of the population lives in the lowlands close to the South African border. Three-quarters of the country consists of highlands rising to nearly 3500 metres in the Drakensberg mountain range. Locations in Lesotho are classified according to four ecological zones: the lowlands, the foothills, the mountains and the Senqu Valley. Its economy is based on limited agricultural and pastoral production and light manufacturing (textiles, clothing and leather), supplemented by large, although declining, remittances from Lesotho miners in South Africa. Recently, there have also been royalties from exporting water to South Africa through the Lesotho Highland Water Project. Major development challenges include poverty, widespread HIV/AIDS, and low-quality education and health care. These development problems are further compounded by a range of environmental problems, including accelerated soil erosion, loss of arable land, periodic prolonged drought and scarcity of water for agriculture, and low levels of environmental awareness among policy and decision makers. Many of Lesotho's two million inhabitants depend on small-scale agriculture for a living. Because less than 10% of the land mass is suitable for farming, Lesotho produces less than 30% of its total food requirement, resulting in a reliance on imported foodstuffs and vulnerability to price fluctuations. Currently, the country is ranked 156th out of 182 countries according to the Human Development Index.

Education

In concurrence with international initiatives, free primary education (FPE) has been a central aspect of educational policy initiatives in Lesotho. This was introduced gradually, one grade at a time, so that by 2006 no standards (classes) were liable for fees. Today, Lesotho has high levels of enrolment. Gross enrolment rates at primary level are over 100%, and greater for girls than boys (Coultas & Lewin, 2002). FPE has raised the primary gross enrolment rate in excess of 100% due to children entering school before the age of 6 or remaining in school beyond the age of 12, and the net enrolment figure to 85% (Ministry of Education and Training, 2008). While access to primary education has been increased through no fees and a school feeding programme, several commentators believe that quality has been compromised. According to the Southern and Eastern Africa Consortium for the Monitoring of Educational Quality (SACMEQ) II report, many children leave school with poor levels of literacy and numeracy (Mothibeli & Maema, 2005).

Urwick (2011) highlights the downside of FPE, which he refers to as a 'crash programme'. In addition to the removal of tuition fees, the government-funded school meals, learning materials and, in some instances, school maintenance, FPE has also led to the recruitment of unqualified teachers and the increased use of in-service training, particularly in remoter areas. According to Urwick (2011), within the national survey of teachers conducted by the Lesotho College of Education in 2005, the unqualified proportion was 45% in the mountains and Senqu Valley, compared to 28% in the lowlands. In national terms, the proportion of unqualified teachers has increased from 22% in 1999 to 36% in 2004, with the great proportion of these based in the mountain areas. While a 'mountain allowance' exists for some mountain areas, it is not sufficiently high to attract qualified teachers to work in the mountain areas for prolonged periods of time. In Lesotho, the number of suitable graduates from secondary schools currently limits teaching-force numbers. Only about 2000 students each year achieve marks on the Cambridge Overseas School Certificate (COSC) examination that would qualify them for pre-service teacher education; up to half of these would need to opt for teacher preparation courses in order to satisfy the demand for teachers (Lewin, 2002). Figure 1 demonstrates the rapid increase of teacher appointments which has taken place during the last decade. The sharp increase in the number of teachers on the payroll in 2003 and 2004 is due to the effort to fill vacancies which have been created since 2000 as an attempt by the government to increase enrolment and to reduce the pupil-teacher ratio (Mulkeen & Chen, 2008).

Teacher quality is also an issue of concern. Moloi et al (2008, p. 620) argue that 'teachers' inadequate knowledge of content, pedagogy and assessment procedures as well as lack of appropriate teaching resources makes it difficult for them and pupils to achieve the set objectives'. This study also raised concerns in relation to the use of English as a mode of communication in the classroom. While the language of learning is officially English for Standards 4 to 7, in practice, Sesotho is used either as the predominant mode of communication or in conjunction with English. As a result, pupil competence in English is poor and, according to the authors, English 'remains a barrier to education in the rest of subjects on the curriculum at this [primary] and higher levels' (Moloi et al, 2008, p. 620). These communication difficulties present particular challenges in the teaching and learning of mathematics.

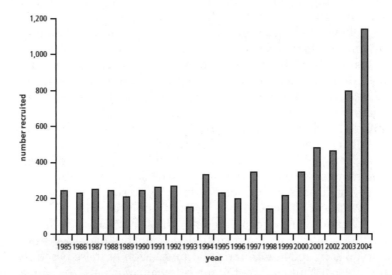

Figure 1. Number of teachers recruited annually, 1985-2004.
Source: Lesotho, Ministry of Education and Training data,
cited in Mulkeen & Chen (2008).

Teacher Education

The Lesotho College of Education – formerly known as the National Teacher Training College (NTTC) – is the only teacher education college in Lesotho. The NTTC was the subject of several evaluations (Daniels, 1985; Sebatane et al, 1987; Burke & Sugrue, 1994), which highlighted a number of issues, including low entry standards to the college, poor standards of English, poor grounding in academic content, a lack of professional preparedness, poor delivery of programmes and a lack of relevant experience of teacher educators (Sebatane et al, 2000). Following these studies, the teacher education programmes have been revised over the last decade. The original Advanced Primary Teachers' Certificate Programme was replaced by a three-year Diploma in Primary

Education for serving teachers and, in 1998, the Diploma in Education (Primary) (DEP) began to replace the Primary Teachers' Certificate as a three-and-a-half-year initial programme (Ntoi & Pulane Lefoka, 2002). The numbers enrolled in initial training for primary teaching have fluctuated between 200 and 400 in the recent past. Typically, over 70% of trainees are female. Selection onto the DEP requires a minimum of four credits (one of which must be in English) and a pass in the COSC. There is little evidence to suggest an improvement in the finding that none of the student teachers achieved an A in the COSC examinations in any of the three core subject areas: English, science and mathematics. Most students achieved an E grade or less, with 62% of these in English, 66% in mathematics and 39% in science (Coultas & Lewin, 2002). The 'low academic calibre' of the entrants to teacher education remains a challenge to teacher education. Ntoi & Pulane Lefoka (2002, p. 281) also note a number of ongoing concerns, including the teacher-centred nature of classes, the lack of reference to the prior experience of students, the absence of interactive dialogue and the limited range of methodologies in use. According to the authors:

> when we looked at the curriculum in action, it was clear that most of the tutors were delivering their lessons in line with the written syllabus as far as content was concerned, but their use of teaching and learning material was minimal, the assessments do not involve the students in much intellectual challenge and the pedagogy was uninspiring. (Ntoi & Pulane Lefoka, 2002, p. 281)

This finding is supported in a study of newly qualified teachers and their perceptions of the training they received in college. The report evaluated the entry requirements of new student teachers, the delivery of the primary teacher education curriculum, career structures and management within the NTTC, means of assessing Lesotho's demand and supply of teachers, and sources of support given to novice teachers (Pulane Lefoka & Sebatane, 2003). Primary student teachers are mostly women in their early twenties from modest backgrounds. Before arriving at the NTTC, a quarter has acquired teaching experience. However, by modelling themselves on the traditional teachers who brought them into the profession, they have adopted teaching styles based on discipline rather than on child-centred education. Many trainees have significant gaps in their own education. The report concludes that the NTTC is sending out primary school teachers who are likely to use teacher-centred methods in their style of teaching and be insensitive to the needs of primary school children. In a study which explores the teaching of primary English and mathematics in Lesotho, the authors found that teachers have poor knowledge of assessment strategies, including the design of tests and assessment tools relevant for measuring objectives;

they note a reliance on 'safe and easy' procedures and the over-reliance on lower-order questions (Moloi et al, 2008). Against this picture, painted largely in terms of teacher deficit, the question is posed: How do DEP student teachers compare with Irish student teachers in relation to mathematical knowledge for primary teaching?

Mathematical Knowledge for Teaching

A highly influential article by Shulman (1987) prompted a considerable body of research in the USA (Ball et al, 2005) and in the United Kingdom, where concerns about deficits in teachers' mathematical knowledge led to the construction of survey instruments to measure the mathematics knowledge required of teachers (Rowland, 2007). In the United Kingdom, a government directive required that teacher educators audit their students' mathematical knowledge and fill the gaps. This audit culture has been part of the UK teacher education scene for more than 10 years and its impact on teacher efficacy has been problematised (Brown & McNamara, 2005). Other research which compared the mathematical knowledge of US and Chinese teachers coined the phrase 'profound understanding of fundamental mathematics' to describe the 'knowledge packages' of mathematics for teaching found among Chinese teachers (Ma, 1999). Interestingly, Chinese teachers had had less schooling and taken less mathematics courses than their US counterparts, yet their pedagogical content knowledge was deemed superior in the four domains tested. Meanwhile, more recent 'situated' theories of knowledge generation have prompted researchers to look more closely at mathematics teaching as a dialectic activity, where the relationships between the mathematics knowledge that a teacher can demonstrate on a test and use in a classroom setting are highly complex and context-specific (Rowland et al, 2005; Ball et al, 2008). While the value of an audit to 'surface and challenge' prospective teachers' mathematical knowledge is widely recognised (Ball, 1990), we are at pains to emphasise that only the mathematics knowledge which can be inferred from student teachers' voluntary participation in an informal mathematics audit is open to analysis. The findings make no claim to generalisability. They offer instead a series of 'snapshots' of aspects of the mathematics subject knowledge of a small voluntary sample of first-year student teachers in the Lesotho College of Education. A situated perspective informs the analysis, where the audit itself is seen as a 'boundary object' at a nexus of 'diverse intersecting social worlds' (Star & Griesemer, 1989, p. 388) and engagement with the audit might be considered a 'field for action' and the student cohort as 'persons acting' in competing settings (Lave, 1988).

The Study

At the invitation of their college lecturer, the mathematics self-audit was presented to 200 first-year students towards the beginning of a mathematics education lecture. A total of 22 audit booklets were distributed from the top of the classroom, and volunteers were invited to participate as the booklets were passed down among them. Freedom to opt in or out was assured, and many more candidates were willing to take the audit than there were copies to distribute. All 22 self-audits were returned completed by the end of the lecture. The self-audit was not envisaged as a high-stakes experience for the student teachers, and the usual lecture continued as the volunteers worked on the audit independently. The audit was administered in a booklet containing 10 items, selected and adapted from the SKIMA (Subject Knowledge in Mathematics) audit designed by Rowland et al (1998). These are coded on a scale of 0-4, where 1 and 2 mean the auditee is mathematically 'insecure', and 3 and 4 mean the auditee is deemed mathematically 'secure'. Because of the limited size of the sample (n = 22), no claims about the mathematics subject knowledge of the first-year Basotho student cohort in general can be made from this survey. Two audits were submitted by male students. The multiple realities of Basotho teacher education result in blurriness in the background to this picture of the mathematical knowledge of pre-service primary teachers on the self-audit and necessitate acknowledgement that findings are from the perspective of a particular mathematics educator/researcher only. Some smudging may occur despite our best efforts to be objectively analytical in reporting (a) the mathematics used by the students in the sample, and (b) certain selected individual students' approaches to working mathematically at the audit. The interplay between confidence and competence at the audit will be examined in an attempt to add light, depth and clarity to the picture.

The Group Photograph

The DEP students in the study were not asked to disclose their final examination Form E mathematics results but research findings from a study by Mpalami & Corcoran (2010) indicate that the majority of DEP students had failed mathematics in the final COSC examination. Of the 22 students who took the audit, none achieved a maximum score of 40, and so none were deemed 'fully secure' on all items of the audit. When this audit instrument was administered in an Irish college of education, there was a 32% response rate (n = 125) and all auditees, with the exception of two, held higher than the minimum entry requirement to teacher education grade D3 in Ordinary level mathematics at the Leaving Certificate level. This is the lowest possible passing grade in the final examination. It is probably not surprising that there was a significant

Dolores Corcoran & Anne Dolan

correlation between strong Leaving Certificate examination results in mathematics and high codes on the self-audit. No such correlation was possible in the Lesotho study.

Identifying Features of the General Picture

Recognition of the connectedness of mathematical knowledge, and the potential for reproduction, transformation or change to participants' cognitive development inherent in the audit process, prohibits arbitrary divisions of the audit items into strict categories. For example, Item 4, grouped under the heading of 'number operations and algebraic thinking', pertains also to the 'shape and space and measures' group. We prefer to think of the 10 items as investigating students' responses to: number and operations on number problems in measures, shape and space, and higher-order mathematical thinking. These three headings were used to structure the analysis: number and operations on number (Items 1, 2 and 3); higher-order mathematical processes (Items 5, 6, 7 and 8); and non-routine and realistic problem solving (Items 4, 9 and 10). This is done for ease of reporting the mathematics used by the students, yet with cognisance of the fact that these categories are inextricably intertwined. There is considerable variation between the mathematical performances of the 22 Lesotho student teachers on the self-audit. There is evidence that some students come well prepared mathematically to teach primary mathematics, but some students performed badly on most of the items in the audit.

Items with Highest and Lowest Facility Ratings

Table I indicates the items in which the Lesotho and Irish students showed highest facility and those in which they showed lowest facility. These percentages represent the number of students who scored 3 or 4 on each item and, in consequence, were deemed mathematically 'secure' on that item. It is predictable that both groups would find the number items easiest. In fact, the order of items of highest facility is the same for both groups of students. A greater percentage of students in the Irish sample got these items correct, although the Lesotho students scored equally on Items 3 and 4, where students in the Irish group performed less well on Item 4 relative to Item 3. The first three items of the audit explored auditees' facility with number. Responses to Items 1, 2 and 3 appear to indicate that Lesotho students are generally stronger on number and operations on number than on other audit items. Lesotho students had a greater facility with ordering fractions, while Irish students had the greater facility with ordering decimals. Items 5 and 6 (reproduced in Figure 2) were intended to test generalisation skills. Item 5 proved

188

relatively easy for the Lesotho students, with 50% of the sample 'secure' on this item, while Item 6 proved too difficult.

Lesotho students

Highest facility		Lowest facility	
Item no. (% secure)	Topic	Item no. (% secure)	Topic
Item 2 (72.7)	Ordering fractions	Item 6 (0)	Generalisation in algebraic terms from three numerical examples
Item 1 (68)	Ordering decimals	Item 7 (4.5)	Reasoning and proof in the context of perimeter and area
Item 5 (50)	Recognising and calculating patterns of squares	Item 9 (4.5)	Perimeter and area of a parallelogram (Pythagorean theorem)
Item 3 and Item 4 (40.9)	Long division with remainder and Calculating value for money	Item 10 (13.6)	Calculating volume of a cylinder
		Item 8 (27)	Justification of generalisation in the context of an arithmagon

Irish students

Highest facility		Lowest facility	
Item no. (% secure)	Topic	Item no. (% secure)	Topic
Item 1 (84.1)	Ordering decimals	Item 9 (14.2)	Perimeter and area of a parallelogram (Pythagorean theorem)
Item 2 (80.3)	Ordering fractions	Item 7 (24.8)	Reasoning and proof in the context of perimeter and area
Item 5 (61.4)	Recognising and calculating patterns of squares	Item 10 (32.2)	Calculating volume of a cylinder
Item 3 (58.3)	Long division with remainder	Item 6 (35.2)	Generalisation in algebraic terms from three numerical examples
Item 4 (46.4)	Calculating value for money	Item 8 (42.4)	Justification of generalisation in the context of an arithmagon

Table I. Items of highest and lowest facility for Lesotho and Irish student teachers.

5. This is a sequence of figures made of grey and black tiles.

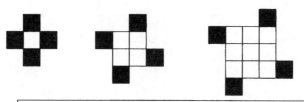

Figure 1   Figure 2   Figure 3
(a) How many tiles will there be altogether in Figure 10?
(b) How many tiles will there be altogether in Figure 20?
(c) Give a strategy for calculating the number of tiles which works for every figure in the sequence.

6. Check that
$3 + 4 + 5 = 3 \times 4$ $8 + 9 + 10 = 3 \times 9$ $29 + 30 + 31 = 3 \times 30$
Write down a statement (in words) which generalises from these three examples.
Express your generalisation using symbolic (algebraic) notation.

Figure 2. Items 5 and 6.

There are undoubtedly language and cultural factors at play here, because while both items ask for a 'generalisation', there is greater support offered in Item 5. In that case, the student is presented with a problem in iconic mode, where it is possible to work out the pattern visually from the three figures of increasing size given. There were many examples of elegant mathematical solutions among the Lesotho students (see Figure 3).

In the case of Item 6, while the numbers are small and the statements are self-evident, the terminology may have been unfamiliar to Lesotho students. Many Irish student teachers also had difficulty with the expression of a generalisation from specific examples such as this. They too appeared to consider that numerical verification was all that was required. Almost all went beyond checking the first case, but did not abstract any generalisation, except that the numerical equations were true (Corcoran, 2008). In order to be deemed 'secure' on Item 6, students had to use inductive reasoning and express a generalisation in both words and symbols that they had derived from three numerical equations. The particular numbers used in the first equation were distracting, so in comparison with other items it appears more difficult to be coded as 'secure' on Item 6, where capturing the precise meaning of mathematical terms like 'generalisation' and 'symbolic (algebraic) notation' may prove an extra barrier to students working in a second language. The three dilemmas identified as inherent in teaching mathematics in multilingual classrooms would appear to have resonances with the mathematics education of pre-service teachers in Lesotho (Adler, 2001).

(a) 4 + 10 x 10 = 104; (b) 4 + 20 x 20 = 404 (c) $4 + n^2$	104 tiles; 404 tiles Figure number, to the power two, add 4.

Figure 3. Two Lesotho students' succinct solutions to Item 5.

Realistic Contexts

Certain mathematics educators make a strong argument that mathematics is learned more successfully in realistic contexts (Dekker, 2007), although concerns have been raised about equity issues in relation to 'making real world contexts accessible to all students' (Boaler, 2002, p. 250). A realistic problem-solving approach is espoused by the Irish primary curriculum (Government of Ireland, 1999a, b). In Lesotho, the curriculum also advocates a child-centred and meaningful approach to mathematics teaching. However, Moloi et al (2008) highlight the continued use of restrictive pedagogies and the absence of real-world examples in primary mathematics. Realistic contexts which offer students opportunities to 'mathematise' real-world problems are the basis for the Programme for International Student Assessment (PISA) definition of 'mathematical literacy':

> an individual's capacity to identify and understand the role that mathematics plays in the world, to make well-founded mathematical judgements and to engage in mathematics, in ways that meet the needs of that individual's current and future life as a constructive, concerned and reflective citizen. (Organisation for Economic Co-operation and Development, 2003, p. 13)

Two items on the audit fit into the realistic mathematics paradigm. One (Item 4) seeks to investigate proportional thinking in a relative value-for-money context, but, since it involves measures of weight and money, may be conceived by students as a 'realistic' problem and approached without recourse to proportional thinking. We will now discuss the Lesotho student teachers' responses to Item 4 as representative of a non-routine problem context, and their responses to Item 7, a higher-order thinking question which seeks to access knowledge of reasoning and proof in the context of perimeter and area.

Item 4 (see Figure 4) was the audit item where there was the least difference in the percentages of students in each sample deemed 'secure'. In answering this item, various arithmetic solution strategies were used. Of the Lesotho student teachers, some appeared to make an incorrect decision based on superficial cues only. For example, one student offered (incorrectly): 'Economy is the best buy because a big box of soap is bought with the small amount of money.' However, there appeared to be a greater affinity for recognising the ratios involved among the Lesotho students, and quite sophisticated reasoning and communication was evident in some answers.

> In a supermarket, there are two brands of soap powder on offer:
> Economy: 2.1 kg for M2.42
> Standard: 840 g for 92c
> Which is the best buy? Explain how you reached your decision.

Figure 4. Item 4: calculating value for money.

Apart from the anticipated confusion of 'g per c' with 'c per g', which occurred frequently among the many Irish students who were unsuccessful, there was another error, where the conflicting calculation of €2.42 ÷ 2.1 (€ per g) was compared for value with 840 g ÷ 92 (g per c) in five cases. This faulty strategy led some students to incorrectly make the correct inference. At a more basic level, the error of confusing the remainder with a decimal value (242 ÷ 210 = 1 remainder 32 being incorrectly recorded as 1.32c) resulted in some students getting the wrong answer. A small number of students made errors in converting 2.1 kg to 210 g, and sometimes displayed a faulty understanding of place value by rendering 2.1 kg equivalent to 201 g.

An interesting response from one Lesotho student shows a sophisticated understanding of ratio coupled with flaws in retrieval of basic division facts. This student appears to choose the Economy option and then sets out to justify the choice, which if the division of 210 by 2 were correctly stated as 105 instead of 150, and the division of 121 by 2 as 60.5 instead of 6.5, would have led to the correct inference that 3 g at 23c is cheaper and better value than 7.5 g at 60.5c, therefore 'Standard is the best buy' (see Figure 5).

There is evidence, too, among the Lesotho students of sound mathematical reasoning in a realistic context (see Figure 6).

A different but equally correct answer was given in pencil by another Lesotho student and followed by a model explanation of how the answer had been found (see Figure 7).

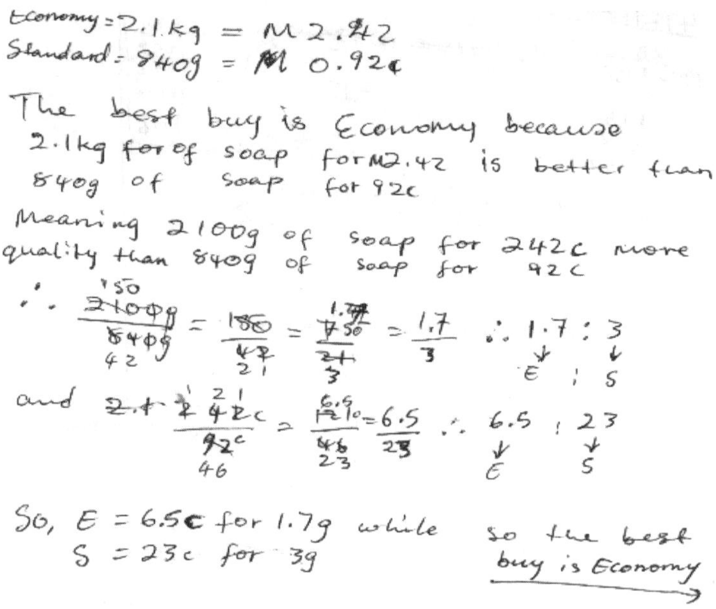

Economy = 2.1 kg = M 2.42
Standard = 840g = M 0.92c

The best buy is Economy because
2.1 kg for of soap for M2.42 is better than
840g of soap for 92c

Meaning 2100g of soap for 242c more
quality than 840g of soap for 92c

$$\therefore \frac{2100g}{840g} = \frac{180}{42} = \frac{750}{21} = \frac{1.7}{3} \therefore 1.7 : 3$$
$$E : S$$

and $2.1 \div 2.42c = \frac{210}{92c} = \frac{6.9}{46} = \frac{6.5}{23} \therefore 6.5 : 23$$
$$E : S$$

So, E = 6.5c for 1.7g while   so the best
    S = 23c for 3g   buy is Economy

Figure 5. Faulty retrieval of number facts leads to incorrect inference.

I think the best buy is when buying
840g of Standard for 92c, because when
changing this grams into kg is 0.84kg and
the amount of buying it it is less

$$1000g = 1kg$$
$$840g = x$$
$$x = \frac{840g \times 1kg}{1000kg} = 0.84kg$$

$$0.84kg = 92c$$
$$2.1kg = x$$
$$x = \frac{92c \times 2.1kg}{0.84kg} = ZAR2.30$$

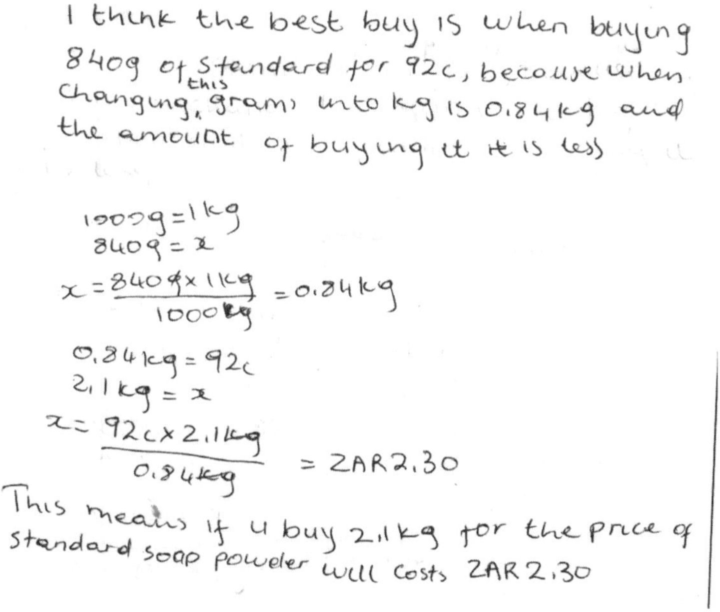

This means if u buy 2.1kg for the price of
standard soap powder will costs ZAR 2.30

Figure 6. Evidence of sound reasoning.

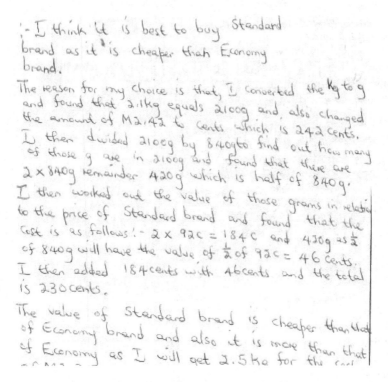

Figure 7. Sound reasoning, well explained.

Snapshots of Reasoning and Proof

UK Circular 4/98 requires that trainee teachers demonstrate '[t]hat they know and understand ... methods of proof, including simple deductive proof, proof by exhaustion and disproof by counter-example' (Department for Education and Employment, 1998, p. 62). This particular emphasis on proof might not be expected in Lesotho, nor is such knowledge explicitly required of Irish primary teachers, but the 'crucial role' of the teacher 'in guiding the child to construct meaning, to develop mathematical strategies for solving problems and to develop self-motivation in mathematical activity' (Government of Ireland, 1999a, p. 5) is highlighted. Explicitly, the Irish primary curriculum requires that children develop the skill of 'reasoning'. It is elaborated that *the child should be enabled to*:

- make hypotheses and carry out experiments to test them;
- make informal deductions;
- search for and investigate mathematical patterns and relationships;
- reason systematically in a mathematical context;

- justify processes and results of mathematical activities, problems and projects. (p. 87)

These aspirations are not listed in the Lesotho mathematics curriculum, yet few mathematics educators anywhere would claim that these are not important mathematical skills which prospective teachers need to develop in order to inculcate them in their pupils. Item 7 (see Figure 8) seeks to access student teachers' facility with mathematical reasoning. Fewer than 18% of Irish students made a fully 'secure' response to the whole question. This figure fell to 4.5% for Lesotho student teachers. However, the 'reasoning and proving' lacuna is not unique to Lesotho student teachers. Stylianides & Stylianides (2007, p. 4) highlight the importance and the difficulty of cultivating US pre-service teachers' mathematical capacity for 'reasoning and proving'. While, from a measurement perspective, a deficit model of mathematics subject knowledge could be construed from the 4.5% 'secure' response on Item 7, this is not, of itself, a particularly helpful finding. A more in-depth understanding of individual responses is required.

---

120 square tiles can be made into a rectangular mosaic. The sides of each tile are 1 cm. The shape of the rectangle can vary. For example, it might be 10 tiles by 12 tiles.

State whether each of the following three statements is true or false. Justify your claims in an appropriate way.

(a) The perimeter (in cm) of every such rectangle is an even number.

(b) The perimeter (in cm) of every such rectangle is a multiple of 4.

(c) No such rectangle is a square.

Figure 8. Item 7: a rectangular mosaic.

Commentary

Of the 22 students who took the audit, all engaged sincerely and many demonstrated a profile that reflects considerable competence in mathematics. Some among the group who engaged equally for the duration of the event warranted much lower codes because of deficiencies in their substantive mathematical knowledge. In some cases, they lacked the kind of mathematical knowledge that has been called 'common content knowledge' (Ball et al, 2008). Common content knowledge has been identified by recent research in the USA as mathematical knowledge present in the population at large, and has resonances with the mathematical literacy assessed by PISA. There was a significant disparity on syntactic knowledge across the group, also (Schwab, 1978). It may be unrealistic to expect these students, halfway through their teaching qualification course, to exhibit 'specific content knowledge' for teaching (Ball et al, 2008). Nor does the audit claim to access this kind of mathematics knowledge. However, misunderstanding and misuse of basic mathematical language would hinder the development of specific content knowledge for teaching in certain students, as would a tendency to offer potential misinformation or mathematically incorrect answers to certain items. Evidence in support of the proposition that student teachers may have to 'unlearn' some of the mathematics (Ball, 1990) they bring to teacher education is to be found in some of these audits. However, the picture is far from bleak. Many students of this sample demonstrated strong, secure mathematical knowledge for teaching and an ability to express their thinking successfully. This could be said to augur well for their future careers as teachers of mathematics in primary schools. However, these snapshots capture some issues which are of interest to the researchers and may be of concern to teacher educators and policy makers in both countries.

Mathematical Misinformation

This research illustrates an apparently negative element of mathematics knowledge for teaching, which we have termed 'mathematical misinformation'. Examples of mathematical misinformation crop up in many of the Irish students' audits and their incidence constitutes a real problem for these students as prospective teachers, particularly in bi- and multilingual classrooms. Students in both data sets sometimes cloak mathematical misinformation in 'pseudo-mathematical terms' by the inappropriate and meaningless use of symbols (see Figure 9).

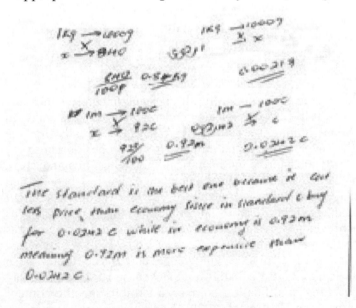

Figure 9. An example of mathematical misinformation.

This student appears to have engaged in a good deal of work to arrive at an answer, but in terms of mathematical problem solving it has not been productive. Were the audit a 'test' situation, the student would have got the answer wrong and not known why. Some sort of feedback loop – or assessment for learning space – would be helpful to students like this. In the teacher preparation courses as presently constituted, there is no mechanism for students to become aware of such pockets of mathematical misinformation in their own mathematics knowledge repertoire. As a consequence, they are not usually in a position to address them.

Audit as an Interactive Exercise

A characteristic common to many of the Irish audits was an attempt to mediate the mathematics by commenting on the problems. We have called this phenomenon 'interactivity' and regard it as an indication of the futility of trying to 'capture' mathematics knowledge as a static, decontextualised commodity that might be measured or labelled. Many of the Irish students who engaged with the audit did so in a spirit of questioning. They used the audit to engage in some sort of conversation about matters mathematical and their own feelings – both positive and negative – about the questions and their ability to answer them. This interactivity resonates with the findings of Schoenfeld (1992), rehearsed by De Corte (2004), that 'regulation of cognitive activities constitutes an essential component of expert problem solving' (De Corte, 2004, p. 5). Such interactivity was less pronounced among the Lesotho students, and may well be because of the setting. It may also be cultural and relate to these students' relationships with their lecturers and with mathematics. The potential to develop expertise in problem solving may be present in the students of both jurisdictions, but may have been hampered by their experiences of school mathematics, which have fostered a stifling rules and procedures approach to getting the only, teacher-decided right answer as quickly as possible (Schoenfeld, 1988). The tendency towards making the audit interactive points to a recognition that mathematical knowledge is social, situated and distributed (Lave & Wenger, 1991), and challenges mathematics educators to design learning environments which facilitate the social construction of 'a mathematical disposition' conducive to expert problem solving (De Corte, 2004). The audit answering patterns tell us something of the various students' approaches to mathematics. It is, however, highly culturally contextual and does not presume to be definitive in any way.

Conclusion

Low educational attainment remains a key constraint to fighting poverty in sub-Saharan Africa (Mulkeen & Chen, 2008). Large pupil-teacher ratios, significant numbers of unqualified teachers, teaching through the medium of English, insufficient teacher education and lack of resources collectively have an impact on students teachers' mathematical knowledge and, furthermore, their ability to teach mathematics. While this study demonstrates positive examples of mathematical knowledge amongst student teachers in Lesotho, serious lacunas exist. To return to the issue of teacher deficit: How do DEP students compare with Irish student teachers in relation to mathematical knowledge for primary teaching?

Firstly, the complex nature of teacher education in Lesotho needs to be recognised. Since the 1990s, participation rates have improved dramatically in schools in Lesotho. However, managing this increase has posed a number of problems for teachers, principals and the Ministry of Education. There has been an increased demand for places on teacher education courses; the number of unqualified teachers has increased (24% of teachers in the lowlands and 51% of teachers in the mountain areas); and students continue to leave school with low levels of literacy and numeracy. In order to mirror progress which has been made in terms of enrolment rates, the issue of teaching quality needs to be addressed – for example, through improved teacher education programmes, more in-service development and support for teachers and teacher educators, the use of improved instructional and pedagogical methods, and better short-term and long-term planning. As the current provision of teacher education is not addressing some of these concerns for a number of macro- and micro-reasons, the reform of teacher education needs to be addressed. A range of international organisations including UNESCO have questioned the effectiveness of current models of teacher education (UNESCO, 2004) in low-income countries. Moon (2007) suggests that the dominant model of campus-based twentieth-century teacher education is insufficient for the needs of the twenty-first century. This study supports commentators such as Moon (2007, p. 355), who call for a new 'architecture for teacher development'. For reasons of cost and logistics, it is argued that effective school-based development might have a greater role to play in teacher education. Moon makes three suggestions: namely, reform of the teacher education curriculum; a rethinking of the period of time for initial training; and an incorporation of new technologies in teacher education, which are now available in Lesotho. These three recommendations have implications for mathematics education.

Secondly, in terms of mathematical knowledge, there is a need to redefine the enterprises of mathematics teaching and mathematics teacher education. In Lesotho at present, student teachers take separate courses in mathematics and in mathematics teaching methods.

Mathematics teaching and learning is highly complex (Krainer, 2005). Dichotomies such as 'content' and 'methods' courses, or 'substantive' and 'syntactic' knowledge, are unhelpful. Here, as elsewhere, public images of mathematics are largely negative and many students (often female) perceive themselves to be weak at mathematics and fearful of mathematics tests, which might highlight their inadequacy. It would be undesirable and counterproductive to perpetuate a deficit model of student teachers' mathematical knowledge, since recent research into learning mathematics highlights the power of focused collaboration in a community of practice to change attitudes to mathematics (Corcoran, 2008). Learning mathematics is best facilitated in a classroom environment which fosters negotiation of shared meaning, and learning to teach mathematics is considerably enhanced by participation in, and the collaboration of, a group of people accountable to the shared enterprise of doing so, over a sustained period. Such 'community of practice' approaches to mathematics teacher education and teacher professional development are flagged by Ma (1999) as being successful in China. The success of Japanese students in international comparative tests of mathematical attainment is attributed to the collaborative practice of school-based lesson study (Stigler & Hiebert, 1999). In an application of lesson study to mathematics teacher education in Ireland, groups of student teachers collaborate to study the curriculum and textbooks, and agree the mathematical ideas or concepts they want pupils to engage with as a result of the particular lesson being planned (Corcoran, 2011). One member of the group teaches the 'research lesson', first to colleagues and then in a primary classroom, while others observe the lesson to study children's responses to the mathematical task(s) during the lesson, with a view to learning about the level of mathematical thinking in evidence in the class. The research lesson plan is then reviewed and revised in the light of learning from the experience of the research lesson. Engagement in this practice has resulted in increased and increasing mathematical knowledge for teaching, and in building a common archive of 'research lessons' which can be tested in other situations. Engagement in a shared practice such as lesson study throws up new ways to answer the question in the title of this chapter: How much mathematical knowledge for primary teaching is enough?

Mathematics is an important cultural practice, to which all children have a right. Mathematics education in Lesotho is not best served by thinking of mathematics in terms of a 'product' to be transmitted or a 'quantity' to be measured. That this approach has worked for some students is undeniable and such thinking gave rise to a body of considerable research and policy initiatives in the United Kingdom and the USA in the past. But research and theories of how mathematics is learned and taught have developed considerably in sociocultural terms, and the emphasis now rests on mathematical knowledge for teaching as situated, social and distributed (Lave & Wenger, 1991). These same researchers who pursued a psychometric approach to mathematics knowledge for teaching – Ball and her associates in the USA, and Rowland and his associates in the United Kingdom – and others throughout the world are now interested in studying *mathematics teaching* and how the dialectical activity can be enhanced (Ball & Forzani, 2010; Rowland & Ruthven, 2011). Yes, teachers need to 'know' mathematics, to hold dispositions open to learning mathematics for teaching and to engage in activities that help them craft identities as 'good' teachers of mathematics, who continue to be interested in improving their mathematics teaching repertoire. But these positive dispositions can be nurtured and dedicated mathematics teacher identities can be constructed when the enterprise is seen as sufficiently important by all concerned. Changes in power relations between lecturers and student teachers will occur as a result of accountability to the enterprise of a collaborative approach to mathematics teaching and through a more relational striving for shared meaning of what it is to learn mathematics, and what is required of teachers to provide suitable mathematics learning environments (Boaler & Greeno, 2000). Indications from this study are that students at the Lesotho College of Education are keen to embrace the challenge of learning to teach 'good' mathematics well.

Acknowledgement

This work was supported in part by a research grant from St Patrick's College, Drumcondra, Ireland.

References

Adler, J. (2001) *Teaching Mathematics in Multilingual Classrooms*. Dordrecht: Kluwer.

Ball, D.L. (1990) The Mathematical Understandings That Prospective Teachers Bring to Teacher Education, *Elementary School Journal*, 90(4), 449-466. http://dx.doi.org/10.1086/461626

Ball, D.L. & Forzani, F.M. (2010) Teaching Skillful Teaching, *Educational Leadership*, 68(4), 40-45.

Ball, D.L., Hill, H. & Bass, H. (2005) Knowing Mathematics for Teaching: who knows mathematics well enough to teach third grade and how can we decide? *American Educator*, 29(3), 14-17, 20-22, 43-46.

Ball, D.L., Thames, M.H. & Phelps, G. (2008) Content Knowledge for Teaching: what makes it special? *Journal of Teacher Education*, 59(5), 389-407. http://dx.doi.org/10.1177/0022487108324554

Boaler, J. (2002) Learning from Teaching: exploring the relationship between reform curriculum and equity, *Journal for Research in Mathematics Education*, 33(4), 239-258. http://dx.doi.org/10.2307/749740

Boaler, J. & Greeno, J.G. (2000) Identity, Agency, and Knowing in Mathematics Worlds, in J. Boaler (Ed.) *Multiple Perspectives on Mathematics Teaching and Learning*, pp. 171-200. Westport, CT: Ablex.

Brown, T. & McNamara, O. (2005) *New Teacher Identity and Regulative Government: the discursive formation of primary mathematics teacher education*. London: Springer.

Burke, A. & Sugrue, C. (1994) *Teaching and Learning at the NTTC*. Dublin: Hedco.

Corcoran, D. (2008) Developing Mathematical Knowledge for Teaching: a three-tiered study of Irish pre-service primary teachers. Unpublished doctoral thesis, University of Cambridge.

Corcoran, D. (2011) Learning from Lesson Study: power distribution in a community of practice, in L.C. Hart, A. Alston & A. Murata (Eds) *Lesson-Study Research and Practice in Mathematics Education: learning together*, pp. 251-268. New York: Springer.

Coultas, J. & Lewin, K.M. (2002) Who Becomes a Teacher? The Characteristics of Student Teachers in Four Countries, *International Journal of Educational Development*, 22(3-4), 243-260.

Daniels, D.J. (1985) *An Appraisal and Critique of Teacher Education in Lesotho: a discussion paper*. Maseru: Ministry of Education.

De Corte, E. (2004) Mainstreams and Perspectives in Research on Learning (Mathematics) from Instruction, *Applied Psychology*, 53(2), 279-310. http://dx.doi.org/10.1111/j.1464-0597.2004.00172.x

Dekker, T. (2007) The Dutch Experience: threat or treat? in S. Close, D. Corcoran & T. Dooley (Eds) *Proceedings of the Second National Conference on Research in Mathematics Education*, pp. 8-20. Dublin, St. Patrick's College.

Department for Education and Employment (DfEE) (1998) *Teaching: high status, high standards*. Circular 4/98. London: DfEE.

Government of Ireland (1999a) *Primary School Mathematics Curriculum*. Dublin: Stationery Office.

Government of Ireland (1999b) *Primary School Mathematics Teacher Guidelines*. Dublin: Stationery Office.

Krainer, K. (2005) What Is 'Good' Mathematics Teaching, and How Can Research Inform Practice and Policy? *Journal of Mathematics Teacher Education*, 8(2), 75-81. http://dx.doi.org/10.1007/s10857-005-4766-0

Lave J. (1988) *Cognition in Practice: mind, mathematics and culture in everyday life*. Cambridge: Cambridge University Press.

Lave, J. & Wenger, E. (1991) *Situated Learning: legitimate peripheral participation*. Cambridge: Cambridge University Press.

Lewin, K.M. (2002) The Costs of Supply and Demand for Teacher Education: dilemmas for development, *International Journal of Educational*

Development, 22(3), 221-242. http://dx.doi.org/10.1016/S0738-0593(01)00060-8

Ma, L. (1999) *Knowing and Teaching Elementary Mathematics*. Mahwah, NJ: Lawrence Erlbaum Associates.

Ministry of Education and Training (2008) National Report on the Development of Education, Kingdom of Lesotho. Paper presented to the UNESCO International Conference on Education, Geneva, 25-28 November 2008. http://www.ibe.unesco.org/National_Reports/ICE_2008/lesotho_NR08.pdf

Moloi, F., Morobe, N. & Urwick, J. (2008) Free but Inaccessible Primary Education: a critique of the pedagogy of English and mathematics in Lesotho, *International Journal of Educational Development*, 28(5), 612-621. http://dx.doi.org/10.1016/j.ijedudev.2007.12.003

Moon, B. (2007) School-Based Teacher Development in Sub-Saharan Africa: building a new research agenda, *Curriculum Journal*, 18(3), 355-371. http://dx.doi.org/10.1080/09585170701590007

Mothibeli, A. & Maema, M. (2005) *The SACMEQ II Project in Lesotho: a study of the conditions of schools and the quality of education*. Harare: Southern and Eastern Africa Consortium for the Monitoring of Educational Quality.

Mpalami, N. & Corcoran, D. (2010) Mathematical Representations as a Means towards Inquiry-Based Teaching and Learning. Paper presented at Science and Mathematics Education Conference, Dublin City University, 16-17 September.

Mulkeen, A. & Chen, D. (Eds) (2008) *Teachers for Rural Schools: experiences in Lesotho, Malawi, Mozambique, Tanzania and Uganda*. African Human Development Series. Washington, DC: World Bank. http://siteresources.worldbank.org/INTAFRREGTOPEDUCATION/Resources/444659-1212165766431/ED_Teachers_rural_schools_L_M_M_T_U.pdf

Ntoi, V. & Pulane Lefoka, J. (2002) NTTC under the Microscope: problems of change in primary teacher education in Lesotho, *International Journal of Educational Development*, 22(3/4), 275-289. http://dx.doi.org/10.1016/S0738-0593(01)00068-2

Organisation for Economic Co-operation and Development (OECD) (2003) The *PISA 2003 Assessment Framework. Mathematics, Reading, Science and Problem Solving Knowledge and Skills*. Paris: OECD Publishing.

Pulane Lefoka, J. & Sebatane, E.M. (2003) *Initial Primary Teacher Education in Lesotho: country report 2*. DfID Educational Paper No. 49c. London: Department for International Development.

Rowland, T. (2007) Auditing the Mathematics Subject Matter Knowledge of Elementary School Teachers. Paper presented at Seminar on Auditing and Assessing Mathematical Knowledge in Teaching, Nuffield Foundation, London, 27 September. http://www.maths-ed.org.uk/mkit/seminar3.html.

Rowland, T. & Ruthven, K. (Eds) (2011) *Mathematical Knowledge in Teaching*. New York: Springer.

Rowland, T., Heal, P., Barber, P. & Martyn, S. (1998) Mind the Gaps: primary trainees' mathematics subject knowledge, *Proceedings of the British Society for Research into Learning Mathematics*, 18(1/2), 91-96.

Rowland, T., Huckstep, P. & Thwaites, A. (2005) Elementary Teachers' Mathematics Subject Knowledge: the knowledge quartet and the case of Naomi, *Journal of Mathematics Teacher Education,* 8(3), 255-281. http://dx.doi.org/10.1007/s10857-005-0853-5

Schoenfeld, A. (1988) When Good Teaching Leads to Bad Results: the disasters of a 'well-taught' mathematics course, *Educational Psychologist*, 23, 145–166. http://dx.doi.org/10.1207/s15326985ep2302_5

Schoenfeld, A. (1992) Learning to Think Mathematically: problem solving, metacognition, and sense-making in mathematics, in D. Grouws (Ed.) *Handbook of Research on Mathematics Learning and Teaching*, pp. 334-370. New York: Macmillan,

Schwab, J. (1978) *Science, Curriculum and Liberal Education.* Chicago: University of Chicago Press.

Sebatane, E.M., Ambrose, D.P., Molise, M.K., Mothibeli, A.S., Motlomelo, S.T., Nenty, H.J., Nthunya, E.M. & Ntoi, V.M. (2000) *Review of Education Sector Analysis in Lesotho 1978-1999.* Paris: Working Group on Education Sector Analysis.

Sebatane, E.M., Bam, V.M., Mohapeloa, J.M., Mathot, G., Pule, S.M. & Otaala, B. (1987) *Consultancy Report of the Internship Programme of the National Teacher Training College.* Maseru: Basic and Non-Formal Education Support Programme.

Shulman, L. (1987) Knowledge and Teaching: foundations of the new reform, *Harvard Educational Review*, 57, 1-22.

Star, S., & Griesemer, J. (1989) Institutional Ecology, 'Translations' and Boundary Objects: amateurs and professionals in Berkeley's Museum of Vertebrate Zoology, 1907-1939, *Social Studies of Science*, 19, 387-420. http://dx.doi.org/10.1177/030631289019003001

Stigler, J.W. & Hiebert, J. (1999) *The Teaching Gap: best ideas from the world's teachers for improving education in the classroom.* New York: Free Press.

Stylianides, A. & Stylianides, G. (2007) Cultivating Pre-service Teachers' Mathematical Knowledge about Proof in Initial Teacher Education. Paper presented at the Annual Conference of the British Educational Research Association, Institute of Education, London, September.

UNESCO (2004) *Education for All. The Quality Imperative EFA Global Monitoring Report.* Paris: UNESCO. http://unesdoc.unesco.org/images/0013/001373/137334e.pdf

Urwick, J. (2011) 'Free Primary Education' in Lesotho and the Disadvantages of the Highlands, *International Journal of Educational Development*, 31(3), 234-243. http://dx.doi.org/10.1016/j.ijedudev.2010.07.004

CHAPTER 11

Teacher Educators and Teaching, Learning and Reflective Practice among the Turkana Nomads of Kenya

THOMAS G. GRENHAM

SUMMARY Drawing upon the writings of the well-known Brazilian educator, Paulo Freire, this chapter describes and explores critically how some of his concepts of education were adapted and applied to the Turkana situation of North-West Kenya. Freire envisioned literacy as being a process of *conscientization* for political, social and economic awareness and freedom of one's self within one's life-world. Education as transformative learning was essential to understanding and critiquing some of the assumptions underlying the Turkana world. In this task, the word of the learner and the world (history, context, culture, beliefs, etc.) in which that learner lived went hand in hand with the process of waking up to being a fully alive person critically conscious of the shaping influences around them. The process of education was key to this wakefulness. The educational effort both formal and informal was designed to empower the Turkana to appropriate the tumultuous cultural, political and economic transformation going on in their midst as a consequence of frequent deadly famine, abject poverty and external cultural, political, economic and religious influences. Mention is made of issues around dependency and independency in relation to the type of education offered in this harsh environment and striking cultural context.

Introduction

My motivation for writing this chapter has been my experience as a missionary among the Turkana people of Kenya for many years. The life and faith of these nomadic people, reflected in the difficult struggle of their daily lives, has become a mainstay of my own insights into teacher education and teaching and learning generally over the years. Currently, I am involved in teacher formation in Ireland and I continue to draw on my lived experience of teaching and learning from the diverse cultural and religious context of the Turkana of Kenya. The interaction of the Turkana's cultural, religious and educational symbols and customs with my own learned Western assumptions about teaching and learning was transformative both for me and for the Turkana.

The transformation is essentially an experience of intercultural education between European missionary perspectives and the Turkana traditional indigenous experience of learning and formation. Teacher education within the Turkana district of Kenya has its challenges and opportunities, all of which were influenced by the reality of pervasive abject poverty caused by persistent and devastating famines. By looking at who the Turkana are and how they belong in their lifeworld, the reader will glean an insight into how a theory of education might assist these people to transform what appears to be a very difficult living environment. The theory of education I offer here is the vision of humanisation developed by Brazilian educator Paulo Freire. Freire's method of education was adapted and used widely in Turkana by missionaries and educators, particularly within the informal education arena, to shape, influence and transform local leaders, teachers, nurses and youth workers, and to encourage adult learning across the society. The underlying assumption is that education can lead people like the Turkana out of dehumanising poverty into a better way of life. Freire's conscientisation approach was essentially intercultural in that European missionaries and the Turkana taught and learned from each other.

Intercultural Education

My experience of intercultural education was between my Irish European culture and the Turkana cultural and religious world view. I learned the significance of intercultural education by uncovering my own embedded assumptions around the nature and purpose of education. My European assumptions had revolved around the idea that education was all about technical knowledge or know-how. Having such knowledge would be beneficial to economic and scientific progress. The Turkana would teach me otherwise. Education was much more than technical or instrumental knowledge – it needs to take into account all aspects of the person-in-relationship with themselves, others and the environment within a cultural, and perhaps a religious, world view. Crossing cultural and religious boundaries of another ethnic group is difficult. Using a theory of education from outside a particular cultural context may be a recipe for failure if it does not take into account the specificity and particularity of diverse meaning perspectives and world views. I like to use a term called *interculturation* to describe intercultural education. I have used this term in relation to crossing cultural and religious boundaries in other writings (Grenham, 2005, pp. 63-87). The same process of crossing or transcending cultural boundaries happens within the field of teacher education and formation.

Basically, interculturation is about a process of education that envisions humanisation as a two-way process of interpretation and cooperation between diverse cultures to awaken consciousness of who people are and how they belong in relationship to themselves, others and the environment. The objective is to offer a life-giving education to discover the intercultural face of being human in the midst of diversely constructed human cultures and religious perspectives. Intercultural education is a partnership among persons and between cultures to mutually discover and awaken the potential and growth of every person in their cultural context. The process of interculturation is respectful of the dignity of the learner within a particular cultural world view. At the same time, the process of teaching and learning enables learners to critically reflect upon themselves and their lifeworld. By lifeworld, I mean the cultural and religious perspective of the people, which is at the heart of meaning-making for the Turkana in this case.

Culture is a set of beliefs, behaviours, customs and traditions shared by a particular group. The components of a culture include language, habits, art, beliefs, customs, music, diet, morals, religion, rules, patterns of behaviour, ways of life, family support systems and philosophy of life. Intercultural education needs to be sensitive to all these areas of culture in order to educate holistically and to teach with integrity and respect for the person-in-context. The teacher educator from outside their own particular culture, such as the missionary from an Irish context within the Turkana context, needs to move from being unaware to being aware and sensitive to his or her own cultural heritage and to valuing and respecting differences. This is a primary ingredient for effective intercultural education.

The striking issue with intercultural education for the Turkana is that the survival of the majority of people depends on livestock. The educational process has to take this into account. The people are essentially pastoralists and their cultural world view centres on their relationship with their animals. For example, the Turkana, who measure wealth in the number of animals a person owns, view people who do not own animals as poor (*ekebotonit* singular and *ngikebotok* plural). The name *ngikebotok* is given to members of a clan who do not own animals and who inhabit the southern part of the Turkana district. They consist of farmers who grow vegetables and fruit, as well as collect honey along the fertile banks of the Turkwel River. Even if one had great wealth in other ways besides owning livestock, the Turkana might consider the person *ekebotonit* and perhaps even a non-Turkana. Such a way of thinking reflects the significance of owning, sharing and taking care of animals for the flourishing of Turkana identity and meaningful belonging. Knowing this about the Turkana would help the intercultural educator to gain a glimpse of what is at the heart of the Turkana world view.

The Turkana People and Cultural Context

Because the Turkana people are primarily nomadic pastoralists, they need to migrate in search of scant grazing for their herds, their sole means of survival. As they move around, they settle for a while near particular villages and towns, and this offers an opportunity to access some informal education. Their herds consist of cattle, which are the pride of the Turkana; camels, which adapt well to the bleak conditions; goats, which survive merely because they are adaptable to eating any kind of vegetation that emerges; and donkeys, because of their innate stubbornness to survive. Livestock are central to the Turkana way of life culturally, economically, religiously and politically. Milk, blood, meat and clothing are provided by the herds. Some animals, like the goat and ox, are used in rituals of sacrifice to celebrate good fortune, as well as when seeking the healing of a sick person and petitioning God (Akuj) to send rain. The relationship with their animals features significantly when applying Freire's concept of literacy and conscientisation. Freire's idea of bringing together the word of the learner and their world is important if education for a better future is going to have any relevant impact upon the lives of the Turkana.

In conjunction with the importance of livestock is the topographical area. The Turkana landscape is striking. The land of Turkana stretches 300 miles from north to south and is about 100 miles from east to west. The region is part of the Great Valley that stretches south through Kenya and beyond. It is bordered to the north by Sudan and Ethiopia, by Lake Turkana to the east, by Uganda to the west and by the Kenyan Cherangani Hills to the south. The area covers approximately 23,000 square miles, consisting of expansive plains of dry land with scattered rocky patches, lava peaks and some mountain ranges (Gulliver, 1963, p. 37). The writer Charles Miller describes the area as:

> A horizonless frying pan of desolation: a sun-dried moon-
> scape of cracked earth harder than iron, grotesque lava heaps
> rising to the height of ten-story buildings, vast plains of
> dehydrated thorn scrub, sightless deserts and scorched black
> mountains. Temperatures often climb to 120 degrees in the
> shade (when shade can be found), and such articles as brass
> buttons and belt buckles will sear the flesh after an hour in the

sun. Thirst is the traveler's closest companion. (Miller, 1987, p. 471)

The climate offers its own problems for all engaged with living and working in this area, and it adds to the struggle to transform in a meaningful way the lives of the people. Much research has been conducted in the region to assist in the process of helping the Turkana overcome poverty. Poverty can be a relative term or concept and, in the Turkana situation, needs further analysis to come to terms with what we mean by abject poverty and its dehumanising effects.

According to the statistics in the *Turkana District Development Plan 2002-2008* provided by the Ministry of Finance and Planning (Republic of Kenya, Ministry of Finance and Planning, 2002):

> the Turkana practise a mixed economy. About 80% of the population derive their livelihood from livestock. Out of these, 64% are absolute pastoralists and 2% are fishermen, while 8% are engaged in basketry and the charcoal trade. The remainder are agro-pastoralists. The poverty level is very high (81% food poverty, 74% absolute poverty and 62% hard-core poverty).

This, then, is the background to a process of teacher formation and to how teachers might teach and relevant learning can happen. Teaching and learning and reflective practice will be greatly influenced by the elements of the lifeworld mentioned above. Some would argue – particularly those from outside the culture – that the purpose of education in this area should be aimed at getting the Turkana out of this harsh environment in order to enable them to access opportunities elsewhere. Others will argue – and I agree – that education should be aimed at helping the Turkana sustain their lifestyle and their culture by providing essential supports within the district. Needless to say, education provides opportunities and choices to stay in the area or to be of service in other parts of Kenya and the world beyond. Education is one of these essential supports that can awaken the Turkana to how best they can be served. Education is a basic human right and yet this is not always apparent to the Turkana. Many aid agencies over the years have provided assistance in areas like health, education and economic development. For example, since 2001, non-governmental organisations (NGOs) such as Oxfam, Great Britain have been helping to provide mobile schools around the Turkana area to cater for the nomadic pastoralists always on the move. There are approximately 163 primary schools in Turkana and seven secondary schools. Other NGO projects have been engaged in rehabilitating the Turkana through various training and formation programmes, especially in the area of teacher education. The United Nations-based organisation UNICEF is involved in enabling the Turkana pastoralists to increase their herds, which have been depleted by severe drought conditions. Faith-based organisations such as

World Vision, the Christian Children's Fund and Catholic Relief Services, among others, play significant roles in Turkana cultural life. Improvement of the Turkana way of life through sustainable modern development inevitably changes Turkana culture and their religious viewpoint. These influences educate and transform the Turkana perspective on the world.

Conscientisation: awakening to personhood

Change for any person or society can be challenging. It is no different for the Turkana people. For the Turkana, change became evident through the introduction and expansion of primary and secondary education for the younger generation, sponsored mainly by the Catholic Church. There are some schools, primary and secondary, sponsored by Protestant groups, and, more recently, Oxfam has been supporting primary education. Further educational transformation was experienced with informal educational programmes like the Development Education Programme, which was instituted in the late 1970s to help the Turkana not only with literacy and numeracy skills, but also to empower them to appropriate the tumultuous cultural, political and economic changes going on in their society. This programme, sponsored by the Catholic Church in Turkana, gave rise to Development Education and Leadership Teams in Action, which was formed to educate the people in their villages. Programmes in adult literacy, family life, community health, savings and credit banking, agriculture and water projects, and women's groups were among the educational activities offered. The overall objective of the educational programmes was to enable the Turkana to attain a critical awareness or consciousness and to participate in their own transformation as they engaged with the political, economic, social and religious influences taking place within their community, culture and religious world view. These programmes generally followed the vision of education developed by the Brazilian educator Paulo Freire. Educators Anne Hope & Sally Timmel (1999) developed a series of practical, illustrated handbooks entitled *Training for Transformation: a handbook for community workers* based on Freire's ideas, which were used as a text for teaching and learning and teacher formation. These handbooks adapted Freire's philosophy of education through practical stories, art, role play, games and symbols grounded in the general African culture. Further adaptation was initiated for the Turkana context.

As mentioned earlier, at the heart of Paulo Freire's work is the concept of 'conscientisation' (*conscientização*; Freire, 1985, p. 160). Conscientisation is Freire's vision of personal and communal transformation towards authentic humanisation. Freire (1985, p. 160) described the conscientisation process as 'cultural action for freedom'. Applying this to teaching and learning, the presence and action of the teacher is towards fostering the inner human freedom of the learner. In the process, the educator/teacher may experience a sense of liberation as well. This is how I perceived my own missionary experience among the Turkana of Kenya. I learned that holistic education is not about mere instrumental or technical knowledge (skills), but includes the emotional, the aesthetic, the cognitive, the spiritual and the moral aspects of personhood.

The purpose of education is to critically awaken the self-in-context and to become conscious to all these aspects of being a whole person. Within the Turkana context, promoting the particular Turkana language and unique cultural world view is both a challenge and opportunity for teachers in this area. The Turkana language is a challenge for outside teachers to learn when English and Kiswahili are promoted within the school environment. Turkana students are not encouraged to use their native tongue in the schools, as assessment is through English and Kiswahili. Both these languages are the official languages of Kenya. The Turkana language is a local or regional language. An opportunity for teachers would be to use the Turkana language more in the school environment, as it makes it much easier for students to grasp ideas, to imagine concepts and to develop a creative disposition for learning. Students will have a better appreciation of their own mother tongue and of the uniqueness and value of their culture. The Turkana language is the key symbol of their culture. Otherwise, if the language has no place in the primary school system, younger Turkana students will develop a negative impression of their own language and culture. Students will tend to favour the language, culture and education that are foreign and imported.

Effective education needs to deal with the reality and danger of cultural dependency. Appreciating and accepting that one's own cultural context contains life-giving aspects which can be shared with others from outside is important. The danger for the Turkana, with so much reliance on outside assistance, is that the people become 'domesticated' according to the prescriptions of outside cultural influences, especially in the area of education.

Being aware of who we are and how we belong is at the heart of a life-giving education. This constitutes knowing something about myself, others and the environment, which shapes my identity and uncovers my potential to be a full human person. To be awakened to the mysteries and potential of self, others and the world is a great thing. Life will never be the same once we grasp the impact of wakefulness upon ourselves, culture, religion, economics, science, politics, the environment, and so on.

Freire frequently spoke and wrote about the concept of literacy in education, defining it as going beyond the mere skills of mechanical reading, writing and numeracy. He envisioned literacy as being a process of conscientisation for political, social and economic awareness and freedom of one's self within one's lifeworld (Freire, 1985, p. 160).

Paulo Freire's Vision: humanisation

Most of my work as a missionary involved education, whether it be the formation of catechists, youth leaders, teachers or political/social leaders. There was also educational formation for those who would deliver various literacy programmes and other awareness campaigns around Turkana to inform about diseases such as AIDS and other dangerous illnesses. I engaged in workshops to facilitate the formation of teachers who would deliver the literacy programmes. In addition, I supervised the programmes in different areas to ascertain how the literacy was 'awakening' the participants. Freire's vision of humanisation was to connect the word of the learner with the world of the learner. This means that the culture and religious perspective, language, symbols, customs and ways of thinking, etc. were pivotal to their education. For the educators, the vision for humanisation constituted the provision of literacy programmes that would open up for the Turkana an option that could free them from the bondage of extreme, debilitating poverty.

Drawing on Freire's wisdom and vision for a transformative and emancipatory education, the political struggle of awakening learners and teachers to life-giving perceptions of themselves, others and the world around them continues. There is the literacy that includes an awakening to the social, cultural, economic, religious and political environments around the learner. For example, in relation to a disease like HIV/AIDS, education included not just information about the disease, but also the social, cultural and economic impact that this disease has on the Turkana. This was a vital element in the education programme. Freire (1987, p. 106) understands this interpretation of literacy as

> the relationship of learners to the world, mediated by the
> transforming practice of this world taking place in the very
> general social milieu in which learners travel, and also
> mediated by the oral discourse concerning this transforming
> practice. This understanding of literacy takes me to a notion of
> a comprehensive literacy that is necessarily political.

The Turkana Religious Vision

For education to be successful in Turkana, it is important to note that the Turkana world view encompasses a spiritual dimension. Their religious world view is symbiotic and integral to how they filter their life experiences within the cultural-meaning perspective. Deep within the Turkana's religious sensibility is an image of Akuj, who takes an active role in all aspects of the Turkana lifeworld. My work as a missionary educator was to create a space for a teaching and learning partnership. This partnership depended upon seeing the Turkana people as having a means through their own traditional religious or cultural perspective to facilitate life-giving transformation for themselves, others and their environment. In other words, from a biblical lens, the Turkana can bring good news to their poor, proclaim liberty to their captives and bring sight to their blind (see Luke 4.18-19).

The Turkana believe strongly in the presence of the ancestors, and their spirits are a powerful symbolic force for those who are still living. These ancestors are referred to as the 'living dead'. Though dead for many years, even centuries, the ancestors have powerful stories of love and fear that continue to influence the way life is lived in the present. The process of contemporary education needs to take this on board within the partnership of teaching and learning, and in the reflective practice that every educator engages. The conscientisation or awakening that Freire suggests happens in this arena of the ancestors. The living, who are the descendants of the ancestors, are made conscious of who they are and whose they are through creatively imagining the past in song, dance, rituals of sacrifice, rites of passage, etc. There is also a desire for the living to be united ultimately with the ancestors and, for this to happen, care is needed to live a good, moral life grounded in the Turkana tradition. With an education system imported from outside by the previous colonial power, Great Britain, there can be a clash between the old and the new. There is a dialectical tension for the Turkana to manage and integrate into their traditions the life-giving aspects of this 'new' tradition from outside.

Because of both informal and formal educational practices and the interaction with outside influences and cultures, the younger generation began to reinterpret their world view. They were no longer wearing the outward signs of their culture, manifested in the way the traditional men and women dressed and behaved. The wearing of skins and the particular bracelets and ostrich feathers that identified their specific moiety was disappearing. The carrying of traditional spears, wrist knives and small stools (*ekicolong*) gave way to adapting to more Western, European fashion and cultural mores of behaviour. The younger generations were awakening to accepting and embracing new cultural and religious ways of life, and were letting go of some of the former traditional ways of life which their parents believed in and practised. A balanced, integrated educational methodology is important to not only having a healthy respect for the past, but also viewing the new as something that builds upon the history, customs and traditions of the past.

Thomas G. Grenham

Methodology for Teaching and Learning

The predominant method for teaching and learning, particularly in the informal literacy education, was the workshop. This means that the teacher and learner were actively engaged in the act of teaching and learning. The participants had an opportunity in the design to offer their comments, questions and ideas. This did not always happen in the formal primary and secondary schools with large numbers and with teachers challenged to move through the content of the curriculum in a timely and efficient fashion. The form of assessment, such as the state examination, usually dictated the shape of the learning environment in the formal educational arena. In contrast, the informal literacy programmes did not have formal assessments and yet learners were able to grasp new ideas through actual participation in role play, discussion, and reading and writing exercises. Most of all, there were opportunities to do practical on-the-ground projects, such as maintaining a small garden or stall or animal husbandry. The acts of reading and writing were related to these activities.

Teacher formation continues in Turkana today, with Oxfam leading a programme entitled Turkana Education for All (TEFA) since 2001. The churches continue to provide the majority of educational services in the area. With the recent creation of mobile schools, the nomadic pastoralist has an opportunity to access education resources. There are approximately 30 such mobile schools that have been initiated and financed by Oxfam. The success of all these efforts at 'awakening' the Turkana and also 'awakening' the missionary and other outsiders is to perceive teaching and learning as a partnership.

The challenge for teacher education in Turkana is that it does not descend into what Freire called a 'domesticating' education. This means that education is perceived as 'banking'. The teacher, missionary or NGO is the depositor of knowledge, while the learner is viewed as a mere receptacle who receives this privileged knowledge and stores it, to be given back at the time of assessment. The issue of power becomes a factor. Those with the privileged knowledge have the power over those who are learning to acquire this knowledge. Then they acquire power and the cycle of privileged knowledge goes on, which still holds the learner as a hostage. Knowledge is seen as 'power over' and not as 'power with'. But this kind of power is not empowering. Rather, knowledge needs to be viewed not as power over someone but as power with others. In other words, when the Turkana critically explore themselves and their lifeworld, they are encouraged to be awake to the paradoxes and privileges that oppress, alienate, limit and marginalise them. These paradoxes and privileges are not only within their own cultural world view, but also among those who come from external political, economic, cultural and religious world views.

Genuine life-giving education for intercultural solidarity occurs when one is able to be *with* people rather than *for* people in their struggle to overcome dehumanisation. This was the objective of our teaching methodology within Turkana. That is to say, no culture should have a superior attitude, reflected through technology, education, religious practices, political ideology and economic development, which can be used to subjugate and domesticate others into thinking, feeling and believing like the 'superior' culture. Freire (1970), in relation to education, observed that 'education thus becomes an act of depositing, in which the students are depositories and the teacher is the depositor. Instead of communicating, the teacher issues communiqués and makes deposits, which the students patiently receive, memorise and repeat'.

The ideal vision of education, both formal and informal, is to create a sense of interdependence of culture and sense of self-determination (self-reliance) that is integrally respectful of what is authentically Turkana. Yet, at the same time, the Turkana people need what comes from outside. We all do as we experience the sense of interdependence in the world. The Turkana have much to offer others as well in the way they can live in harsh conditions, respect the environment around them and develop meaningful spiritual connections with their dead. Interdependence needs mutuality. Without this mutual respect, one culture can dominate the other, which is perceived to be a vulnerable culture and people. Then, one culture becomes dependant upon the other in an unequal way. Hence, the 'vulnerable' culture becomes domesticated according to the prescriptions of the dominant culture. Teachers have a huge role in avoiding this dilemma. Their own assumptions and prejudices need to be examined as to how they see themselves as holistic educators. The inner capacity of an educator to mediate care, compassion and empathy to those who seek meaning and understanding of their life situation is crucial. For an educator to realise that he or she can learn from those who are poor, ill, disadvantaged or marginalised reflects a literacy of care, deeply rooted in human vulnerability and fragility.

Action and reflection, as Freire points out in much of his writing, becomes a significant aspect for growing in wisdom through an education process that values the integrity of the person-in-context. It is the methodology from which 'awakening' can take place within the educator, who, in turn, assists or facilitates the awakening of the learner. This is because the teacher or educator is in touch with his or her humanity. Being grounded in a particular tradition, religious or non-religious, enables the educator to assist others like the Turkana in their context to claim who they are and how they belong in their own community and beyond.

The action and reflection methodology is about conversation. This is not a superficial conversation. Rather, it is an intentional and focused conversation that is generated from a specific theme. This theme is generated within the context in which the Turkana live. A pressing aspect or need of their lives is explored to see what can be understood and integrated, and perhaps to see what action, if any, can be augmented for the betterment of that specific issue. This conversation is an evolution of six stages. The six stages of an evolving conversation are, briefly:

1. A centring theme, such as poverty, corruption, access to food, and so on, which emerges from the needs of the participants.
2. The engaging and naming of issues within that theme.
3. Critical reflection – questioning, such as 'Does this happen here and why?'
4. Accessing the culture and religious world view to explain the current experience.
5. Appropriation of meaning into lived experience.
6. Decision making for renewed action (Grenham, 2005, pp. 245-253).

This conversation needs to take place in a conducive and safe environment so that the power dynamic is also balanced for the process to work. However, the conversation can get interrupted by various obstacles that impact on the quality of the teaching and learning.

Obstacles to Teaching and Learning

Poverty is the major obstacle to teaching and learning in Turkana. Lack of food security in many families causes children to be distracted. They are unable to concentrate at school. Because of a nomadic lifestyle, many parents deny their children a chance to go to school as the children are needed at home to take care of animals. The ravages of diseases such as malnutrition, AIDS, malaria and other deadly infections impact on the health of the learner.

Famine is a constant companion for the Turkana. Inasmuch as famine is perceived as problematic, cattle rustling also forms part of the Turkana consciousness and causes conflict and stress for the community. Such a violent situation compounds the rehabilitation of the Turkana as well as sustaining education formation services and resources (Henrickson et al, 1998, pp. 14-17).

Extreme climatic conditions, coupled with poor availability of resources, hinder teacher education and teaching and learning generally. Teaching and learning within the Turkana District relies heavily on outside aid, especially foreign aid. Missionaries and other expatriate agencies provide most of the services in the area. While the Kenya government does provide some services in health and education, these are sketchy and unreliable. Government schools in Turkana are poorly maintained and lack basic resources for teachers and learners. Frequent famines caused by persistent droughts have led to abject poverty and death.

Conclusion

I am keenly aware that when I teach someone else, I am being educated as well. The complexity of education is such that through it we discover the gift and the truth about ourselves, others, the environment and something greater than ourselves. It is through this web or network of relationships that the potential for boundless life is discovered and sustained. This is the dream. Freire (1992, p. 90) wrote that: 'Dreaming is not only a necessary act, it is an integral part of the historico-social manner of the person. It is part of human nature, which within history, is in permanent process of becoming'. We, as teachers and educators, invite and challenge each other in the process of teaching and learning and reflective practice to be who we are as well as who we are called to become. The Turkana people taught me well and perhaps they learned something from me, too.

References

Freire, P. (1970) *Pedagogy of the Oppressed*. New York: Continuum.

Freire, P. (1985) *The Politics of Education: culture, power, and liberation*. South Hadley, MA: Bergin & Garvey.

Freire, Paulo (1992) *Pedagogy of Hope: reliving Pedagogy of the Oppressed*. New York: Continuum.

Freire, Paulo & Macedo, Donaldo (1987) *Literacy: reading the word and the world*. Westport, CT: Bergin & Garvey.

Grenham, T. (2005) *The Unknown God: religious and theological interculturation*. Bern: Peter Lang.

Gulliver, P.H. (1963) *A Preliminary Survey of the Turkana*. Cape Town: University of Cape Town.

Henrickson, D., Armon, J. & Mearns, R. (1998) *Conflict and Vulnerability to Famine: livestock raiding in Turkana, Kenya*. Drylands Issue Paper E80. London: International Institute for Environment and Development.

Hope, Anne & Timmel, Sally (1999) *Training for Transformation: a handbook for community workers*, Book IV. London: Intermediate Technology Development Group.

Miller, C. (1987) *The Lunatic Express: the building of an impossible 600 mile railway across East Africa*. Nairobi: Westlands Sundries.

Republic of Kenya, Ministry of Finance and Planning (2002) *District Development Plan, 2002-2008: effective management for sustainable economic growth and poverty reduction*. Nairobi: Ministry of Finance and Planning.

CHAPTER 12

An Account of the Alternative Education Experience Africa Programme in Transition: Irish pre-service teachers' experience in Zambia and the Gambia

FIONA BAILY & DEIRDRE O'ROURKE

SUMMARY This chapter presents a summary of the key findings of a 2008 research report entitled 'The Impact of Student Teaching Placements in a Developing Context', and examines the changes made to such placement programmes based on these findings. The aim of the research study was to explore the impacts of a Mary Immaculate College student teaching placement programme in an African context, specifically in relation to student participants' engagement in development education as teachers. This investigation identified that teachers who have participated in African placement programmes demonstrate a higher level of engagement in development education than those teachers who did not. However, this study also highlighted the potential for improving the quality and depth of the programme. The issues raised in the report have been addressed in more recent placements. These changes have been extremely beneficial to programme participants.

Introduction

This chapter focuses on the ways in which Mary Immaculate College (MIC), University of Limerick is moving to further develop the quality and depth of its African student teacher placement programme, Alternative Education Experience Africa. In 2008, a research project, funded by Irish Aid, was carried out by MIC in partnership with

Development Education: '80:20, Development in an Unequal World'. The research study was entitled 'The Impact of Student Teaching Placements in a Developing Context', and its aim was to outline and assess the impacts of an MIC student teaching placement programme in Africa. While the research highlighted a varied and rich range of personal and professional impacts on student teachers, it also highlighted specific areas within the programme, such as the further development of a placement programme based on sustainable principles of equality and mutuality. MIC is currently in the process of adapting specific aspects of the programme in line with the aims highlighted in the report.

This chapter begins by providing a brief overview of the MIC teaching practice placement programme, the Alternative Education Experience (AEE). It will then go on to outline the context, aims, objectives, findings and recommendations of the research study and conclude by illustrating the changes that have been made to the placement programme in relation to the research findings.

Overview of the Alternative Education Experience Module

Within the AEE module, third-year Bachelor of Education (B.Ed.) students in MIC are provided with the opportunity to select and spend time in an educational setting 'which is normally outside the range of experiences of students on teaching practices' (Mary Immaculate College, 2009, p. i). The purpose of the programme is to afford student teachers the opportunity to experience an educational sphere of which they have little or no practical knowledge.

A typical alternative educational setting could be a school catering for children with special needs or an early language unit. Some students take the opportunity to travel abroad to complete their placement in a foreign educational context.[1] The role of the student 'is that of assistant/observer' (Mary Immaculate College, 2009, p. iv). The module is assessed on a pass or fail basis. In order to pass, a student must complete 10 days in their chosen setting under supervision and complete a student response report.

Alternative Education Experience Africa

Since 1997, over 300 students have chosen to complete their AEE teaching practice placements in primary schools in developing countries. Over 220 of those students completed their placements in primary schools in Africa, more specifically in Zambia and the Gambia – placements which are organised, facilitated and conducted by MIC staff. These placements have come to be known as 'AEE Africa'. The AEE Africa placement is subject to the same academic requirements as any other placement within the AEE module.

The majority of AEE placements take place in the final two weeks of the autumn semester, immediately before Christmas break. Due to the requirements of the academic calendar, AEE Africa is completed in the inter-semester break.

Students travel to their placement country as a group, accompanied by a lecturer. The first few days on the ground focus on acclimatising to the surroundings and the local culture as well as school orientation. Once familiarised, the students begin their placement in the schools. Attending the 'morning shift', students complete a mixture of observation, pair, group or individual teaching. Afternoons and weekends are spent visiting educational and cultural organisations such as colleges of education or local museums and markets.

The AEE Africa placement provides students with the opportunity to partake in some or all of the following:

- spend time in the classroom both observing and teaching;
- meet with members of the Ministry of Education in their host country;
- visit initial teacher education institutes;
- meet with peers – i.e. student teachers from their host countries;
- visit schools for the hearing- and visually impaired;
- teach in Islamic faith schools;
- volunteer in education or child-focused organisations.

Research Study Context and Rationale

Development education (DE) is a key concept within the Irish formal education sector. Irish Aid defines DE as:

> an educational process aimed at raising public awareness and understanding of the rapidly changing interdependent and unequal world in which we live ... it seeks to engage people in analysis, reflection and action for local and global citizenship and participation ... It is about supporting people in understanding and acting to transform the social, cultural, political and economic structures which affect their lives at personal, community, national and international levels. (Irish Aid, 2007, p. 9)

Student teaching placement programmes in developing countries can be an effective method for teacher education colleges to introduce their students to development issues and, in doing so, motivate and equip them to engage in DE with their future pupils in the classroom (Willard-Holt, 2001; Roberts, 2003; Fullam & Dolan, 2005). Such placements can also be a way of developing an awareness of and respect for cultural diversity in student teachers, which, in the multicultural Irish schools of today, is also very relevant (Merryfield, 2000; Villegas & Lucas, 2002; Fullam & Dolan, 2005; Purdy & Gibson, 2008).

However, such placements can be the cause of many destructive impacts. The difference in material wealth between the global North and South [2] can result in

> power imbalances ... a sense of dependency in the partner in the South ... [which can] negatively affect their sense of dignity, limit genuine communication, interfere with the process of self-reflection and obscure a deep understanding of the causes and consequences of poverty. (O'Keefe, 2006, p. 5)

Regan (2007) argues that many placement programmes are based on colonial attitudes and perceptions, resulting in the maintenance of an aid or welfare approach to programme development.

'The Impact of Student Teaching Placements in a Developing Context' research study built on the assessment offered by Patrick Fullam & Anne Dolan, of MIC, in their 2005 study *Impact of Study Visits on Student Teachers*. This study explored the short-term personal and professional impacts of the AEE placement programme on 28 participants who travelled to the Gambia and Zambia in 2004. It also sought to investigate how the programme could contribute to the development of 'culturally responsive teachers' (Villegas & Lucas, 2002). The study concluded that: 'On a professional level several students expressed an interest in returning to work in a different culture and the commitment to teaching intercultural and development issues in their classroom was expressed in clear terms' (Fullam & Dolan, 2005, p. 27). The current research study was concerned with discovering if students had proceeded to engage in DE, in the long term, as a result of the AEE Africa experience.

Research Aim and Objectives

The overall aim of the research study was to explore the relationship between student teachers' experience of a teaching practice placement in a developing country at pre-service level and, in this context, the inclusion of DE in their current practice as teachers. The objectives of the research included:

- To identify how AEE Africa placements impacted on the knowledge, attitudes, skills and behaviour of student teacher participants on a personal and professional level.
- To identify ways in which MIC can develop the quality and depth of the AEE Africa placement programme for all programme participants.

Research Methodology

A structured questionnaire was devised targeting the 222 past MIC B.Ed. students who had completed AEE Africa placements between 1997 and 2007. In addition, a structured questionnaire was also distributed to a control group of 222 past B.Ed. students of MIC who did not complete their AEE placement in a developing country.

Focus group discussions were held with past MIC students who had completed AEE Africa placements since 1997 and are all currently teaching. Semi-structured interviews were conducted with MIC staff involved or previously involved with the programme, and with representatives from teacher education colleges in Ireland running similar programmes.

Key Findings

The research findings have clearly indicated a number of positive and consistent personal and professional impacts on student teachers. The research findings were analysed and presented under the following headings: personal and professional impacts in terms of the knowledge, attitudes, skills and behaviour of AEE Africa participants. The following is a summary of the key research findings.

Personal Impacts

Throughout the research, it became clear that the majority of AEE Africa participants had experienced considerable personal growth and development at a variety of levels, as evidenced by their comments and descriptions. Two dominant responses emerged from the research:

1. Personal growth and development in terms of increased self-reflection and self-knowledge; more open, altruistic and giving in their attitudes and behaviour towards others; and changed perspectives as to what is important in their lives.
2. An appreciation in a realistic and renewed way of how fortunate they, the students, are to have the lives and opportunities they have been afforded. This was a very strong outcome throughout all aspects of the research.

Professional Impacts

The research has clearly indicated a number of consistent impacts in terms of the professional knowledge, attitudes, skills and behaviour of AEE Africa participants on the following levels:

- An increased awareness, knowledge and understanding of the African education system and of general development issues in

223

Africa. The questionnaire findings highlight that 40% of AEE Africa respondents stated that they had a very high and 40% stated that they had a high level of interest in/awareness of the issues in developing countries. In comparison, 12.3% of the control group respondents stated that they had a very high and 31.5% stated that they had a high level of interest in/awareness of the issues in developing countries. Sixty-nine percent of the AEE Africa participants strongly agreed with the statement: 'My understanding of development issues deepened/improved/broadened as a result of my AEE placement.' Relevant issues highlighted here include that whilst participants' 'awareness' of development issues in Africa has been raised, their 'understanding' of the same issues is debateable, and also that a number of participants felt that their main objective was to learn about education in Africa, as opposed to development-related issues.

- Participants' professional behaviour, particularly in relation to engagement in DE in the classroom. The questionnaire findings highlight how 81% of those who completed AEE Africa are currently teaching DE and related issues, in comparison with 67% of those who did not complete their AEE placement in a developing context. Seventy-two percent of AEE Africa respondents stated that their motivation to engage in DE as teachers was influenced by their AEE Africa experience, and 62% stated that the placement had influenced the nature and content of DE topics they engage in.

- Improved skills and capacities in the context of teaching in multicultural classrooms; in terms of a more holistic approach to teaching; and in their opinions towards the role and use of teaching resources.

- A feeling of increased connection and solidarity with Africa and the work of development agencies. Seventy-nine percent of the AEE Africa respondents answered 'yes' to the question: 'Has your AEE placement influenced your decision to/not to associate financially or otherwise with other development-related organisations, charities, solidarity groups, etc, either at home or abroad?'

The Role of Mary Immaculate College

The research respondents were also asked to provide suggestions on the future role and function of MIC as regards the development of the AEE Africa programme. Among the suggestions offered by the AEE Africa participants and college staff were:

1. To improve preparation and follow-on activities for the AEE Africa programme. Particularly relevant here is the importance of preparing participants to teach appropriate aspects of the Gambian and Zambian curriculum and, on return, enabling participants to gain a

deeper understanding of the complex development issues they will have witnessed.

2. To develop a programme based on sustainable principles of equality and mutuality and, in doing so, minimise any charitable or aid aspects of the programme. Other issues highlighted here include aspects of the placement programme which run the risk of maintaining a sense of 'dependency', rooting the programme in an aid or charity model; post-colonial attitudes; and economic inequality between counterparts.

Research Conclusions and Recommendations

The main aim of this research was to examine the impacts of AEE Africa on student teacher participants, specifically in relation to participants' engagement in DE as teachers. The research has identified that teachers who have participated in AEE Africa engage in DE more so than those teachers who have not participated in the programme. There have also been significant impacts in terms of participants' skills and abilities as teachers, particularly in relation to teaching in a multicultural classroom. The research has also highlighted that participants who have participated in AEE Africa have a higher level of interest in and knowledge of global development issues than those who have not participated in the programme. For the majority of AEE Africa participants, the experience has remained with them and has influenced their understanding of and commitment to the development issues affecting African countries and their involvement in and support of the work of development agencies at home and abroad.

How the programme is managed and administered has an effect on how students and the host community experience the placement. Before the placement, it is necessary that students are sufficiently prepared and informed on the subjects that they will be teaching, and that they have considered their role, their motivations and expectations, so as to maximise learning opportunities and minimise destructive impacts, particularly for the host community. Participants also need to be sufficiently debriefed so as to help them process and share their experiences of development issues, and guide them in ways to use this experience positively in the future. Best practice in placement programmes of this nature advises a basis of equality and mutuality. It is important to be aware of aspects of AEE Africa which may promote and sustain a programme which is rooted in charity and aid, and to work towards minimising those aspects. The following section illustrates the changes that have been made to the programme based on the research findings outlined.

Changes to the Programme

The commencement of the study outlined above coincided with staffing changes in MIC. In late 2007, as part of the restructuring of the Development and Intercultural Education (DICE) Project [3], Irish Aid funded a part-time lecturer in DICE in each of the five initial teacher education colleges. The funding of a dedicated DICE lecturer means the AEE Africa placement is now designated as a member of staff's core responsibility.

The responsibilities of the DICE lecturer include preparation and accompanying of students on their AEE placements in a developing context, as well as the debriefing of participants upon their return. This is significant from the point of view of the future development of the programme and in terms of a response to the findings of 'The Impact of Student Teaching Placements in a Developing Context' report.

The main issues identified in the report have been addressed to varying degrees. This section focuses specifically on four individual areas: superficial understanding of development issues; building on principles of equality and mutuality; aspects of the teaching element of the placement; and, finally, the debriefing process. The changes implemented in relation to these areas are outlined below.

Understanding of Development Issues

The main objective of the AEE programme is to experience an alternative educational setting. However, for those completing their placement in either Zambia or the Gambia, fully comprehending the educational setting they are to operate in is not possible without an understanding of the complex problems which face countries of the global South, and the structural inequalities that create and maintain them. Neither would it be possible for participants to realise one of the strongest intended learning outcomes of AEE Africa – engagement with DE.

While information on development issues formed part of pre-departure training in previous years, it is now being more clearly identified to the students within preparation sessions. A dedicated section on development issues has been timetabled, which encompasses areas such as the Millennium Development Goals and the Human Development Index. These topics are discussed with a particular emphasis on education so as to give the students a framework within which to understand the issues.

At this point, however, discussing development issues is merely awareness-raising. Adequately conveying the depth of poverty the participants will be exposed to and its structural nature is a challenge. Bryan et al's study of student teachers' perspectives on social justice and DE clearly demonstrates the scope of the problem:

> Forty percent of respondents, for example, identified a lack of
> education and training as one of the most important reasons
> for poverty in developing world countries, whereas only 7%
> saw a relationship between poverty and these countries'
> colonial pasts, and only 21% viewed the nature of
> international trade and economic policies as one of the most
> important reasons for poverty. Respondents were more likely
> to attribute poverty to factors like overpopulation (28%) and to
> natural disasters, such as floods, earthquakes and droughts
> (30%). Moreover, less than 4% viewed the lifestyles of those
> in the West as being one of the most important reasons for
> poverty in developing countries. (Bryan et al, 2009, p. 35)

Issues of development are usually new to participants, the majority of whom will not have studied development previously or travelled to a country where these issues are so prevalent, therefore this part of the preparation is very theoretical for them. Simply conveying the pervasiveness of the poverty they are about to witness is challenge enough. The time available for preparation is in itself limited owing to the constraints of the academic timetable.[4] An added difficulty is that, at this point in the programme, participants are preoccupied by the practical aspects of the trip – i.e. vaccinations, flight times, etc.

Andreotti warns of the dangers of a superficial understanding of underdevelopment and the structural nature of poverty, emphasising the need to provide a space for learners

> to reflect on their context and their own and others'
> epistemological and ontological assumptions: how we came to
> think/be/feel/act the way we do and the implications of our
> systems of belief in local/global terms in relation to power,
> social relationships and the distribution of labour and
> resources. (Andreotti, 2006, p. 49)

Therefore, in order to compensate for the aforementioned time constraints within which AEE Africa has to operate, a lot of the work on cultivating in-depth understandings of development issues is carried out informally on the ground. This is delivered on an ongoing basis by both the accompanying lecturer and the individuals and organisations the students interact with in their host country. Such in-country learning is invaluable as it can be directly linked to the types of issues the students are experiencing. For example, in the Gambia, students meet with FEMIGAM, an indigenous non-governmental organisation dedicated to increasing female participation in education at all levels. Such meetings provide an opportunity for students to integrate what they have observed in the classroom and in wider Gambian society with the aims and work of Gambian-based non-governmental organisations. Links with such organisations are highly effective in facilitating the students' understanding of the issues they are being faced with for the first time.

Much use is also made of the return period. Students have, by this stage, started to ask questions themselves of the connections between the global North and South. They have frequently raised these questions in the group debriefing as they reflect on their experience. At this point, they are fully aware of the magnitude of the poverty people of the global South struggle with. Similarly, they are aware of the resources these countries posses and the work ethic of the people they met with. It is at this point in the programme that students are ready to explore the underlying reasons for the existence of poverty and the role that the global North plays in this.

Developing a Placement Programme
Based on Principles of Respect and Equality

Best practice recommends that the relationship between the host community and the programme participants should be one based on mutual respect and equality (O' Keeffe, 2006; Regan, 2007). There is a danger in any sending programme of participants developing post-colonial attitudes (Regan, 2007), a term explained by Andreotti (2006, p. 44) as 'a discourse of modernisation in which colonialism is either ignored or placed securely in the past, so that we think it is over and does not affect – and has not affected – the construction of the present situation'. In other words, 'the North's superiority over the South is assumed' (Kapoor, 2004, p. 629). Lissner found much evidence of this attitude in her study of the message church-based aid agencies were communicating in the 1970s. She spelled out the beliefs resulting from such an attitude as follows:

> The development problem is all 'out there'. It is caused by
> endogenous factors inside the low-income countries. We in the
> high-income countries are outside spectators; our present
> standard of living is as a result of our own efforts alone. The
> only, or most important, thing we can do to reduce poverty
> and human suffering in the third world is to provide more aid
> resources. (Lissner, 1977, p. 158)

An unexamined sense of superiority, combined with a belief that the underlying reason for poverty in countries of the global South is entirely due to internal factors, can lead to post-colonial attitudes.

'The Impact of Student Teaching Placements in a Developing Context' report found that the students were acutely aware of the economic inequality between them and their host community, treating it as a fact to which they felt the obvious response was donating money. This then casts the relationship between the students and the host community as that of 'giver-receiver', reinforcing feelings of superiority among the students:

> For northern partners particularly, exposure to significantly lower levels of material wealth can result in the (perhaps understandable) desire to prioritise fund-raising and aid donation. This risks converting a linking relationship, characterised by equality, mutuality and reciprocity, into a one-way donor-beneficiary relationship. (O' Keeffe, 2006, p. 10)

While the 'charity model' of development and all that goes with it is to be avoided, from the point of view of the placement organisers it is very difficult to dissuade the students from fund-raising for their 'host community'. Participants are advised that this is not a requirement of the programme and the college does not enquire into how much students have raised for donation. Instead, the programme organisers view their responsibility as highlighting alternative responses to the poverty the participants will encounter – for example, by engaging in DE in their professional capacity and advocacy/campaigning. Although the report found that the students recognised that economic inequality hugely influenced the relationship they had with the host community, it is not evident from the report or from personal interaction with participating students that a feeling of superiority permeated any of the interactions between the students and their hosts.

Another route taken in trying to tackle any post-colonial attitudes is through emphasising relationships with the host community other than those characterised as 'giver-receiver' in order to promote a more balanced rapport. Meeting with officials from the Ministry of Education and the Gambian Teachers' Union, visits to initial teacher education colleges and observing teachers in the classroom ensures the respect and admiration of the students at a professional level for those they are interacting with.

Using the newly complied 'AEE Africa Information Booklet' [5] and *Volunteering and Information Charter* (Development and Intercultural Education Project, 2009) [6], pre-departure training now openly explores the issue of post-colonial attitudes. Both documents address respecting the host community through sensitivity to local culture, an awareness of local languages and acting in a professional manner at all times. Accentuating the attitude that they are 'here to learn' rather than the narrow-focused 'here to help' is also stressed. Coupled with the in-country training on issues of poverty and structural inequality, the danger of post-colonial attitudes begins to recede and the attitude of a learner gradually becomes more prevalent. One participant put it well:

> For the first day we observed the class, saw what the teacher did, how she coped with so many students, what subjects were

being taught, etc! I honestly can say I was amazed!! The
teachers in the Gambia are so resourceful! There is no such
thing as Mary I's beloved 'fearas' [7] ... don't underestimate the
standard of the students! I was amazed with how advanced my
class were in maths and English![8]

Teaching in the African Setting

Up until 2009, students embarked on their placement without knowledge
of the specific classes they were to be placed in, or the subject areas they
were to teach. Typically, classes were allocated to the student teachers in
the first few days of the placement, after agreement had been reached
between the head teacher in the host school and the accompanying
lecturer. Class selection was based on a number of considerations: (1) the
children's proficiency in the English language; (2) whether or not the
class was due to undertake a state examination; and (3) if the class had
had a student from Mary Immaculate College the previous year.

The uncertainty surrounding the grade and the subjects students
were going to be asked to teach had practical as well as psychological
implications. Without knowledge of the exact situation they were to be
facing, the student teachers were unable to prepare either in terms of
lesson planning or the type of resources to bring with them. This
therefore became a source of unnecessary stress. Added to this was the
general anxiety of teaching in a completely new educational system. In
response to the concerns expressed in the report, the process of class
allocation has been altered and the pre-departure training in this area
improved upon.

Class/subject allocation. Classes are still selected using the same
considerations as before. As much as possible, however, classes and
subject areas are agreed on in advance of departure from Ireland and
students are also apprised in advance of any specific requests a school
has in terms of subject area. This takes a lot of ongoing communication
with the host schools. However, the change allows both the student
teachers and the class teachers on the ground the time to prepare
adequately.

Whereas in previous years participants moved from observation to
pair teaching, to individual teaching, it is now the norm for students to
complete the placement through pair teaching. This allows participants
the opportunity to plan together and support each other's teaching.

Setting the educational context. As previously outlined, students are
exposed to the issues facing less developed countries as part of the pre-
departure preparation sessions. These sessions are carried out through
the lens of 'education' – in other words, the problems of poverty and

development are illustrated through the particular challenges they create in terms of education. Through focusing on the second Millennium Development Goal – universal primary education – and UNESCO's Education for All, students gain a greater understanding of the context in which they will be teaching. These sessions are helpful in preparing students for the physical realities of the school, for the potentially wide range in ages within their class and for the pressures on the school administration.

Goodwill on the part of the ministries of education in both countries has also helped in familiarising the students with the educational environment they will be operating in. Both groups of students now receive orientation from the local Ministry of Education during their first days in the country. This provides information on the most current teaching techniques, methodologies and schemes in use in their host schools.

A large part of planning is awareness of the curriculum and the textbooks in use in the host schools. As part of pre-departure training, participants have the opportunity to better inform themselves through reading the curriculum outline and samples of textbooks currently in use in the schools.

Students are also given the opportunity to speak with former programme participants. This gives students the opportunity of hearing first-hand about the lessons and teaching methodologies which proved popular in previous years and the resources that would be of most value. Immediately prior to departure from Ireland, the students are engrossed in a five-week teaching practice. The opportunity for compiling lessons for their AEE Africa placement is emphasised to the students. They are encouraged to work with their Irish class to build up a profile of life in Ireland to share with the students in Zambia or the Gambia. This is to include examples of Irish legends, music, sport, food, etc. The intention is for the students to then share these with their African class and create a similar African profile to be shared with their Irish class on their return. Students are provided with a sample lesson plan and image pack with which to do this.

Debriefing

The debriefing process is essential for a number of reasons (Lovell-Hawker, 2008), including the well-being of the participants, planning for future placements and in order to complete the learning experience:

> Through each experience we may gain new understandings
> and skills, and our beliefs about ourselves, others and the
> world are challenged, changed or reinforced ... Simply to
> experience, however, is not enough. Often we are so deeply
> involved in the experience itself that we are unable, or do not

have the opportunity, to step back from it and reflect upon
what we are doing in any critical way. In any planned activity
for learning, debriefing provides an opportunity to engage in
this reflection. (Pearson & Smith, 1985, p. 69)

In 'The Impact of Student Teaching Placements in a Developing Context' report, the students were vocal about the importance of debriefing. It was even suggested that debriefing was of more importance than preparation. While vital, in this instance the debrief process is complicated by the fact that due to the pressures of the college calendar, participants usually only have one full day in between returning from their placement and starting their final semester. The needs of a robust debriefing process must therefore be balanced with the academic demands being placed on the students in their final semester.

The debriefing process has been strengthened in response to the findings of the report. The staff member immediately involved in debriefing has up-skilled in this area, recently completing a course designed to meet the needs of participants of either long- or short-term placements abroad, based on the most up-to-date methods in debriefing participants. This debrief process has now been scheduled across the whole semester, ensuring that it is an ongoing and gradual process. Specific sessions are to be dedicated to debrief only to the exclusion of professional sessions on DE or preparation for Africa Night.[9] Debrief is held in groups of 8-12 people and lasts for between 90 minutes and 2 hours per session. Participants are also offered individual debrief sessions at a time of their choosing, should they wish to avail themselves of these sessions.

Conclusion

AEE Africa has been found to have a significant impact on the programme participants both personally and professionally. While the overall aim of 'The Impact of Student Teaching Placements in a Developing Context' report was to examine the effect of AEE Africa placements on teachers' inclusion of DE, the report has also served to highlight areas of the programme which could be further developed. Many of the issues raised within the report have been addressed and the college continues to strive to improve all aspects of the programme.

Notes

[1] A smaller number of students have organised their own AEE placements in a developing context, and have travelled independently. However, these students were not the focus of the research study.

[2] For the purpose of this discussion, the global North/South refers to the divide between the predominantly economically rich countries of the northern hemisphere and the predominantly economically poor countries of the southern hemisphere.

[3] The DICE Project works to address the need for global and social justice perspectives within primary education in Ireland. See http://www.diceproject.org.

[4] Participants are off-campus for the majority of the semester preceding the placement.

[5] Internal to Mary Immaculate College (2008).

[6] A shared document of the five teacher education colleges.

[7] *Fearas* means 'equipment' or 'resources', in this instance for use in the classroom.

[8] Taken from the student response report of a programme participant in the Gambia (2009).

[9] Africa Night is held annually and is an opportunity for AEE Africa participants to present to the college community on their experiences.

References

Andreotti, V. (2006) Soft versus Critical Global Citizenship Education, *Policy and Practice*, 3, 40-51. http://www.developmenteducationreview.com/issue3-focus4

Bryan, A., Clarke, M. & Drudy, S. (2009) A Study of Student Teachers' Perspectives on Social Justice and Development Education, in M. Liddy & J. O'Flaherty (Eds) *Ubuntu Network: action research and other projects to integrate development education into initial teacher education*. Limerick: Ubuntu Network. http://www.ubuntu.ie

Development and Intercultural Education Project (DICE) (2009) *Volunteering and Information Charter*. Dublin: DICE.

Fullam, P. & Dolan, A. (2005) *Impact of Study Visits on Student Teachers: report on Developing Links Symposium*. Limerick: Mary Immaculate College.

Irish Aid (2007) *Irish Aid and Development Education: describing, understanding, challenging the story of human development in today's world*. Dublin: Irish Aid.

Kapoor, I. (2004) Hyper-Self-Reflexive Development? Spivak on Representing the Third World 'Other', *Third World Quarterly*, 25(4), 627-647. http://dx.doi.org/10.1080/01436590410001678898

Lissner, J. (1977) *The Politics of Altruism: a study of the political behaviour of voluntary development agencies*, 2nd edn. Geneva: Lutheran World Federation.

Lovell-Hawker, D. (2008) *Debriefing Aid Workers and Missionaries: a comprehensive manual*. London: People in Aid.

Mary Immaculate College (2009) *Additional Educational Experience*. Limerick: Mary Immaculate College.

Merryfield, M. (2000) Why Aren't Teachers Being Prepared to Teach for Diversity, Equity and Global Interconnectedness? A Study of Lived Experiences in the Making of Multicultural Global Educators, *Teaching and Teacher Education*, 16(4), 429-443. http://dx.doi.org/10.1016/S0742-051X(00)00004-4

O'Keefe, C. (2006) *Linking between Ireland and the South: good practice guidelines for north/south linking*. Dublin: Irish Aid & Suas Educational Development.

Pearson, M. & Smith, D. (1985) Debriefing in Experienced-Based Learning, in D. Boud, R. Keogh & D. Walker (Eds) *Reflection: turning experience into learning*, pp. 69-84. Abingdon: Routledge.

Purdy, N. & Gibson, K. (2008) Alternative Placements in Initial Teacher Education, *Teaching and Teacher Education*, 24(8), 2076-2086. http://dx.doi.org/10.1016/j.tate.2008.05.007

Regan, C. (2007) Lies, Spin and Colonialism. Paper presented at Irish Development Education Association national conference on Linking and Immersion Schemes with the Global South: developing good practice, Dublin, 20 September.

Roberts, A. (2003) Proposing a Broadened View of Citizenship: North American teachers' service in rural Costa Rican schools, *Journal of Studies in International Education*, 7(3), 253-276. http://dx.doi.org/10.1177/1028315303251398

Villegas, A.M. & Lucas, T. (2002) *Educating Culturally Responsive Teachers: a coherent approach*. New York: State University of New York Press.

Willard-Holt, C. (2001) The Impact of a Short-Term International Experience for Preservice Teachers, *Teaching and Teacher Education*, 17(4), 505-517. http://dx.doi.org/10.1016/S0742-051X(01)00009-9

CHAPTER 13

Teacher Educator Exchange Partnership in Uganda and Ireland: closer perspectives on teacher education in sub-Saharan Africa

PATRICIA KIERAN, CARMEL HINCHION, DORIS KAIJE, RUTH KYAMBADDE & PADDY BRADLEY

SUMMARY This chapter outlines the origin and development of a North–South Teacher Educator Exchange Partnership (TEEP) programme located in two Ugandan and seven Irish universities. The main feature of TEEP was a series of exchange visits designed to further capacity building among teacher educators in Uganda and Ireland through cross-fertilising pedagogies, professional expertise and scholarly research in a professional exchange. The chapter overviews the educational system in Uganda and explores Peer Observation of Teaching (POT) as a central methodology in the TEEP project. The importance of striving to create an egalitarian, mutually enriching partnership which enabled the sharing of different approaches to teaching and teacher formation was fundamental to sustaining TEEP. While TEEP was not without its challenges, both Ugandan and Irish participants reported a development of their repertoire of teaching, research and professional skills by working with their TEEP colleagues.

When I was young, I used to hear that, if you think your mother is the best cook, then wait until you eat food cooked by another person's mother. I think this was the birth of the TEEP [Teacher Educator Exchange Partnership] exchange programme, providing people with the opportunity to share different ideas and cultures as well as learn new knowledge and experience a new way of doing things. TEEP enabled us to share ideas about how to teach, what to teach, how to assess teaching, sharing pedagogical ideas around curriculum content, teaching methodologies, teaching resources and assessment techniques. (Ugandan participant, Kieran & Bradley, 2011, p. 1)

Introduction to the Teacher Educator Exchange Partnership and Its Role in Teacher Education

The Teacher Educator Exchange Partnership (TEEP) is an innovative ongoing project conceived, designed and sustained by the Centre for Global Development through Education (CGDE) in Ireland. The CGDE was established in 2008, and all of its programmes, including TEEP, have been funded by Irish Aid, Ireland's official programme of assistance to developing countries under the Programme of Strategic Cooperation between Irish Aid and Higher Education and Research Institutes 2007-2011. The Millennium Development Goals (MDGs) require the international community to work to eradicate extreme poverty, empower women and promote gender equality, achieve universal primary education and create a global partnership for development. Ban-Ki Moon states:

> The Goals represent human needs and basic rights that every individual around the world should be able to enjoy – freedom from extreme poverty and hunger; quality education, productive and decent employment, good health and shelter; the right of women to give birth without risking their lives; and a world where environmental sustainability is a priority, and women and men live in equality. (United Nations, 2010, p. 3)

As a means of furthering these goals – in particular, that of promoting quality education – the CGDE embarked on a North-South partnership programme designed to support teacher educators and their pre-service teaching programmes in Uganda and Ireland. TEEP was a small-scale pioneering programme which focused on developing partnership between nine Ugandan and nine Irish teacher educators, located in two Ugandan and seven Irish Universities. TEEP's explicit aim was to further capacity building among teacher educators and their host institutions through cross-fertilising pedagogies, professional expertise and scholarship in a professional exchange. The main feature of TEEP was exchange visits by teacher educators in Uganda and Ireland. The two Ugandan universities involved were Kyambogo University and Makerere University, both based in Kampala. In Ireland, the seven institutions involved were based in Dublin (University College Dublin and St

Patrick's College), Belfast (St Mary's College), Sligo (St Angela's College, University College Galway), Cork (University College Cork) and Limerick (Mary Immaculate College and the University of Limerick). The Irish participants visited Uganda from 11-25 April 2010 and the participants from Uganda visited Ireland from 9-24 October 2010.

Uganda

Uganda was identified as a TEEP partnership country as it is one of Irish Aid's 9 partner and priority countries. In 1997, the Ugandan government introduced a policy of universal primary education and, with a population of over 32 million, which is expected to double in the next 20 years, this brought many opportunities and challenges. Uganda has over 5 million children of primary-school-going age (5-12) and, with over 33 native languages and dialects, the rate of literacy for females of 15 and over stands at 57.7%, while for males it is 76.8% (Nakabugo, 2010). There are undoubtedly multiple challenges for teacher formation in this sub-Saharan country where there is an insufficient supply of qualified teachers. Since the introduction of a policy of universal primary education in Uganda,

> Demand for places in the primary teachers colleges has been rising in recent years, and the qualifications required for admittance have been made more stringent ... over the medium term, the quality of applicants to primary teachers colleges has steadily improved. (Mulkeen & Chen, 2008, p. 101)

Further challenges concerning teacher retention, most especially of female teachers in rural schools, are a major issue in a country where 87% of the population live in rural areas. TEEP engaged in a teacher educator exchange programme in Uganda and Ireland precisely because the issue of teacher formation and continuing professional development has been identified as crucially important in Uganda (Mulkeen & Chen, 2008). The TEEP programme was designed as one aspect of the international, inter-institutional programmes supported by the professional development programme of the CGDE to enhance the teaching, learning and research skills of educational practitioners, North and South, through research seminars, collaborative research projects, doctoral and postdoctoral work, as well as teacher exchange partnerships. TEEP specifically targeted poverty reduction in Uganda by contributing to the quality of its teacher education programmes.[1]

Education is central to poverty reduction and the government of Uganda's *Education Sector Strategic Plan 2004-2015* (ESSP) stresses the need to improve curricula and pedagogy in teacher education institutions. Its strategy is to help primary pupils achieve their education goals through 'the continuing improvement of teaching. This includes a continued effort to recruit teachers and teacher-trainees' (Ministry of Education and Sports, 2004, p. 18).[2] While the CGDE initiated TEEP as a bilateral process to enhance and support the quality of teacher education programmes in Uganda and Ireland, this chapter will primarily explore this process as it relates to Uganda.

The CGDE was cognisant of existing programmes within Uganda which focus on teacher development and curriculum reform, and which are spearheaded by the ESSP. While access to education is crucial for poverty reduction, it is important to emphasise that the nature and quality of educational provision is critical if poverty reduction is to be achieved. The solution is not simply to fund more students to attend primary, secondary or tertiary levels of education. Research has shown that the quality of educational provision is a key factor in student retention and completion in developing countries (Mulkeen & Crowe-Taft, 2010). TEEP seeks to explore the interdependent relationship between the quality of teacher formation and pupil performance through enabling teacher educators to reconceptualise and improve the teaching and learning process. Existing research from Uganda shows that teacher qualification has an impact on student achievement. In one study looking at pupil performance in English at Grade 6, 'relative to pupils of teachers who did not complete secondary education, students of teachers who completed secondary education scored 2.52 points higher' (Nannyonjo, 2007, p. 38). Quality of teacher preparation and performance impacts on the learning experience and outcome of pupils. With this in mind, TEEP decided not to focus initially or exclusively on capacity building through investing in physical infrastructure, but to focus rather on teacher educators and to capacity build through an exchange programme with peer observation of teaching (POT) as its cornerstone. This led to a model of international cooperation in the field of teacher education and educational research through a person-centred approach which focused on the professional development of teacher educators in Uganda and Ireland.

Phase One: TEEP in Uganda

In the first phase of the TEEP process, the CGDE furthered its existing research links with Makerere University and Kyambogo University (KYU) in Kampala, where a new Bachelor of Teacher Education had been designed and was in the initial stages of implementation. In November 2009, the director of the CGDE published an outline of the TEEP programme and invited interested parties in university faculties of education and colleges of education and the liberal arts in Ireland and Uganda to apply to participate in the programme. A number of teacher educators volunteered for the programme.

This first phase of the programme involved Irish members visiting Uganda in April 2010, with the second phase of the return visit to Ireland taking place in October 2010. While the travel and other practical arrangements were organised through the CGDE, the most important element of preparation was a full day of briefings, discussion and meetings held at Mary Immaculate College, Limerick, and KYU, Kampala, in April 2010. The planning day offered a first opportunity for many of the TEEP volunteers to meet and share opinions. This was of great benefit and a precursor of the valuable introductions that would take place once participants met their exchange partners. TEEP's planning day provided an opportunity to reflect upon the genesis and objectives of the TEEP process, articulate anticipated outcomes, and explore logistical and practical issues, as well as methodologies that might be applied to TEEP. In Ireland, following an introduction by the director of the CGDE, the Irish participants were given a briefing on 'Insights into Uganda's Current Education System' (Nakabugo, 2010). The programme then moved to a discussion of TEEP's objectives and how they might best be met through the project's design and implementation.

Preparation for the TEEP Exchange in Uganda

In Uganda, the CGDE coordinator invited interested CGDE members at Makerere University and KYU, in the primary teachers colleges and national teachers colleges to apply to participate in TEEP. Through the CGDE coordinator, KYU lecturers who lectured students on the Bachelor of Teacher Education programme were also informed about the TEEP opportunity and encouraged to apply.

Three preparatory meetings were attended by all the Ugandan participants and were held in March and April 2010 at KYU. At these initial meetings in Kampala, TEEP was introduced and explained to the volunteer participants. Members shared their fears about and expectations of the partnership. A tentative programme for the two-week teacher educator exchange in Uganda was drawn up. This included introductions to and briefings from the KYU vice chancellor, deputy vice chancellor and registrar. Arrangements were made for the Irish TEEP participants to visit selected primary and secondary schools, as well as a school for the deaf and primary teachers colleges. Visits were to be made to places of amazing natural heritage, including the source of the Nile and the Bujagali Falls in eastern Uganda.

Some Ugandan lecturers took time to prepare specific classes for their partners. Students whose lectures were being observed by TEEP participants were briefed about TEEP, its objectives and Ireland. This was done to avoid students' possible diversion of attention on seeing a 'new face' in the lecture room. Students were quite amused during the POT because some of them mistakenly viewed TEEP as a peer supervision of their own supervisor. This is unsurprising in a system where lecturers routinely supervise pre-service teachers during their school/college practicum.

TEEP was an inter-institutional exchange and lecturers in some of the TEEP participants' departments were also briefed about the activity. A large meeting was held on the second day after the Irish TEEP participants arrived in Uganda on 12 April 2010, when the Dean of the Faculty of Education at Mary Immaculate College, Limerick, Professor Teresa O'Doherty, presented an outline of the TEEP programme to all the Irish and Ugandan participants at KYU. This presentation and the ensuing discussion increased the Ugandan participants' appreciation of the programme and ensured that all partners were on an equal footing. The two teams collaboratively agreed on the practical logistics of implementing the TEEP process in a manner which supported teacher educators' professional needs while supporting the quality of teaching and learning in diverse contexts.

Peer Observation of Teaching

During phase one of the TEEP process, the nature of the professional relationship between the Irish and Ugandan participants was discussed, with a particular focus on the protocols and purposes of POT. This focus on observing a peer teacher educator teaching, and subsequently giving peers structured, supportive feedback, was identified as a means of nurturing partnership and mutuality between the Irish and Ugandan partners. Through a joint enterprise of observing another person teach and giving feedback, teacher educators were given a voluntary opportunity to reflect critically on their own teaching as well as to learn from their partner's teaching styles and content delivery. Through POT, teacher educators were enabled to articulate and extend discourses on styles and repertoires of teaching and learning. The TEEP volunteers were briefed on the procedures adopted for POT in sample universities and were familiarised with supporting academic literature and documentation which suggested that POT could enhance teacher performance. In Ireland, the TEEP volunteers began with a working definition, where '[p]eer review of teaching is informed colleague judgement about faculty teaching for either fostering improvement or making personal decision' (Van Note Chism, 2007, p. 3). However, the notion of an overly systematic, restrictive or judgemental approach to the observation of another's or one's own teaching was deemed inappropriate for TEEP. TEEP was not designed to facilitate making judgements on the quality of another colleague's teaching for the purpose of quality assurance, or for external audit. The model selected for TEEP was a collaborative model of POT:

> Collaborative peer review of teaching is about finding ways of
> creating and sustaining conversations about teaching which
> are constructive and purposeful and which open problems in
> teaching to public debate and discussion. It shares ... the
> ultimate goal of enhancing the students' experience of higher
> education ... collaborative peer review emphasizes mutuality
> of benefits between observer and the observed (Gosling, 2005,
> p. 13).

The TEEP volunteers were committed to partnership from the initial
stages of the project and unease was expressed that one teacher educator
might make unilateral arrangements about POT in the absence of their
partner. It was therefore agreed that any protocols, approaches and
documents concerning POT should be flexible and mutually agreed upon
by the Ugandan and Irish participants.

As with any type of international exchange, the TEEP participants
were interested in the important matter of practical arrangements
regarding passports, visas, accommodation, food, medical procedures,
etc. Since this would be a first visit to sub-Saharan Africa or Europe for
most participants, and the first visit to Africa or Ireland for some, such
details were of major interest, and colleagues who had taken part in
previous trips were cross-questioned with enthusiasm.

TEEP in Uganda

The work of collaboration between higher education institutions in
Ireland and Uganda was premised on the belief that teacher educators are
agents of change and cultural workers (Freire, 2005). The concept of
culture is a contested one and can be understood from many stances. The
TEEP participants understood culture as the practices which prevail in
the world as people structure and give meaning to their lives. There is an
inevitable link between the texture of the cultural world and the
structures and processes of education. The TEEP programme was an
action towards, or an entry point into, poverty reduction in sub-Saharan
Africa, by targeting professional educators positioned to make an impact
from the perspectives of their cultural contexts. Essentially, the TEEP
participants were involved in a type of reflective inquiry, which can
reveal

> important valued benefits at the core of professional education
> and learning: uncovering needed perspectives; identifying
> critical moral and ethical dimensions of practice; encouraging
> collaborative inquiries; deliberating about underlying
> professional purposes and possibilities – all valued aspects of
> professional education that might otherwise be missed if

reflective inquiry were lacking, not endorsed and practiced.
(Lyons, 2010, p. 8)

Where possible, the programme was organised to work with an exchange partner who had comparable administrative, professional teaching and research portfolios. In the subject-specific teaching areas, there was a key focus on pedagogical content knowledge, where subject content, effective teaching methodologies and assessment procedures were shared between participants. For example, a Pedagogy of English lecturer in Uganda was partnered with a Pedagogy of English lecturer in Ireland. Furthermore, a Religious Studies lecturer in Uganda was partnered with a Religious Education lecturer in Ireland, and a dean of the Faculty of Education in Ireland was partnered with a dean of the Faculty of Education in Uganda. While it was not always possible to match each partner's academic or professional profile identically, the organisers of the TEEP exchange made a considerable effort to form partnerships where there were strong areas of commonality.

Phase Two: Ugandan TEEP participants visit Ireland

In October 2010, the nine Ugandan participants arrived at Dublin Airport and were welcomed by the director of the CGDE. The day after their arrival, they were reunited with their Irish partners and were given a full day's briefing and induction on the Irish educational system and the nature of teacher formation programmes in Ireland. This session also included an overview of the work of Irish Aid, as well as a discussion on how participants might document and report on the TEEP process. In a sense, this meeting was a follow-up and consolidation of previous partnership work in Uganda. Immediately after this meeting, the Ugandan TEEP participants travelled to seven university colleges to shadow their partners and engage in POT.

The participants not only engaged with their exchange partners in their place of work, but were invited also to Irish homes to share meals and meet family and friends, just as the Irish participants had been invited to Ugandan homes during their TEEP exchange. The Ugandan participants visited important geographical and historical locations in Ireland such as Bunratty Castle, the Cliffs of Moher, the karst landscape of the Burren and Viking Dublin. All of these activities enriched the relationships among the teacher educators, and this enhanced understanding of place and culture ultimately added value to the endeavour of building professional capacity and collaborative educational links.

The library facilities in Ireland were commented upon frequently by the Ugandan TEEP participants, as they were deemed to be well stocked with a variety of recent and relevant resources for educational disciplines. The first day that the Ugandan TEEP members were on the university campus in Limerick was Open Day 2010. On Open Day, post-primary students visit the university to acquaint themselves with university programmes and services. This was a learning experience for many Ugandan TEEP members. Open Day brings schools closer to the university and helps young people to make informed decisions about their future career. This visit has the potential to motivate post-primary students to study in school. One TEEP participant noted: 'In Uganda, schools are completely detached from university activities.'

The Ugandan participants also noted that lecturers in Ireland were able to share resources with their students freely as a consequence of information and communications technology. These included web pages, book extracts and references, which were given to the students at the end of lectures. Students were encouraged to read materials and explore resources after the lecture. Through the use of memory sticks, the intranet and Moodle, students had a capacity to access information independently while ensuring participative learning and up-to-date knowledge. The Ugandan participants also commented on the overall emphasis on making learning interactive through a range of activities including group work, paired activities and student presentations. Also of note was the use of artefacts in the lecture to illustrate key points and provide a multi-sensory approach to learning.

Inter-Country Exchange: first impressions of Uganda

On arrival in Uganda and Ireland, the participants' first impressions were interesting. From Irish eyes, the colours of Uganda were stunning – the green lushness carried in the heavy heat and the red earth was different to the dark-brown Irish soil. From Ugandan eyes, the Irish climate was cold and the pace of life was fast. The streets of Kampala were full with people bustling about their work at fruit and vegetable stalls. The young men sat on their motorbikes waiting to engage in taxi service. There was a notable young population, which is confirmed by the statistics: 50% of Uganda's population are under 14 years of age and 2.1% are over 65; life expectancy is 52.72 years and the country has the second-highest birth rate in the world at 47.84 births per 1000 (Nakabugo, 2010). These statistics became a notable reality as the TEEP participants immersed themselves in a new environment. Indeed, the Irish participants were experiencing a sense of cultural and geographic dislocation which provided much learning. The initial days in the partner countries involved welcomes and visits. The Irish team made a visit to the Irish Embassy in Kampala and met the Irish Ambassador, Kevin Kelly. The ambassador and his colleagues outlined their diplomatic mission and stressed that education is a priority in their agenda of eradicating poverty. These meetings were essential for cultural orientation and group

Patricia Kieran et al

planning. The TEEP participants gained an overview of the contextual realities which impact teaching and learning.

At the initial TEEP meeting involving all the participants in Kampala, partners discussed the meaning of professional collaboration and POT. There was consensual agreement that POT was a shared enterprise of opening the door of one's classroom, inviting a peer in to observe, and holding one's teaching up to scrutiny for the purpose of developing teaching repertoires which would lead ultimately to the improvement of student learning. However, TEEP involved more than classroom-based POT. It also involved shadowing partners as they went about their daily work. Both shadowing and POT were embedded in a dialogic process, where dialogue is an educative process that, among other things, 'involves the ability to question, listen, reflect, reason, explain, speculate and explore ideas ... it involves a willingness and skill to engage with minds, ideas and ways of thinking other than our own' (Alexander, 2006, p. 5).

The participants were invited to compose a personal and professional portfolio for their partner in order to facilitate the sharing of biographical and academic histories. This emphasis on integrating, as far as practicable, personal and professional data meant that POT only took place after a detailed, extended, bilateral exploration of both partners' philosophies of teaching and learning. All steps in the procedure were open to negotiation and revision. Clear boundaries were established between partners and partners regularly checked in with each other to ensure that both were in agreement about the process. Prior to the first POT, partners held informal interviews which were designed for them to get to know each other and build trust. Conversations followed a schedule of prompting questions such as: 'Tell me a bit about you – your background, family, community'; 'How did you become a teacher?'; 'How did you become a teacher educator?'; 'Do you like being a teacher educator – why, why not?'; 'What would you change if you could?'

As the relationships developed and became more relaxed and 'safe', approaches for working together were agreed. Peer observation was shaped in the form of three stages: (1) a pre-observation meeting; (2) the classroom/lecture observation; and (3) post-observation conversation and feedback. In the pre-observation stage, the partner being observed indicated to the observer any particular area of their teaching on which they would like observation and detailed feedback. Sometimes this was quite specific, where the observed partner, for example, might request feedback on levels of classroom interaction, assessment strategies or use of teaching resources. At other times, no specific area for comment was identified and POT was more generally focused. During the lesson/lecture the observing partner sat in the classroom and took relevant notes. After the class or lecture a dialogue between both TEEP partners focused on the teaching and learning styles and outcomes of the class. For example, the observer may give feedback on teacher–student interaction as requested and a pedagogical conversation would follow, comparing and contrasting different approaches. The flexibility of the TEEP process facilitated an organic, needs-based development where the observation of the peer teaching became part of a whole range of activities for TEEP partners, including practicum visits to schools, library use, research seminars and attendance at meetings and formal events on campus.

In classes participants experienced many of the same challenges in both Uganda and Ireland: management of large-group teaching, the use of relevant and engaging materials and methodologies, effective assessment of student work and inclusive education structures and approaches. Many of the Irish participants remarked on how the Ugandan education system dealt with the issue of hearing and visual impairment in a much more effective way than the Irish system:

> I was extremely impressed to see that sign language interpreters were available within lectures and tutorials on the campus at Kyambogo and that it was normal to integrate students with hearing impairments within education lectures. Equally at Bishop Willis Core Primary Teacher's College, in Iganga, I met blind students who were enrolled in the teacher education programme and was informed that Braille printing facilities were available to these students. Structures for the inclusion of student teachers with visual or hearing impairment are not available in Irish teacher education at the moment. (Irish TEEP participant)

Another Irish participant remarked on how a visit to the Gender Education Centre in Makerere University showed her a model of inclusion that would be valuable in the Irish context:

> It opened my eyes to what is possible in correcting gender imbalance and it planted a seed that could be nurtured in the future in my own practice and institution. As a member of Limerick Fairtrade City and as Coordinator of the One World Awareness Society in Mary Immaculate, I exchanged insights with Ugandan academics and producers on how Fairtrade and sustainable tourism can be incorporated into academic disciplines and lived practice in Uganda and Ireland.'(Irish TEEP participant)

The professional partners shared subject knowledge and resources, dilemmas and achievements, and prepared for future connections and collaborations. Scholarly work emanated from the TEEP exchange. TEEP partners co-wrote papers and co-presented at seminars and conferences such as 'Education in the Developing World: a closer look at Africa'

(CGDE Lunchtime Seminar Series, Ireland, 14 October 2010) as well as the 'Capacity and Confidence Building in Teacher Education' symposium in Limerick (30 August 2011). Research has resulted in abstracts being submitted for the 11th UKFIET (UK Forum for International Education and Training) International Conference on 'Global Challenges for Education: economics, environment and emergency' at the University of Oxford, 16 September 2011 and also for the Educational Association of Ireland Annual Conference, 15 April 2011.

TEEP Findings

TEEP embodied a commitment to mutually empowering partnerships and emerged from a worldview which did not envisage capacity building in KYU and Makerere's teacher formation programmes exclusively through the provision of physical resources. TEEP involves building partnerships not only at institutional level but at a personal and professional level. In the first instance, planning for the programme emphasised developing relationships between Irish and Ugandan partners involved in teacher formation. As TEEP developed it became apparent that there was a need, not just for South–North partnerships, but also for South–South partnerships linking Ugandan teacher educators and institutions with colleagues and institutions in other African nations. TEEP provided an open environment where the sharing of good practices became a continual ongoing process which lasted long after the initial teacher educator exchange had ended. TEEP provided not only a glimpse into another teacher educator's professional sphere but also into the lifestyle of the participants.

A key element in the development of a productive professional exchange for all participants was the experience of being a cultural stranger in another country. The experience of and critical reflection upon unfamiliar experiences led to an enhanced understanding of and empathy for the work of teacher educators in radically different educational settings. Unanticipated outcomes of TEEP included the participants' attachment of great importance, not only to academic fieldwork through visits to university campus lecture rooms or school settings, but to visits to colleagues' homes. What was unanticipated here was that participants' capacity to see professional and academic situations from multiple perspectives was enhanced by their personal engagement with TEEP members' lives outside of the lecture room or classroom. From its inception TEEP was latitudinarian in its approach and it placed the peer review of teaching in a broad personal, cultural and social context. While in some settings POT can often 'be handled very poorly and lead to unwarranted judgments' (Van Note Chism, 2007, p. 19), this was not the experience of TEEP members. Objections to peer review range from 'anxieties about openness and possible threats to academic freedom, the difficulty of defining a peer, problems with finding time to devote to peer review, concerns about the validity and reliability of peer review, and concerns about undesirable aftereffects of the approach' (Van Note Chism, 2007, p. 19). It is remarkable that no such objections were registered during TEEP in the informal feedback sessions and in participants' formal written reports. TEEP partners commented instead that the sharing of pedagogies and subject expertise occurred in a non-judgemental manner which fostered respect, trust and friendship. The following comments are testament to the success of the higher education institution exchanges: 'I have really grown professionally and personally since joining TEEP programme' (Ugandan TEEP participant). Another (Irish) participant stated:

> This has been a very positive personal, professional and
> academic experience. Both parties appreciate the privilege it
> has been to learn from each other's teaching, learning and
> research. We identified multiple common teaching areas and
> exchanged lots of ideas, approaches and resources.

TEEP set out to establish a mutually negotiated, egalitarian, bilateral process that challenged the notion of POT as a threat. Participants were briefed that peer review was not a clandestine form of surveillance, inspection, mentoring or tutoring. The importance of an egalitarian, mutually enriching sharing of different approaches to teaching and teacher formation was fundamental to sustaining the process. Both Irish and Ugandan participants reported a development of their repertoire of teaching, research and professional skills by working with their TEEP colleagues.

One cannot underestimate the importance of interpersonal as well as inter-institutional contact in the process. Person-to-person contact proved most effective as partnerships developed. TEEP members from Uganda and Ireland were invariably more likely to respond to personal contact through email or telephone when they came from a familiar colleague rather than from a large institution. TEEP partnerships were also more productive and had an increased longevity when the partners shared the same academic discipline or had similar professional or administrative duties (e.g. Mathematics, Special Educational Needs, Religious Education). Partnerships with a distinct common academic focus or professional orientation were more likely to flourish and lead to further bilateral collaboration through conference presentations, publications, exchange of different teaching methodologies as well as course content and assessment strategies.

As the professional partnerships developed, key themes concerning teacher formation in Uganda emerged. The role of library facilities in supporting teacher formation programmes as well as the identification of existing library strengths and lacunae became a critical aspect of the TEEP programme. In all formal educational contexts, library provision is a foundational catalyst and crucial support for the academic and professional development of critical, reflective teacher educators and teachers. Well-organised, resourced and used library facilities enable the development of research, teaching and scholarship for teacher educators and their students. In Uganda TEEP participants noted that, relative to their partners in Ireland, students and staff had less access to recent and relevant publications and to online journals and library resources:

> Unlike the library in an Irish university that I visited, which encouraged the development of research, scholarship and teaching, my own University library in Uganda is unable to meet these expectations. The available books are very old. Publications dating from 1990 are still considered to be relatively new. Physical space for scholarship and research is limited. Students and teaching staff compete for the same desks and reading material. International journals are in short supply. Journals tend to be local and when available, are not received regularly. As teacher educators, there is not much incentive for scholarship and professional development. Many therefore resort to using the internet for research despite its shortcomings and its limited availability at the University. (Ugandan TEEP participant)

The difficulty of sustaining undergraduate and postgraduate research in education where the tools of scholarship are not readily available or accessible is a major challenge. The TEEP Report (Kieran & Bradley, 2011) placed an emphasis on maximising the use of existing library and research provision to support teaching and learning and began to identify strategies to enable further capacity building such as the use of e-books. However TEEP's findings illustrated the considerable differences in computer networks and provision for information and communications technology (ICT) in Ireland and Uganda. This resulted in the development of different styles of teaching in both countries.

> Every teacher educator needs resources (technology, books, stationery …) in order to have lessons that are not entirely abstract and theoretical. One of the advantages teacher educators in Ireland certainly have is access to a wider array of resources including interactive technologies like Smart Boards and web technologies. Students also have access to resources on Local Area Network (LAN) which enables them to access resources in a flexible manner. (Ugandan TEEP participant)

Greater infrastructure and support for ICT in teaching in Uganda was recommended as an important target for institutions involved in teacher formation. Ugandan academics were not as well resourced with up-to-date library materials or ICT equipment. One of the Ugandan academics remarked, 'Use of ICT in lectures would ease our energy in trying to be audible to the large classes that we normally handle at the University'. Indeed, Ugandan TEEP participants drew frequent attention to the level of provision of interactive white boards, visualisers, and PowerPoint facilities not only in Irish universities but also in Irish primary and post-primary schools. They commented on the opportunities and range of choice that ICT provided for students and teachers in terms of teaching styles and content delivery and the benefits for students, particularly in situations where there are large numbers of pre-service teachers in a lecture hall or classroom. Ugandan participants also suggested that greater use of online library links and resources for pre-service student teachers could greatly enhance the quality of teaching, learning and research. It was interesting to note that some Ugandan TEEP partners noted an over-reliance on ICT and PowerPoint in Ireland, in some of the teaching they observed:

> there is a possibility that PowerPoint is actually abused rather than innovatively used. This is the danger I see in some of the lessons; dense text on the PowerPoint with no discussion, debates or analysis is likely to be unattractive.

The availability of technology in the teaching and learning environment needed to become part of a larger, more interactive repertoire of learner-centred teaching approaches and not the exclusive methodology used by some teacher educators. One Ugandan participant stressed, 'there is a need to be conscious of PowerPoint presentations being a tool and not a method'. In general, TEEP members reported the benefits of opening the classroom door to others as they observed and gained feedback on a variety of interactive teaching styles as well as high levels of pupil participation in small and large group teaching and learning situations which they observed. This was particularly evident in some classes observed in Uganda, where student numbers were large, with a lecturer to student ratio of over 1:300, yet it was evident that the high quality of pedagogical interaction was not always dependent on the availability of resources to support teaching and learning. In teaching and learning contexts where the teacher educator explicitly linked academic subject areas to life skills that were of immediate relevance to the students, TEEP partners observed increased levels of student engagement and participation. One Irish participant commented:

> In a lecture on gender and education, the teacher educator did not begin with the academic literature on theories of gender or studies of gender and education. Instead she skilfully deconstructed diverse understandings of gender in contemporary Ugandan society, by simultaneously providing

multiple illustrations of gender theory from everyday life. She
did this in a skilful manner which challenged and provoked
lively debate among students. It was evident that this teacher
educator had adopted a learner-centred, interactive
methodology which combined theory with practice and
encouraged multiple critical readings of a complex issue.

It was interesting to note that any assumption that a deficit of technology
and resources resulted in a teaching and learning deficit in Uganda were
challenged. TEEP members from Ireland with a particular interest in
special educational needs and inclusive education noted that lectures in
the Faculty of Education at KYU were signed for hearing impaired
students, while in Bishop Willis College provision was made for Braille
printers for eight students on teacher education programmes who were
registered blind. No such level of investment in infrastructure or
inclusive practice was available for pre-service teachers in the Irish
colleges of education.

The TEEP Report (Kieran & Bradley, 2011) indicated that there had
been considerable interest in different models of school-based work,
often referred to as 'practicum'. Colleagues discussed the benefits and
disadvantages of different models in the light of the different
infrastructure and support mechanisms in the different countries. Some
colleagues identified practical matters in administration and preparation
that could be implemented immediately. Colleagues also shared their
experiences of the continuing process of revision and updating of
programmes of teaching, learning and assessment in teacher education.
This process can be supported by learning from and observing the
practice of peers in international contexts. The TEEP programme
provided partners with an incentive and also with support to help them
revisit and redesign familiar teaching and learning approaches as a
consequence of seeing things done differently, and sometimes more
effectively, elsewhere. The introduction of student evaluation of
teaching, learning support for students, and systems which articulate and
incorporate findings from the student voice is a vital aspect of quality
teacher formation.

TEEP as a Window on Teacher Education in Uganda

TEEP provided a window into the world of teacher education in two
premier Ugandan universities and primary teachers colleges. It revealed
the commitment and professionalism of teacher educators in Uganda,
often in a context of a very high student–lecturer ratio as well as limited
resources. Ugandan teacher educators involved in TEEP suggested that
their capacity to research, teach and further their own professional
development was impeded by the inadequacy of library and ICT
facilities. Inevitably, this impacted on their style of teaching and the

manner in which they assessed their programmes. Often they did not have the freedom to use microphones in teaching large groups or to use PowerPoint presentations or to recommend recently published texts to their students. Inevitably, the quality of the formation of pre-service teachers in Uganda is impacted by the lack of recent and relevant resources and library materials. However, it is important to note that the teacher educators in TEEP exhibited an huge appetite for research, scholarship and contact with the international educational community, North and South. Ugandan teacher educators had a great deal to contribute to their Irish counterparts, who learned much from their educational expertise and range of teaching skills. Ugandan TEEP participants voluntarily and readily opened their lecture room door to their peers and willingly invited them in. They were committed to programme review and ready to reconceptualise course outlines, programmes of learning, assessment strategies and administrative procedures. They engaged in POT with great generosity of spirit.

Recommendations

It was evident that different levels of access to modern tools of communication can have an inhibiting effect on the initial stages of developing partnerships between individuals and could be detrimental to long-term activities. Investment in additional ICT infrastructure in some African institutions to give increased access to facilities such as email, Skype and the Internet would make communication easier and more reliable and would therefore facilitate enhanced cooperation on joint programmes and activities. Such facilities would also simplify practical arrangements for travel and planning of programmes on exchange visits. The same argument applies to library resources. Ugandan participants were emphatic in identifying this as a key area for development. Library provision is fundamental to development and study for both staff and students.

Efforts should be made to build upon the success of the programme in building professional partnerships, and personal friendships, between teacher educators in the contributing universities. Such partnerships need to be nurtured. They have tremendous potential to contribute to the professional development of colleagues in Ireland and Uganda and could be enlarged to bring more people into small working groups. On the other hand, we all know from personal experience how easily such friendships can wither when genuine promises of contact get swamped by the pressures of day-to-day work. Relatively modest amounts of money could provide a framework to encourage further development of joint activities between professional colleagues with measurable benefits for the students in both countries.

TEEP and the Centre for Global Development through Education have been innovative and productive. Their programmes arise from the far-sighted goals of Irish Aid in developing the capacity and capability of people in partner countries. Irish Aid is to be commended for identifying capacity building in teacher education as a key target in its work and we hope that it can enable this important work to be taken further to the benefit of both of countries. It was apparent that priorities and proposals for development arising from such partnerships must be based on a realistic awareness of the context in Uganda and Ireland. Programmes must start from the existing situation, realistically appraised, and plan for what can realistically be achieved in a defined time frame. The programme directly addressed this issue by promoting a deeper understanding and empathy than can be achieved from a simple analysis of education statistics.

Conclusion

TEEP was an overwhelmingly positive professional and inter-institutional partnership which had definite outcomes and led to capacity building among teacher educators and their institutions. It involved cultural and pedagogical dislocation. It went far beyond a geographical relocation, or the experience of being a cultural stranger in a new educational context. TEEP participants were deeply challenged to reconceptualise the very acts of teaching and learning as a consequence of the cross-fertilisation of pedagogy, administration and scholarship. Seeing others teach, in different contexts, forced participants to look again at their own teaching and learning environments. While partnership involved an exchange of ideas, it was fundamentally a sharing of pedagogical and research praxis surrounding teaching and learning. Numerous aspects of teacher formation were observed. These ranged across administration, student services, course design, pedagogy, assessment, teaching practicum and library provision, among others. TEEP resulted in change. Participants moved from seeing things done differently, to beginning to think about and talk about doing things differently themselves. Lacunae were identified. The need for modification of existing pedagogies or resources or systems became evident. Participants and institutions gained the support and insight of partners, who provided subject area knowledge, valuable experience and practical wisdom which not only challenged orthodoxies but gave support and encouragement to enable a change of practice to occur. This was not a unilateral change of practice. All partners were challenged. All partners learned. All were invited to reconceptualise their own and their institution's practice on the basis of what they experienced and observed. The multiplier effect of this positive process, as it impacts on students and wider learning communities, can only be conjectured about.

Notes

[1] In Uganda, Irish Aid has provided €2 million for a teacher training college in the Rwenzori area and is now in the process of supporting the college to introduce information and communications technology as a learning tool. J Minister Conor Lenihan (Irish Aid website: http://www.irishaid.gov.ie/article.asp?article=644 [accessed November 2011]).

[2] Irish Aid (2009, p. 26) states that its support for Uganda's education sector contributed to an increase in primary school enrolment in 2009.

References

Alexander, R. (2006) *Towards Dialogic Teaching*. York: Dialogos.

Freire, P. (2005) *Teachers as Cultural Workers*. Boulder: Westview Press.

Gosling, D. (2005) *Peer Observation of Teaching*. SEDA Paper 118. Birmingham: Staff and Educational Development Association.

Irish Aid (2009) *Irish Aid Annual Report: focus on poverty and hunger*. Dublin: Irish Aid.

Kieran, P. & Bradley, P. (2011) *Teacher Educator Exchange Report*. Limerick: Centre for Global Development through Education.

Lyons, L. (2010) Reflection and Reflective Inquiry: critical issues, evolving conceptualizations, contemporary claims and future possibilities, in N. Lyons (Ed.) *Handbook of Reflection and Reflective Inquiry*, pp. 3-22. New York: Springer. http://dx.doi.org/10.1007/978-0-387-85744-2_1

Ministry of Education and Sports (MOES) (2004) *Education Sector Strategic Plan 2004-2015*. Kampala: MOES.

Mulkeen, A. & Chen, D. (2008) *Teachers for Rural Schools: experiences in Lesotho, Malawi, Mozambique, Tanzania, and Uganda*. Washington, DC: World Bank.

Mulkeen, A. & Crowe-Taft, N. (2010) *Teacher Attrition in Sub-Saharan Africa: the neglected dimension of the teacher supply challenge*. Paris: Secretariat of the International Task Force on Teachers for EFA, UNESCO.

Nakabugo, G. (2010) Insights into Uganda's Current Education System. Unpublished Report, Mary Immaculate College, Limerick.

Nannyonjo, H. (2007) *Education Inputs in Uganda: an analysis of factors influencing learning achievement in grade six*. Washington, DC: World Bank.

United Nations (2010) *The Millennium Development Goals Report*. New York: United Nations.

Van Note Chism, N. (2007) *Peer Review of Teaching: a sourcebook*, 2nd edn. San Francisco: Jossey Bass.

Notes on Contributors

Fiona Baily is a PhD scholar at Mary Immaculate College, University of Limerick, Ireland.

Eimear Barrett is a Public Health Intelligence Officer at Queen's University Belfast, Northern Ireland.

Paddy Bradley is a Senior Lecturer in Teacher Education at St Mary's University College, Belfast, Northern Ireland.

Colin Brock held the UNESCO Chair in Education as a Humanitarian Response and was a Senior Fellow and Senior Lecturer in the Department of Educational Studies at the University of Oxford, United Kingdom.

Maria Campbell is a Lecturer in the Education Department at St Angela's College, Sligo, Ireland.

Paul Conway is a Senior Lecturer in the Department of Education at University College Cork, Ireland.

Dolores Corcoran is a Lecturer in Mathematics Education at St Patrick's College, Drumcondra, Dublin, Ireland.

Peadar Cremin is the former President of Mary Immaculate College, University of Limerick, Ireland.

Anne Dolan is a Lecturer in Education at Mary Immaculate College, University of Limerick, Ireland.

Thomas G. Grenham is a Lecturer in Religious Education at Mary Immaculate College, University of Limerick, Ireland.

Rosarii Griffin is a Lecturer in the Centre for Adult Continuing Education and a Researcher in the Centre for Global Development at University College Cork, Ireland.

Clive Harber is an Honorary Professor at the University of South Africa, Pretoria, and is an Emeritus Professor of the University of Birmingham, United Kingdom.

Carmel Hinchion is a Lecturer in Teaching, Learning and Assessment in the Department of Education and Professional Studies at the University of Limerick, Ireland.

Marty Holland is a Lecturer in Special Education at Mary Immaculate College, University of Limerick, Ireland.

Doris Kaije is a Lecturer in the Department of Religious Studies and Philosophy at Kyambogo University, Kampala, Uganda.

Matemoho Khatleli is a Lecturer at the Lesotho College of Education.

Patricia Kieran is a Lecturer in Religious Education at Mary Immaculate College, University of Limerick, Ireland.

Sarah Kisa is a PhD scholar and a Lecturer in Mathematics Education at Kyambogo University, Kampala, Uganda.

Ruth Kyambadde is a Lecturer in the Department of Teacher Education and Development Studies at Kyambogo University, Kampala, Uganda.

Louise Long is a Lecturer in Education at St Mary's University College, Belfast, Northern Ireland.

Stella Long is a Lecturer in Special Education in the Department of Special Education at Mary Immaculate College, University of Limerick, Ireland.

Bob Moon is Professor of Education at the Open University, United Kingdom, and the founding Director of Teacher Education in Sub-Saharan Africa (TESSA).

Ann Mugwera is the Academic Registrar at Kyambogo University, Kampala, Uganda.

John Musaazi is the Principal of the College of Education and External Studies at the University of Makerere, Kampala, Uganda.

Mary Goretti Nakabugo is a Senior Lecturer in Higher Education Studies in the School of Education at the University of KwaZulu-Natal, South Africa.

Elizabeth Oldham is a retired Senior Lecturer in Education at Trinity College Dublin, Ireland.

Veronica Opendi is a Lecturer at Kyambogo University, Kampala, Uganda.

Laura Regan is a Lecturer in Educational Psychology in the Department of Education and Professional Studies at the University of Limerick, Ireland.

Jacqui O'Riordan is a Lecturer in the School of Applied Social Studies at University College Cork, Ireland.

Deirdre O'Rourke is a PhD scholar and a Lecturer in International Development and Education at Mary Immaculate College, University of Limerick, Ireland.

Justine Otaala is a Lecturer in Science Education at Kyambogo University, Uganda.

David Stephens is Professor of International Education in the Education Research Centre at the University of Brighton, United Kingdom.

James Urwick is a Senior Lecturer in the East African Institute of Higher Education Studies and Development at Makerere University, Kampala, Uganda.

Freda Wolfenden is the Associate Dean of the Faculty of Education and Language Studies at the Open University, United Kingdom, and the Programme Director of Teacher Education in Sub-Saharan Africa (TESSA).